Praise for *They Cannot Take the Sky*

'In the richly woven polyphony of this book, we hear asylum seekers—both those who made it past all obstacles and those still imprisoned in hell-holes in the Pacific—tell of their hopes and fears, of the horrors they fled from and the soul-destroying tedium of the limbo state, of the deliberately inhuman treatment they have suffered in the camps, and the many kindnesses of individual teachers and volunteers. They emerge as brave and resourceful people who ought to have been welcomed with open arms but instead have become pawns in an obscure game played between the political parties. As a matter of policy they have been turned into non-people, their names erased, their images blanked out, their voices silenced. The interviewers, editors and translators who put together *They Cannot Take the Sky* are to be thanked for enabling them to emerge into the light and break the silence.'

J.M. Coetzee

'I welcome *They Cannot Take the Sky* as an urgent and much needed addition to the canon of Australian literature. These stories of perilous journeys from dangerous homelands to rightfully and justly seek asylum in Australia, and our rejection and brutal treatment of refugees—the men, women and children who only dream of having a chance to live a safe life like you and me, will be remembered in the history of the world as being among the most important stories of rejection of those in most desperate need of our times. These are the stories you will read and never forget. All Australians must read this book. We can and must do better than this.'

Alexis Wright

'We have waited too long for an anthology like this. Deftly drawn, wide-ranging, and painstakingly edited and collected, these engaging stories from immigration detention are desperate and passionate; harrowing and inspirational; beautiful and forlorn. This book will boil your blood, break your heart, and trawl the darkest recesses of your mind. It will make Australians ask—again—of ourselves: *what kind of people are we*, and how did we possibly let it come to this?'

Maxine Beneba Clarke

'To understand ourselves as a society it is vital that we listen to and read the stories of others; the stories of people who are suffering, people with stories of courage, people living lives of hope under extreme difficulty. The generosity and bravery contained in the stories presented in *They Cannot Take the Sky* offer us, here in Australia, the potential to be better, to be accepting and open. It is time for us to read and listen.'

Tony Birch

'Read this book—it will make you ashamed to be an Australian, but proud to be part of a humankind that can cope so imaginatively with unjust imprisonment. There are great people in these stories—sometimes, Serco guards—as well as bad—the Christian politicians who, if there is a hell, will burn in it for the suffering they have caused to these innocents. These authors can be witty, sometimes hilarious, always insightful, loving and even, *mirabile dictu*, forgiving—and boy do we need forgiveness for mandatory detention.'

Geoffrey Robertson

'These haunting stories, narrated by asylum seekers, are breathtaking in their honesty, the intensity of their lived-experience and their depth of feeling. Epic in scope, and in their attention to searing detail, I read them with a sense of surprise at the many twists and pendulum swings, from hope to despair, from acts of brutality to unexpected kindnesses. And with a sense of wonder, that such insight, eloquence, and paradoxical moments of love and beauty, can emerge from so much suffering.'

Arnold Zable

'So many Australians have such strong opinions on asylum seeker policy, despite never hearing from asylum seekers themselves. The importance of reading these voices and first-hand stories cannot be underestimated. This should be mandatory reading for every voting-age Australian.'

Benjamin Law

'By turns, raw, defiant, eloquent, tragic, angry, hopeful, despairing and funny, these voices from behind the wire bear compelling witness to the human cost of Australia's border protection policies. To pay attention to these stories is to know we must do things differently and to remember that the universal aspiration to a dignified life is the essential human quality that should guide our thinking.'

Peter Mares

'This book is testament to the resilience and honour of human beings. How is it that people—sometimes teenagers, alone—who have fled persecution and mortal danger only to find torture at Australian hands can react with humour, humanity, insight, concern for those they've left behind, and even sometimes for their guards? This book is extraordinary and humbling and necessary. Australia has gone rogue at international law. Behaving illegally, our politicians have the nerve to call people fleeing persecution 'illegals'. This must stop. As one of the contributors, Amir Taghinia, puts it, in words that might apply to our sense of what it is to be Australian, as well as to an individual being persecuted: "There might not be a reset button."'

Anna Funder

'I could quote all the philosophers and prophets in the world to urge the Australian public to remember their humanity, but it won't make the people seeking asylum any more real. Only the people themselves can do that, which is why the Australian government has gone to such lengths to silence asylum seekers and the people who work with them. But in this overdue collection, Australia's imprisoned refugees finally speak. They describe the island prisons journalists are not allowed to visit, the lives they left behind and the lives they want so much to begin. There are curious and unexpected revelations too, a growing love of place in Christmas Island, a refugee learning to herd huge crabs off a road, a connection made with an old woman in a Manus Island jungle. There is a longing for connection, be it sex and touch, or expression as one young woman's weekly newsletter is shut down. Who would have thought? The detained refugees the Australian government has spirited away to island prisons are human.'

Anna Krien

'This is a book whose human, frank, illuminating voices the government does not want to hear from. In the end Australia will hear and honour these life histories, and honestly acknowledge Australia's shameful part in them. *They Cannot Take the Sky* brings that day so much closer.'

Tom Keneally

THEY CANNOT TAKE THE SKY

Stories from detention

Editors: Michael Green and André Dao
Associate editors: Angelica Neville, Dana Affleck
and Sienna Merope

ALLEN&UNWIN
SYDNEY · MELBOURNE · AUCKLAND · LONDON

First published in 2017

Copyright © Behind the Wire Incorporated, 2017

All rights reserved. No part of this book may be reproduced or transmitted in any form or by any means, electronic or mechanical, including photocopying, recording or by any information storage and retrieval system, without prior permission in writing from the publisher. The Australian *Copyright Act 1968* (the Act) allows a maximum of one chapter or 10 per cent of this book, whichever is the greater, to be photocopied by any educational institution for its educational purposes provided that the educational institution (or body that administers it) has given a remuneration notice to the Copyright Agency (Australia) under the Act.

Allen & Unwin
83 Alexander Street
Crows Nest NSW 2065
Australia
Phone: (61 2) 8425 0100
Email: info@allenandunwin.com
Web: www.allenandunwin.com

Cataloguing-in-Publication details are available
from the National Library of Australia
www.trove.nla.gov.au

ISBN 978 1 76029 280 5

Internal design by Christabella Designs
Set in 12/16.5 pt Sabon by Midland Typesetters, Australia
Printed and bound in Australia by Griffin Press

10 9 8 7 6 5

The paper in this book is FSC® certified. FSC® promotes environmentally responsible, socially beneficial and economically viable management of the world's forests.

Contents

Foreword: Christos Tsiolkas — ix
Introduction — xiii

Prologue
For six months I was Jesus: Behrouz — 3

Part I
When I become famous, I'll give Tony Abbott a job: Hani — 29
The funny thing is, they didn't care: Benjamin — 48
I felt I had magical power: Donna — 57
My face is plastered to the window: Jamila — 67
She said, 'You can be my son': Taqi — 79
It was a strange, alien land: Aran — 90
Voices: On leaving, arriving and a song about the homeland — 104

Part II
I wore a black shirt to my ceremony: Ali — 123
I still love the mountains more than anywhere else: Neda — 148
I had a cause and I was fighting for it: Wahid — 160
They took me to gaol and that was heaven: Munjed — 172
They didn't like us to sleep on one bed: Nima — 181
I thought I would leave detention, but my heart is there still: Lina — 190
Voices: On boredom, freedom and blockading the gates — 200

Part III

When I was a kid I had heaps of dreams in my mind: Aziz   221
I learnt all people are equal: Sajjd   237
Education is light: Omar   243
One day the torturer will get tired and you will win:
    Ariobarzan   248
Now I don't have the heart for girls: Sami   253
I have been tortured and I have been loved: Imran   257
We are all convicted to live on this planet: Amir   272

Epilogue
I can also tell a story: Peter   287

Afterword   305
Contributors   307
Acknowledgements   315
Behind the Wire   317

Foreword

We read for pleasure and we read for knowledge. And there are some books we read because we must, for in not reading them we are in danger of not understanding our world and our own place in the world. Over the last century such books have included *The Diary of Anne Frank*, Primo Levi's *If This is a Man*, George Orwell's *1984*, Hannah Arendt's *Eichmann in Jerusalem* and Aleksandr Solzhenitsyn's *The Gulag Archipelago*. There are others, of course there are, from every continent on this planet but I mention those five because they were crucial in creatively and purposefully giving voice to the obscene injustice and anti-humanity of totalitarianism. It is no accident that three of them have as their subject the Holocaust and the others that of the Stalinist purges and the murderous Soviet system of forced exile. Such books break free of their geographic, cultural and historic boundaries, and in doing so they smash the borders we humans erect to keep ourselves separate from one another. In forcing us to confront the evil we are capable of they also ask us to acknowledge our shared humanity. I love literature, I love so many books, but I know that very few are necessary. That isn't to somehow diminish the function of art and creativity. I'm not someone who believes criticism involves a ledger where you give a book a mark for utility. Some of the greatest works of art are purely pleasurable. But the books I mentioned above are both works of art and also works of witnessing. They are necessary.

In Australia in 2017, *They Cannot Take the Sky* is also necessary. For nearly two decades now, Australian politics has been corrupted by a toxic and destructive national debate about asylum seekers and refugees. Unfortunately, fought out as much across media—traditional and digital—as it has in our parliament, the issue of asylum has become inexorably entwined with our security and existential fears arising from the threats of international terrorism. Our leaders, across the political spectrum, have failed in the democratic imperative to ensure a cogent and humane approach to the issue. In fanning the hysteria of partisanship they have betrayed our trust. That great leveller, history, will ultimately judge us on what kind of country we created for ourselves at the beginning of the twenty-first century. This isn't the place for political analysis. All I want to suggest is that in all the screaming across the parliament floor or on social media, we forget that the asylum seeker and the refugee is a real person, with a real body and a real consciousness, that they are as human as we are. We know that the detention centres we have built on our continent, on Nauru and on Manus Island, are not places we would ever countenance imprisoning Australians. We know what we have done. We don't need history to instruct us on that.

The stories in this book—these accounts, these testaments—they are all a form of witnessing to what occurred during our watch over the last twenty years. There are moments of brutality and incomprehension; how can it be else? But there are also moments of great humour, of inspiration and of almost heartbreaking generosity. Time and time again, a voice will offer thanks to the individual kindness of an Australian that dared to visit a refugee in prison, that offered assistance as the newcomer tried to navigate their way in a foreign and perplexing country. These stories also act to break down the cumulative and dangerous stereotyping of refugees as having always the identical and same experience. These storytellers are not only Muslim or Afghani or Tamil; they are also, and just as importantly, mothers or fathers, brothers or sisters, artists or students, workers or scientists, lovers both straight and gay. Some of them embody the rawness and fury of youth and some the wisdom and caution of age. The cumulative effect is one of a great and powerful chorus that sings the possibility of a hope that Australia has been denying itself, the enrichment that comes from openness and charity. Hani writes, 'I realised that freedom is not walking free. It means to be free mentally and physically.' Chained to policies that we all know in our hearts to be destructive and inhuman, can it be said that we Australians are truly free?

Many years ago now, I was having a drink with a cousin in Athens. We were talking and drinking late into the night and as it will always be with a Greek, we were furiously discussing politics and history. She was reflecting on the White Australia Policy and arguing that if we had not had such a racist attitude to the immigrant in the late 1930s, there would have been a generation of Jewish artists, scientists and intellectuals who might have made Australia their home. 'Think of it,' she said, grabbing my hand and holding it tight, 'Think of what your country could be if you had not had such stupid laws.'

They Cannot Take the Sky is full of great writing. I hope that in the future that many of the narrators will be the writers of a great new wave of Australian literature. Their experiences as refugees cannot be forgotten, that will always inform the work that they do. But I can't wait to hear their stories of Australia and their stories of the world. I wish my country were not beholden to stupid and wicked laws that gutless men and women created out of fear and ignorance; and yes, out of venality and the lust for power. There is darkness in this book but there are also great pleasures to be had, such as the thrill of a new language and the rush of eloquent storytelling. There is much knowledge to be gleaned and I am grateful to every single one of the narrators for sharing their world with me. And of course, there is witnessing and testament. The witness to what we have done and the testament to what we could be. This is why this book is absolutely necessary.

Christos Tsiolkas

Introduction

Speaking on a smuggled phone from inside the Australian-run immigration detention centre on Manus Island, Papua New Guinea, Abdul Aziz Muhamat related an anecdote about his day. He'd been standing near the gate when a security guard had called someone's name three or four times. The man was standing nearby but he didn't reply. Aziz told the guard to call his ID number instead—the man responded immediately. 'Look, man, no one is pretending here. Why should he pretend?' Aziz told the guard. 'We forgot our names.'

At that time, mid-March 2016, Aziz had been on Manus for two and a half years. He was 21 years old when he left Sudan. As we write, more than half a year later, he remains in the detention centre, with no end in sight.

This book exists for Aziz to speak his own name, to tell us about his life and what is happening to him—to tell us about his toothache, about the smell of the breeze, and about the regret that fills his heart. It is a record of Australia's mandatory immigration detention system from the point of view of the people it incarcerates. It is more than a record, however, and it is about much more than detention.

Some people talk about love: love lost, love found, love imagined, love desired. Desire itself. The loyalty of friends. An unfathomable love, like Lina's: 'I thought I would leave detention, but I couldn't leave it. My heart is there still,' she says. Many dwell on their families, the wisdom passed down by their parents. Their hopes for their children. Almost all talk of death. Their stories are taut with defiance and resistance. They differ on the matter of hope.

Since 1992—and in many cases earlier than that—Australia has locked up people who arrive here fleeing persecution. Refugee policy is a national obsession; no day passes without a news story. Politicians and commentators of various stripes are outraged by one another, and everyone is certain that they hold the moral high ground. But only very rarely do we read more than a short quote from the people in question.

This book comprises stories from 35 people, from young children to adults with families of their own. They were born in nine different countries—although for many, their country of birth did not recognise them as citizens. They arrived in Australia by boat or by aeroplane between 1997 and 2013. What happened to them next varied radically depending on the date of their arrival; in some cases, just a matter of days made all the difference. They speak about their experiences in more than a dozen different detention centres, onshore and offshore. They do not represent anyone else, but we know that thousands of other people have these stories to tell, too.

Some of our narrators have chosen to remain anonymous, but most have used their real names. Some have spoken out at great risk to themselves. All of those who have shared their stories have done so despite the lack of transparency about how refugee claims are assessed and the regime of secrecy surrounding detention centres. The fear of retribution—from the Australian government or foreign governments—has prevented some narrators from publishing their stories in full. Some narrators chose not to publish their stories at all. We hope they will feel safe to do so one day.

Introduction

The book's title, *They Cannot Take the Sky*, is drawn from a line in Behrouz Boochani's story, which opens the collection. What follows is the work of the narrators, together with a small group of interviewers and a larger number of people who have volunteered their time and skills in interpreting and transcribing interviews. It has been a work of trust, dedication and care.

When she was in detention on Christmas Island, Hani Abdile—who was then seventeen years old—began her own newsletter, the *CC Weekly*. Among other regular spots, it featured a segment called 'Refugee of the Week', interviews with officers and an update on policy announcements. It lasted six weeks before the detention centre's management shut it down. 'I think the truth is small, you know. Bitter,' Hani says. 'Nobody ever wants to hear the truth.'

In Hani's story, and in them all, sometimes the truth is small and bitter. Sometimes it is surprising, sometimes hilarious, sometimes devastating. Often it is large and sweet. All the narrators in *They Cannot Take the Sky* have something to say, and they want to be heard.

Amir Taghinia is another young man indefinitely imprisoned in the Manus Island detention centre. He spoke to us at length, over several conversations, telling us about the blinding glare in the compound, of his desire to study international law, and of how, for six months, he prayed for death every night. At last we asked, 'Is there anything else you want to say?' Amir replied, 'I think I have told you enough about what is going on in here. And I hope there is someone who hears these things, you know?'

Michael Green and André Dao

Prologue

For six months I was Jesus

Behrouz

Behrouz Boochani works tirelessly from detention on Manus Island. Every day he wakes, smokes, and begins his job—conducting interviews, updating his Facebook page, writing articles or working on his book. He landed on Christmas Island on his birthday and exactly three years later, still in detention, he told this story.

Literary language

My name is Behrouz Boochani. I am a Kurdish journalist and writer, but I left Iran about three years ago.

I publish a lot of stories in the newspapers and in the media about Manus, but people, really, they cannot understand our condition, not in journalistic language. Where we are is too hard. I think only in literary language can people understand our life and our condition.

You know, a father crying for his small daughter, you cannot find this story in any newspapers or media. A lawyer never can understand this. A judge never can understand this. I saw a lot of people, on the darkest nights in this prison, trying to find a corner and cry for their son, or their wife or their daughter. Only in literary language you can describe this man and his feelings and why he is crying.

I never use the government's words, the government's concepts. For example, they use the word 'camp' for this prison. But I never say that this prison is 'camp'. When I write anything in Facebook or in a newspaper, or when I do an interview with a journalist, I always use 'prison'. And we are prisoners. When you say 'camp', people think that our condition is better than a prison. But this place is more than a prison, because a prisoner has some rights. Family members can come to visit a prisoner. A prisoner can have a lawyer. A prisoner knows how many years he must stay in the prison. A prisoner was in a court and a judge made an order. A prisoner committed a crime.

But on this remote island, we cannot have any lawyer, nobody can come to visit us. And we don't know how many years we must stay here. This prison is more than a prison. I always use 'Guantanamo'. And I believe that 'Australian Guantanamo' is not enough for this prison, not enough. But I don't have any other words.

The old woman

I think I told you about the old woman. Did I tell you that?

The old woman, she was living in the jungle on Manus. And I had a connection with her. When I was in Foxtrot prison, in the first months, I became friends with one of the local officers and he told me that his mother lives in the jungle in Manus: 'Sometimes she is crying for you, that you are in this prison.'

We sent each other some messages, through her son. And I found out that the old woman, she had never left Manus. She said, 'I am praying for you. And I always feel you.' She didn't know any more about us, she only knew that we were here . . .

Just a few messages, like love messages. And I sent her that, 'I love you, and I feel your heart.'

Yeah . . . the effect on me . . . I . . . [*Sighs.*] . . . That old woman, after few months, she died. And I found out . . . that the human is human. And there is no difference between a woman or man in a village in Kurdistan, or in New York City, or in Sydney or Melbourne, or an old woman in a remote island . . . in a small village in the jungle.

It's not different to what I thought before. When I was in Iran, I knew that all people are same, but not like this, deeply. I thought that education can affect people . . . but this old woman, she didn't go to any school.

The big problem is not local people or refugees. The big problem is Australia. People always forget that when we say 'Manus hell prison' we mean our prison, not this island or the people. The local people think that the refugees are criminals because Australian Immigration says to them a lot of times that we are criminals. And the refugees think that the local people want to kill them. But this is not true and there are a lot of kind people on Manus.

The Papua New Guinean High Court made the decision that Manus prison is illegal. That decision made some changes in our life. They opened the gates, allowed people to use the buses to go to Lorengau* town for few hours. It's not full freedom, but it's a little, and that is good. I myself came outside just for few days and I have to go back.

Right now I don't have cigarettes, I have to go buy cigarettes. But it's night, and it's dark, and it looks dangerous. You know the Manus people are so kind, but Manus Island is not safe. Some people can be kind and still do violent actions. We cannot go outside at night, and we don't feel safe during the day also.

---

* Lorengau is the main town on Manus Island. It is about 24 kilometres from the detention centre, which is located in a naval base at Lombrum.

The big problem is that we don't want to live on Manus. And Manus people, they are living tribally, and they have a very poor economy. Really, Papua New Guinea has no capacity to accept us.

On the dark ocean

My village is a small village, near Ilam city in Kurdistan in Iran. It's near the border, between Iraq and Iran, but the land is Kurdistan, and I was born in that village. I am writing a book, and I started it with these words: 'I was born in a war.'

I was born in 1983. At that time there was a big war between Iran and Iraq, but on Kurdistan's land. I describe Iran and Iraq as two big animals that are fighting in our garden. Kurdistan is very beautiful, and they destroyed our village, our houses. Everything. I was in that village for about eighteen years, and after that I went to Tehran, the capital city. I was at university for about seven years and I got a masters in political geography and geopolitics. I started work as a journalist in Tehran and then after a few years, on 13 May 2013, I left Iran.

I was in Indonesia for about four months. I had such hard days in Indonesia because I was scared of the Indonesian police. I was always in a room and I didn't go outside. After four months I left Indonesia for Australia but our boat sank. Suddenly I found myself on the dark ocean. I had to swim about 30 metres to reach a piece of wood. I was holding the wood on the ocean for about half an hour and then a small boat came. They were fishermen and they saved me. Then the Indonesian police came and put me in gaol for about a day. That night I escaped from gaol and went to Jakarta. And after two weeks I started again to go to Australia.

On my second journey, one of the guys with me was from Ilam city. And he made a big mistake, because he called his family and said, 'Me and Behrouz, we are on the boat, and we are going to Australia and we will arrive there in the next two days.' So our family expected that we would call them after a few days. Our boat was lost for about a week and we didn't have any water or food. Really, we were dying. A big British ship found us. They made contact with the Australian navy who came to us after about six hours. And they took us to Christmas Island. That was very special because on that last night, when I thought I was dying, it was my birthday, 23 July. It was very special.

I arrived at Christmas Island and at that time I was about 53 kilograms because I had a big journey and most of the time I was hungry.

They didn't allow us to use the phone for about ten days. So for about seventeen days I couldn't make contact with my mother, and she was crying. She said, 'We were accepting that you lost your life.'

After a month, they exiled me by force to Manus Island. And on that first day on Manus, I called her and I told her, 'My mum, we are here. We will be here for two years.' At that time, I . . . I thought that two years is too long. I told her that so she would be ready for anything to happen for me. And three years have now finished. We are going into four years.

Sometimes I talk with her, but not too much. She's worried about me. She didn't go to school and she cannot write. When I was in Iran she always felt that I was working against the system, but she couldn't understand what I was doing. When I talk with her she always tells me, 'Please, don't do anything against the government. Be very quiet.' I don't give my family any information about my work here. Nothing. I only sometimes talk with them to say I am alive, and that I am on Manus. I . . . I don't . . . They don't know anything about me.

I always forget that I am a refugee
When I arrived on Christmas Island I told them that I was a political journalist and I believe in liberal democracy and I couldn't live in religious dictatorship in Iran and I came to your

country because Australia is a Western country, a free country. But they didn't care.

It was very hard for me to make contact with Australian journalists or newspapers. We didn't have much access to the internet, only two times during the week for about 40 minutes, and it was too slow. When we wanted to open, for example, our Facebook, we had to wait for about ten or fifteen minutes for it to open. But at that time I started to write.

After two months I gave the local people cigarettes and they brought me a recorder and I started to make interviews. I tried to send my voice recordings but sometimes I couldn't because the internet was very slow and I became angry.

You know, really, I always forget that I am a refugee and I am in this prison with these people, because I always think of myself as a journalist and a reporter and human rights activist. I am always watching and monitoring people and monitoring the system. And just sometimes I find that I am a refugee and I have thongs and I have shorts and my name is MEG45.

For six months, when we first came to Manus, all the officers called me Jesus, because when I have a beard, my face looks like Jesus. Manus people are religious people, and some of the local officers loved me because when they saw me they felt that I am Jesus.

I don't believe in any religion, but at that time I was very happy about that name because now the officers and this system never call us by our names. All people are called by number. The officers say 'MEG45', 'GDD42', 'QAN64', all like this. When the G4S company* left Manus after the riot,† those first officers

---

* G4S is a British-based multinational security services company, which specialises in managing corrections facilities. It was contracted by the Australian government to run the Manus Regional Processing Centre from February 2013 to March 2014.
† On 17 February 2014, there were violent clashes in the Manus Regional Processing Centre, following weeks of protests by detainees. One man died—a 23-year-old Iranian asylum seeker named Reza Barati. Another detainee lost his right

left and I lost my name. After that I became MEG45, but for six months I was Jesus.

My duty as a journalist

This system is trying to take people's personalities by calling them by a number and humiliating them. After a long time they think they are not human. But fortunately I didn't lose my personality—I think I became a better man. I didn't forget that I am Behrouz, I am a Kurdish journalist. I didn't forget where I came from, and what my mission is, my duty as a journalist.

You know, I think suffering can make people bad or good. Suffering can change people's personalities. I know a lot of people, they became better people in this prison, they grew in humanity. I could find some beauty in this prison—and I am glad of that. But it is too much for me to say I am a good man. I can say that when I was in Iran I was a bad man, and now I am a little less of a bad man. [*Laughs.*]

Any prisoner thinks about how they can escape from prison. Any prisoner has the right to try to escape from prison. When they first sent me to Manus the fences were small. There were a lot of officers around the prison, but several times at night I jumped the fence and went outside, walking on the beach and listening to the ocean and smoking there. And that was a very big crime in this system, but I did it several times. It was amazing really. But after

---

eye after being bashed, and a third was shot in the buttocks. Scores of detainees sustained injuries, including broken bones and lacerations. The violence ended early in the morning on 18 February. A review into the incident was conducted by Robert Cornall, a lawyer and former secretary of the Attorney-General's department. In his report, Cornall stated that police, local men and some expatriate service provider employees entered the detention centre and 'started bashing detainees'. He concluded that Barati 'suffered a severe brain injury caused by a brutal beating by several assailants and died a few hours later'. However, only two Papua New Guinean men were charged with murder. They were found guilty and sentenced to ten years' gaol. No government officials faced any sanctions over the clashes.

the riot in February 2014, they made big fences and after that I couldn't go outside.

But I thought a lot about how I could escape from this prison. I imagined escaping from Manus and going to some embassies in Port Moresby, or going to Indonesia. I thought about going to New Zealand, but if you see the Pacific map, it's really hard. The first big problem is how to escape from the prison. The second problem is how to escape from Manus Island, because hundreds of kilometres around is ocean, it's too dangerous. And if you escape from the island and go to Port Moresby, how can you go to a third country? The nearest country is Australia, and if you go to Australia they send you back to Manus.

After two years I thought that if I escape from this prison I cannot help people—if I am inside the prison I can do more to help—and I forgot it.

I know that Australian history has a lot of episodes like Manus. For example, Aboriginal people were put in prison without any crime. I know some refugees that have been in Australian detention for seven years. But I myself feel that I have a mission, and this is my duty, to write and write about Manus and about Nauru, and tell the next generation in Australia how your government tortured people and put children and women, and men, in prison without any crime.

I am not a normal journalist. Some journalists in Australia sit in their office and drink coffee and do their work as professionals. But I am in prison with other prisoners. I need to forget that I am a prisoner. I need to accept that I am a journalist and writer and I have a mission—I have a big and important duty, and I must do my best.

When I feel upset or sad, I try to resolve it within myself and I try to make sure that people don't know. Sometimes, when you talk with your girlfriend or with your mother, with your friends, with your brother, sister, it's natural that you might sometimes be upset or angry. Sometimes you feel that you want to be with your mother, you know? Sometimes I miss my mother, but I cannot show my sadness.

I know a man, he once wanted to talk with his father because his father was dying. And the officers said, 'No, this is against our system.' They checked the list: 'You must come to use the phone in three days at three o'clock.' After three days he went and used the phone but his father had died three days ago. And he said, 'I cannot forgive myself, because I couldn't talk with my father.'

When I am working I feel better. I found out in this prison that we must work and work and work. I found life's meaning in working. I don't mean that you must go to an office or something. I mean, each day you must create something that makes your life lighter, more beautiful. If you play soccer, it's working; if you listen to music, it's working. Yeah, working for me is like food. And sometimes more important than food.

It is hard writing in prison

Today is my birthday. I always forget my birthday but Facebook helped me. Yeah, today is my birthday on a remote island. A beautiful island. I am sure that when I left Iran I was 28 and I have been in this prison for three years. That means I am 31. But on my ID card I am 33. I lost two years, I don't know where. This is a big question, really, and I think about it a lot. Where did I lose the two years? It's a question. [*Laughs.*] I am sure it's because of prison, but it is a mystery for me.

When I started to work under my real name, I started to publish work on Facebook too. Sometimes I'd write something about Manus prison, just as fun, because I thought that Facebook was social media, not too important. My Facebook suddenly got bigger and a lot of people sent me messages. And after few months my Facebook became a media. Some newspapers don't talk with me; they take my post and use it in their report. Sometimes I post some short pieces about my political opinions, about the Australian immigration system. Or sometimes I introduce some refugees, showing that they have skills: they are engineers, or they are artists, or they can play guitar. Because the Australian government is making propaganda that these people are terrorists, or they are dangerous. And I try to change this imagination.

I describe Manus prison as like a street with a lot of people walking on it. Imagine that you are a writer on a street. All the time people are around you and they want to talk with you. For example, one of them talks with his wife, or his daughter, or his son, or his father, and he becomes nervous or feels pressure and comes to ask me, 'Behrouz, when will we go outside?' And I say, 'Very soon, you must be strong, don't worry! We are not the first persons in history that are in prison. And we are not first persons that are in prison without any crime. We must be strong, my brother!' And every time I lose my energy because of people.

It is hard writing in prison because people are always around you and you cannot focus. But sometimes I write about the people that bother me. And I describe them. [*Laughs.*]

People in Manus prison they know me more as a singer because all the time I am singing. Not in a loud voice, only for myself. I listen to classical music. Imagine me in a long line for food, in small shorts and a big T-shirt, under the shining sun, listening to Beethoven, Mozart. I could stay in the longest lines with this kind of music. I can say that I resist Manus prison by music.

And myself, I wrote eight Kurdish songs here. A few months ago I recorded a short video and sang a Kurdish song. I published it on Facebook and a lot of people sent me messages because of that song. Yeah, from France, Iran, Brazil, and Australia especially. Even from Laos, even from Laos. It was wonderful, yeah. I'll never forget that song.

I always write on my phone, on WhatsApp. I send it to my friend and he keeps it and prints it . . . I cannot edit. My big problem in writing is that I don't like to edit my writing, I just like writing. When I want to write an article I think a lot, think a lot, then I start to write . . . smoking and writing, smoking and writing, smoking and writing, and when I finish I read it.

You know, when I want to write articles in journalistic language, it's easy. It makes me happy. But writing in literary language is too hard. When I write that way I feel angry and I cannot talk with people. It's too hard. Really, sometimes I feel too scared to write. I have to sleep in the day and wake up at night, and wait for people to sleep, and only from 2 a.m. until the morning I have some time. Sometimes I become angry with people, and I cut all my relationships, because I need to keep my aloneness.

Very complex torture

Sometimes I am tired. But I would like to talk about detention, and about prison, and I will continue to talk about Manus prison all of my life, and I will talk and I will write, because this happened. It was in the twenty-first century, in a Western country.

You know that they are torturing us. I always use the words 'systematic torture'. Imagine a person, a prisoner in Manus. When he wakes up in the morning he must stay in the line for the toilet. After that, he wants to eat breakfast, so he must stay in the line for an hour, with such humiliation, because an officer is there, and he says, 'Okay, next five people, and you must stay there.' And after ten minutes, 'Next five people, and you must stay in the line.' For only food. And after that you must stay in the line to buy a cigarette. After that you must stay in the line for lunch, for dinner. And you don't have any facility to do anything, only backgammon, only talking with people. How much can you talk with people?

Some people every day must go to IHMS* to take tablets for their depression. And they must give their ID cards to the officer and stay in the line and when you go to IHMS they search your body. And then you go outside and at the next gates they search your body. During a day they search your body about twenty times, only to get tablets.

Sometimes the Wilson guards,† or G4S when they were here, they beat people. And the Australian newspapers sometimes write a story about G4S or Wilson guards beating people. But they never write anything about how they are torturing us. This system is focused on our minds. And it's very complex torture.

A big taboo

You know, there is a big problem for any prisoner: sex. I know a lot of organisations—like Amnesty International, like Human Rights Watch—came to Manus and published some reports about Manus. And there are a lot of stories about Manus prisoners in the newspaper and in the media and they mentioned a lot of problems, but nobody ever talks about sexual problems, and how lack of sex affects people's minds, and affects people's memories. It's a big taboo. I just talk with journalists and try to convince them to write about this subject.

I can talk about this because I saw a lot of young boys in Manus prison who sometimes say, 'Oh, I need to have sex, I need to have sex.' I saw people hit their head on the wall. This is Manus reality. I saw a lot of people who, when a woman came to the prison, they

---

* International Health and Medical Services (IHMS) is the healthcare company contracted to provide medical assistance in Australia's immigration detention centres on the mainland and on Christmas Island, Manus Island and Nauru.
† Wilson Security is an Australian private security company. It has been operating as a subcontractor for Broadspectrum in the offshore detention centres at Nauru (since late 2012) and Manus Island (since February 2014). In September 2016, it announced that it would stop working in the detention centres at the end of its contract in October 2017.

were watching the woman like she was a very special thing.

You know, these are my experiences. I don't talk about myself. I am a prisoner like other prisoners. I saw a lot of things that convinced me that we need to talk about this problem. I saw a lot of rape in prison. People got crazy and raped young boys.

The important problems in Manus prison are the constant lack of sex, and rape, violence and mental problems. I expected that in a modern country like Australia the media would be free and people—some activists or some journalists—would write about this. Or psychologists. This is a prison reality, and it's big part of the systematic torture.

This is more than racist

I wrote a statement for a rally in Australia and I wrote that the Australian government is a fascist government. One of the advocates sent me a message: 'Behrouz, please if it's possible, do you want to take out "fascist" because if we read this for people in the rally, people will feel bad.' I was thinking for two days, *How can I take out this concept?* It was hard for me, because I deeply believe that the Australian government is fascist. I finally sent a message to her and said, 'Okay, take it out.' That was very hard for me.

I don't want to talk about all policy, but I want to say that they are fascist because of this policy. They are fascist because they torture some people, some children. There was a baby, he was in Nauru and they sent him to Australia for treatment for a few weeks. The government wanted to send that baby back to Nauru. They were exiling a baby . . . to a remote island . . . and this is fascist. This is more than racist.

They are torturing people, torturing children. They are making propaganda. The Australian people have a big problem: they are waiting for the government to give information. For a modern country this is not good. It is hard to accept that from people in universities, or people who are writers or journalists or poets—they have a responsibility for humanity, and they must take action and put pressure on the government. But they are quiet and they are silent.

I think that in Manus prison my political opinion has changed and I've become, like, an anarchist. I've lost trust in any government. [*Sighs.*] I thought a lot about justice when the Australian High Court made a decision about offshore processing centres. We were watching on the monitor. At that time, I completely lost trust in the Australian system. I know the Australian government exiled people here, but I expected that one day the Australian High Court would make a decision against the government.

We are here because of the whole of Australia, not only because of the Liberal Party, or the Labor Party. I know, a lot of people in Australia are fighting for change. But the whole of Australia made this trouble: Australian courts, Australian universities, all of Australia put us here. I think Australian civil society is defeated, completely, because they couldn't change anything. And I think history will make a judgement. I know a lot of Australian people are trying to help people in Manus and Nauru, and they are amazing, but I think the big problem is that the majority of Australian people are only hearing or watching the prime minister or the government.

I myself saw three prime ministers in Australia: Kevin Rudd, Tony Abbott and Malcolm Turnbull. And I saw Scott Morrison as immigration minister, and Peter Dutton. You know, the Australian political space changed three or four times and we are still here. The Papua New Guinean Supreme Court made a decision that Manus prison is illegal and we are still here. People in Australia had a lot of rallies and we are still here. International organisations like Amnesty International and Human Rights Watch published several reports about Manus and we are still here. A lot of things happened around us, but nothing changes, and we are still here.

Each day I receive a lot of messages from people saying, 'Sorry, Behrouz, sorry. We really want to help you and other refugees.' But the big problem is the majority of Australian people don't research about Manus and Nauru. It is hard to be in Manus prison or Nauru and not hate Australia and not hate this system.

[*Pauses, listening to a loud bird call.*] This bird is the chauka. [*Listening.*] It's singing. I don't know what it's saying. When the chauka is singing I can only try to feel whether it means bad or good. Today I think it's good, yeah, like it came to us to say hello. [*Laughs.*]

I would like to talk about this. The chauka is a very special bird in Manus because you can only find it in Manus. You cannot find it in other islands or anywhere in the world. The local people love the chauka. I once published a short story about the chauka when I was in gaol, the Chauka gaol.*

I don't know why they gave that name to that horrific place. I don't know why. Sometimes when the system wanted to punish some people they transferred them to Chauka, and put them under such pressure.

I was there for four days. When I was in that gaol a chauka bird came and started to sing. When the chauka is singing, it is because of one of three reasons. First, if chauka comes to your village and starts singing it means you are lying or some other people are lying. You know? It's amazing. And the second reason is that a man and woman, they are having sex. And third, the reason is that a person will die tonight or on the next days. Death, birth and honesty.

---

* Chauka was the name of an isolation unit in the Manus Regional Processing Centre, located away from the other compounds. It consisted of three converted shipping containers, without windows or ventilation, arranged in a triangle.

THEY CANNOT TAKE THE SKY

I found I am a crazy poet

The big torture for any prisoner is to change his place. It's too hard. Immigration's plan was to transfer people who got negative [refugee] results* to Foxtrot and Mike compounds, and positive people to Delta and Oscar.† I was in Delta prison at that time and they transferred me to Foxtrot. Then after a week they came to me and said that I was positive. And I said that I didn't give Papua New Guinea my case and I don't want to live in Papua New Guinea. And they said, 'You are positive, and you must go back to Oscar or Delta, we will use the police.' After few days they gave me a paper that said I must transfer to Oscar or Delta at eight o'clock in the morning.

There is a huge tree inside Foxtrot. And in the morning I climbed to the top of that tree and I started to protest. I didn't wear anything, only a pair of shorts I had. When I was on top of that tree I found I was a crazy actor, a crazy poet.

When I was in that tree, a lot of people were watching. The refugees were supporting me. And a lot of police, a lot of immigration staff and a psychologist. First, I read my political statement about why I climbed the tree: because I didn't want to go to Papua New Guinea, and I left my country because of my political opinions, and I would never accept their positive [refugee] result.

I told them that I needed music. I said, 'If you don't bring music for me, I will kill myself.' And an immigration officer said, 'Don't give him anything.' I yelled at him: 'You are a stupid man because

---

* Negative result refers to the Papua New Guinean Immigration department's assessment of a person's application for refugee status. In Manus Island, men are given an initial positive or negative assessment, which they can appeal if negative, or, if positive, must be confirmed. The men use the following terms to explain the status of their refugee claim: positive, double positive, negative or double negative.
† Foxtrot, Mike, Delta and Oscar are separate compounds within the Manus Regional Processing Centre. In mid-April 2016, at the time Behrouz is describing, the men were not allowed to move freely between the compounds.

you cannot understand that when a crazy poet is protesting on top of a tree, inside a prison, on a remote island, and wants to listen to Beethoven, he can kill himself if you don't give it to him. He can kill himself only because of music.'

I will never forget that. Yeah, I felt free at that time. I was completely crazy. But philosophical crazy.

He said, 'Okay, give him music.' And they sent my MP3 player. I was listening to Beethoven and Mozart. And I said, 'I am a poet and I need cigarettes' [*laughing*]. Yeah, and they sent me cigarettes too. [*Laughs.*]

After that I wrote a poem about the birds and the beautiful sky, because on top of that tree I could see the ocean. I wrote a letter saying that today I am a free man because I have enough power and I am outside this system. On top of this tree I was above the fences, and I was outside the prison. Suddenly it was raining and some of the refugees who were with me, they took off their T-shirts and were in the rain.

I was up there for about ten hours, and at five o'clock I said, 'I will come down, but you must write a report that this protest was a political protest and was not because of mental problems.' But the psychologist said, 'No, first come down and we can have a discussion.' And I said, 'You cannot tell me to come down because I have power while I am on top of this tree. If I come down I will lose my power and you don't have enough power to tell me to come down.'

At that time, really, I wanted to kill myself. When the psychologist came to me I really wanted to kill myself. I couldn't accept that this stupid psychologist, after only a few minutes, could say that I wouldn't kill myself. I was angry, because I think people are very complex and nobody can understand whether someone can kill himself or cannot. I was so close. But sometimes I think the psychologist saw through it, because I didn't kill myself. But, really, I wanted to kill myself. I don't know.

I told Immigration, 'I don't want anything. Just you must promise me you won't cut down this tree. And second thing, when I come down I want to take a shower, and not talk with you. After a few days I will come to you.' And they said, 'Okay.' And I came down and took a shower.

Before that protest I wrote a lot of poems only for myself. Poetry, in my opinion, is the greatest concept and I didn't accept at that time that I was a poet. But after the protest I felt myself as a poet, and I am a poet now. Yeah, I am a poet.

The coconuts are my lovers

When I was outside prison I knew that the sky was beautiful, nature was beautiful. But I found nature power and nature beauty in Manus. The sky is like a friend for a prisoner, because around you everything is metal fences, but the sky, they cannot take the sky.

I think the Manus moon is too special. Sometimes the moon is crazy because the clouds are moving, and sometimes it's calm, quiet. Once I described the moon as a pregnant woman because on that night the moon was so quiet and, like, heavy. I always find the moon to be a woman. I wrote another poem that described the moon and Manus Island as two sisters, in the sky and the blue ocean.

Sometimes, it's too hard to have a relationship with people, because you always see them. During the day you see people—'Hi, hello, hello, hello'—and the space is too small and you cannot say hello to people each time and the best way to escape is that you make direct contact with nature.

We had a lot of beautiful coconut trees and they cut all of them down. The Transfield company,* they cut down a lot of the

---

* Broadspectrum (formerly known as Transfield Services) began providing catering and building maintenance services in offshore detention centres in 2012, then took over as the major contractor running both facilities in 2014. It is now owned by trees inside and outside the prison because they wanted to make roads. I want to tell you, especially, a story about a big tree near the fence. The company wanted to cut it, but the local people protested, and they said, 'We won't allow you to cut this tree because is a tree for love.' They had this story, that many years ago a fisherman was on the ocean near that tree and suddenly a beautiful woman like an angel came down from the tree and called him to come to her. The fisherman felt scared and went away. The next day, the fisherman came and the angel came down again and he went to her and found a lot of fish there. The angel went with that man to his village and they were married. The people in that village believed that this tree, it's like a holy tree, and they didn't allow the company to cut it.

There are four prisons in Manus. I was about eighteen months in Foxtrot, about thirteen months in Delta and few months in Oscar and Mike. In Delta, there is one coconut tree, they forgot to cut it down, and a lot of other coconuts you can see from inside the prison. Once, I wrote a poem about the coconuts and I described them as my lovers. Every morning when I wake up I start my day by smoking, and always I go near the fences and I sit there and every day I say, 'Hello beautiful, my lovers.' I always say that the coconuts are my lovers.

Sometimes some animals came to our prison, like snakes, or crabs. Sometimes some migrant birds were flying and they were very beautiful because we could see them from inside prison and they were flying from far away.

I think this is my experience, after three years in this prison: that life is beautiful even inside a hell prison.

Spanish infrastructure company Ferrovial. When Ferrovial bought Broadspectrum in May 2016, it announced it would not tender to continue running the detention centres; however, the Australian government exercised its option to extend the contract to October 2017.

Some of my secrets

A girlfriend? You know I don't like to talk about . . . [*Laughs.*] Love, ah, love can make some beauty and it's too hard to live without any love. I think that love can be the base of life and I think, yes . . . too hard question, really. I love love [*laughing*].

Any prisoner in prison has free time to think—to think about everything, especially about love and life, meaning and deep meaning. Everything. I think a lot about my relationships with people, especially that I had with women. In a deep way, I could find my mistakes and my wrongs, and how I could be a good lover and how we can protect our relationships.

Imagine a house. Love is like a garden for that house. I think that love can make life like a celebration. Only love can do that. One of my friends, he is a journalist working in Australia. He wanted to write a story about love relationships between refugees in Manus and Australian women. He made contact with me. He also made an interview with a psychologist about prison and love. That psychologist explained to him that it's not good for a prisoner to be in a love relationship with a woman outside prison. I really don't believe that psychologist, because I think any prisoner needs to have love and has the right to have a lover. To sometimes write or talk with his lover.

Some people in the prison, they have lovers, and they can endure this suffering with love. Love can also destroy everything, but it's how you understand love, and it's not important whether you are a prisoner or a free man. I want to say that any prisoner has this right, to have a lover. Because love can bring some beauty to the hell prison.

I have a big problem with keeping numbers in my memory. After they put us in Lorengau gaol and transferred us to Charlie compound, after a few days they brought us a phone and said,

'You can call your family.' I forgot my family's number. I just remembered a number and that number was for my lover, my girlfriend. At that time I hadn't talked with her for a long time, for about five or six years. I said, 'Okay, give the phone to me.' And I talked to her [*laughing*] . . . Yeah, it was wonderful. She said, 'Oh, it's incredible that you called me!' And we talked to each other for about ten minutes. But I didn't tell her that if I had my family's number I would not have called her. We talked to each other and I told her that I was in prison now and I was talking to her from prison. We talked about some wrong things in our relationship and I told her, 'Please forgive me for some of my wrongs.' Yeah, I just remember that. She was happy and she said, 'Yes, I made mistakes too,' and that was last time we talked to each other.

No, it's too hard a question really, in prison especially, about love . . . Oh, you are so dangerous, you are revealing some of my secrets! I cannot censor myself. Don't ask me questions like this [*laughing*]. Yeah, I have some love letters. When I was writing those poems, yes, I can imagine someone, I just . . . describe prison and some of my days and describe nature. And I send them to someone. I have some replies and I keep the replies, just for thinking. I just wanted some replies from women.

Even in prison, every day my heart beats some new thing. Ten years ago, I thought about love so differently. I think that we can never be perfect in love. I think love is scary sometimes. Love is like Manus nature, because when you are walking in the jungle you feel scared, and the same time you also feel enjoyment. It's like that.

You know probably some women after this interview will want to kill me. [*Laughs.*] A woman, if she says 'I love you,' I say 'Yeah, okay, you love me.' I believe in freedom in love. I don't have a right to say to people, 'Don't love me.' Anybody can love me. [*Laughs.*] Next question.

We have something for the world

Death. During my life I have been close to death three times. The first time was when I was a teenager. I was climbing a mountain in Kurdistan and I fell down. But I was so young that I didn't find any special meaning in that. It didn't affect me.

The second time, was when I suddenly found myself under the dark ocean and I was swimming. I found the incredible feeling at that time because I was enjoying swimming, just for a moment, just for a second. After that a big wave fell down on me and I thought, *Yeah, I am going to die.* I was close to death. And I found it beautiful. Yeah, I can say that was beauty. But now, when I think about it, I feel scared.

On the hunger strike I felt death again, because my body became weak.

I only know that the death is a part of life. Probably a lot of people don't accept this, but I am talking to you about my experience because I was close to death three times. I don't claim that I understand the meaning of life and death and love. But I claim that I understand something for myself: I can find some beauty. And I don't believe in any religion or god, or even something like god. I don't believe in that. I must believe in nature.

You know, prison can have a big effect on anybody. The people in Manus prison, they have learned a lot about life because of such pressure on them and because of much suffering. If they survive, they have something for the world. You can write a book about anybody in Manus prison.

The Manus prison has affected me... I must live in the moment and enjoy life only in the moment and not think much about the future because we don't know anything about the future. The prisoner, most of the time, he thinks about the present or the past, but the future—it's too hard. You can always enjoy the rain.

When we think about the future, we lose the rain. It's best that we enjoy the rain now.

Sometimes I have a dream—I have had this dream for a long time, from when I was a child. It's like something sacred because this dream is only for myself. In my dream, always I am climbing a hard mountain and I feel scared. But I am climbing. It's a very hard mountain. And sometimes I find some rivers . . . so clear that you can see everything in the river. I am on the mountain, I feel fear, and I am trying to climb.

On Manus, I have more nightmares. In the first months, when I was on Manus, one of my big nightmares was that I was in Iran. When I woke up, I felt comforted to know I was not in Iran, I was on Manus . . . And I heard from some other people that they had this nightmare too. They told me, 'Oh, last night my nightmare was that I found myself in Iran and when I woke up I found that I was in prison. And I become happy.'

I had another nightmare several times: I was in a place where builders were working. I said hello to the workers and I asked them . . . 'Which way should I go, that I can go outside of this place?' And they told me, and I went that way, and I found another building, and a lot of workers there. And I asked them, 'Which way should I go?' and they said, 'That way.' And I went to there . . . and again I found some workers. 'Which way?' And I finally found that I never could go outside from this place. I am used to this nightmare. I can be strong.

PART I

When I become famous, I'll give Tony Abbott a job

Hani

Hani Abdile grew up in Somalia. She came to Australia by boat in 2013 and spent eleven months in Christmas Island Detention Centre. She is now in Australia on a bridging visa. Since being released from detention she has performed her poetry at the Sydney Opera House and been given an award for Civics and Citizenship by her state member of parliament.

They got a lot of crabs and chickens and refugees

We will never know the fire is really bad until we touch it. I never knew something terrible was happening in my land until it came, until the moment faced me. So yeah, I left home. I didn't want to leave home but home was happy for me to leave.

   I remember when I was on the sea, I was like, *God, please, only one time, just take me out of this water, just put me on land*. And then later, when I came out of the water, they put me in detention, I was like, *God, I promise, if you take me out of this detention I will never ask you anything*. And then I came out of the detention and I was like, *God, I went to community detention, if you take me out of this community detention, I will never ask you anything else.* Now I have a visa and I'm like, *God, if I get permanent residency I will never ask you anything*, and when I get permanent residency I will be like, *God, if you make me citizen, I will never ask you anything.*

I came to Australia in August 2013. I was on the boat for eight days.

When I got to Christmas Island, everything was different. The first thing I could see was crabs and chickens, 'cause they got a lot of crabs and chickens and refugees. My funniest thing was when my case manager told me, 'You are an asylum seeker,' and I was thinking it was somebody's name, and I said, 'No, I'm sorry, my name is Hani.'

I was thinking all the refugees were just coming from Africa. I knew Iraqi people were refugees but I never knew they were coming to Australia. That was my first shock when coming into detention. So at that moment I have to change my attitude. I have to be someone else because I lived in a country of one people, one culture, one religion. Walking into that camp, there were more than 800 people and everyone had their own religion, their own perspective—everything was different, like, totally different. I was speaking very little English but living in the camp was like language school for me. Everyone got something positive in there.

First, when we came from the airport they took us to this big tent where Serco* welcomed us really well. They took us to a big tent, and they gave us a phone so that we could call our

---

* Serco is a British company that operates public and private transport, schools, call centres and prisons, among other things. Since 2009 it has been contracted by the Australian government to run the detention centres on the mainland and Christmas Island.

families. I called my sister. My sister, she just thinks every day I'm on a new continent. 'Cause last time I called her I was in Asia, and then I call her and I was like, 'I'm in Australia.' She's like, 'Where is Australia?' I'm like, 'One day you will know, just relax.'

I told her that I was safe, and that I reached Australia, and everything was okay with me. But she couldn't believe it. She really couldn't believe that I was in Australia until I went for a medical in Darwin and I could call her on Skype so she could see me. It's something that she couldn't actually believe.

After the phone calls, Serco brought food. This was, like, the best moment on the first night. There was Goodie, from Serco. Goodie was the best human that I met on Christmas Island. On the first night, I remember, she couldn't find clothes for us. She went to the other centre, until she found five trousers and two T-shirts.

It was a very remarkable moment because all of us—the 45 people who were on the same boat—were together in that big tent. So we start singing, crazy stuff. And then one lady, Nadifa, a Somali mother, started dancing, and then we all started dancing. We ate food, it was so happy. The Serco officers, they brought speakers and music. So we could have just like lots of fun on the first night, and Goodie was there, we were dancing, actually it was just so good. Everyone was just shaking their heads and their bodies. Everyone was doing whatever they were capable of, because the night before we were on the boat, and we were just, you know, lying on the water. It's just like, a different world.

And then, when it was about ten o'clock, Serco came and they said, 'Okay, single males have to go, and then the females,' and anyone who was under eighteen, like me, they said would remain in the same camp. So they put us in a tent. We slept in the tent on military beds.

The next morning when I woke up I had different expectations. People kind of looked happy. It was a new place, new people, everything was good shit. It was kind of orientation week. We played a lot of volleyball in the first week. We played badminton, a lot of games.

I remember my first day the officer knocked, and so he was like, 'Yeah, you have to go and get breakfast.' There were oranges, apples, there was everything you really wanted. There were noodles. So you go there, and you eat.

Then I remember the first and second weeks, we used to clean the compound. Because you're really enthusiastic, you want to do something. So we'd wake up in the morning, we'd go for breakfast, and then we'd start cleaning the centre. Then we'd do activities like English classes, different activities. We'd do running, we'd do basketball sometimes, and we got another sewing activity. You'd be like, so enthusiastic—happy you're learning new things, you know?

I think two weeks later we did our medical checks, then after that they took us from Charlie to Bravo. We stayed at Bravo two days and then they took us to Aqua* which is like, maybe, 20 kilometres away. For example, from Parramatta to Lidcombe. So we stayed there for six weeks.

But this, here was the reality. You had, like, orientation week, you had the introduction to how things worked, but now you came to the real thing. This is where real life was starting. This is where you enter hell.

---

* Charlie and Bravo are compounds in the Phosphate Hill Processing Centre, which is used to house people when they first arrive on Christmas Island, usually for only one or two days. Aqua compound is located on the edge of the Christmas Island immigration detention centre, which is in a national park area about 17 kilometres from the island's town. Aqua is a series of demountable buildings containing bedrooms, bathrooms and a dining area.

They don't want you to be here, but they still give you food

They drove us to Aqua. The main immigration office is maybe ten minutes' drive from Aqua. So before they took us to the camp they took us to the immigration office. We were seated, everyone seated. So this lady came, she's got a miniskirt and a blue shirt, and she's got sunglasses. This lady looked really heartless. She looked as if she'd never smile even if you tickled her. [*Laughs.*]

Then she got a Somali interpreter, a Kurdish interpreter and a Tamil interpreter—she had all these interpreters beside her. The interpreters, it was like they were in front of God and they were being judged. They were all looking down. There were all these Serco officers—they don't smile, they look very angry, they drink a lot of protein to get the muscles. And this lady just started reading all these laws and she's like, 'You have to remember you guys will never be settled in Australia. You have to contact your embassies, and let us know if you wanna go back to your home country. We're gonna send you guys to Manus Island and Nauru. There will not be processing in Christmas Island.'

She was talking for almost one hour. She was just speaking like a radio. It's like you turn it on, and you can never turn it off. You'd think that before she walked into the room she took out her heart and put it in a locker. Because she never smiled. She was like, 'Listen, you will never settle in Australia. Why did you come to this country? We don't need people. If you want to come, go back and come by plane.' And she was saying all these horrible things and everyone was crying. It was so bad—it was really, really heartbreaking.

Then they took us to Aqua. There were almost two thousand people. The rooms were full. There were double-decker beds.

Underneath was a woman, and on top there was a man sleeping. But it was better than the camps in Africa, like Dadaab, because those people don't have anything to eat. At least here, they don't want you to be here, but they still give you food.

There was this big hall where everyone was sleeping, boys and girls. Then slowly, slowly, they started doing age interviews. If you passed the interview you went to another camp. If you were a female but under-age you went to another camp with families that have kids. Most of the time, they changed your name into a number—they called you ABC1, ABC2. By the time I finished eleven months, even if you call me Hani all the day, I would never say yes. If you called my boat number, I would say yes. Or they would call you Detainee, like that is your name.

So we finished our time in Aqua then we moved to Camp CC.* So this camp totally became my home.

I met amazing officers

At CC I met amazing officers who worked there. They were really positive people. They were really good people who were ready to share your pain, who were ready to give you positive energy, who would say, 'It doesn't matter, one day you will be out of here.' Even though their job is to be grumpy, they have a heart. They are still in my life, and these are people I can call for advice. They listened. When you are sad and you find someone who listens, that means the world. When I went to activities, all I got was positive energy. Like, if I went to English classes, the people who taught me were all good.

---

* Construction Camp is a low security detention facility, which was formerly accommodation for construction workers. It was used primarily to detain families and unaccompanied minors. It is across the road from the Phosphate Hill facility.

I used to sleep all the day, and they used to be like, 'Why are you sleeping? You better learn English, that's much better!'

The effect of detention is not only on the people who are detained but also on the people that work there. I used to feel sad for the people that worked there. Most of them are young, like they are 20, 21, 23. They are people who finished school and they wanted to go to Bali and Immigration said, 'We gonna give you this money,' and they would be like, 'Fine, I'm gonna get this money and I'm going to go to Bali'—but before they get to Bali they are going to get mental illness! [*Laughs.*]

I will keep my CC clean

CC is my home, all I have known, where I started my life. CC was good, good officers, good accommodation. Good food, good everything. Only it was stressful sometimes. I started learning English. We used to have English classes. We used to go two weeks on, two weeks off. It was across the road. The first teacher was called Miss Barbara. She was also a music teacher. She used to be a really hopeful teacher. She used to have all these people coming to school, but nobody actually wanted to learn, because everyone was stressed. So instead of teaching English she used to teach music.

CC has some facilities, it has TV. There's a lot of plastic there. Heaps of plastic. I mean most of the things there are made up of plastic. There's no garden. The garden you can see is only the oval, which is outside the centre. And then they got a basketball court. Behind the basketball court is the fence, and then there's the forest.

We used to do cleaning. I love cleaning. In the night-time, I would be awake all night cleaning the compound. I just thought, *I wanna keep my Australia clean.* I used to watch these videos called *Keep Australia Beautiful,* and I used to think it's a good thing to watch while you're on Christmas Island. It's pretty much these people who volunteer to clean the cities—I think Queensland, Gold Coast and somewhere else. And I loved it, I loved the program and I just thought, 'I will keep my CC clean.'

I used to clean the whole compound, and then one of the bosses used to give me phone cards so I could call my family. I used to take the hose, and wash the pathways, clean my room. That's all I could do, you know, that's all I could do.

Same shit but different smells

My room had a beautiful painting. It was a tree, and then it had this big flower in the middle. I used to have a lot of poems on the wall. I used to have a lot of encouraging quotes on the wall. I got a lot of books.

One day I went to my case manager and she said, 'Listen, if you feel tired of staying in this place, we can send you home. We can do that for you . . . or otherwise wait and we're going to send you to Nauru . . . But you have to remember, there is no processing here.'

So I went to my room and wrote a poem called 'Born in Endless War'. When I wrote that poem I posted it on my Facebook, and this lady wrote to me and said, 'Hey, are you a poet?' Then she started sending me exercises, like how to write. This woman is really important in my life, her name is Janet Galbraith. She started a writing group called Writing Through Fences, and she changed my life into poetry. If someone didn't tell me, 'Your writing is beautiful, keep writing,' I couldn't be where I am today. If I am sad I write a sad poem. If I am happy I write a happy one.

When I become famous, I'll give Tony Abbott a job. Me and him, like, he came by boat when he was young and I came by boat when I am young, so we have a common thing. I used to write to him because I wanted him to know that I was here, still waiting for freedom. I kept sending him letters to tell him, 'Prime Minister, I'm still here waiting,' you know? And explaining to him why I came to this country and what I want to do. Just telling him my plans, pretty much.

He didn't ever write back. But one day, his office wrote back and said, 'You will never settle in Australia,' and it was so bad.

Each day has the same shit but different smells. It's boring because there's only four walls and it's like, what can you do? Like, if you go to that wall, or that wall, or that wall. There's nothing else. But again, it depends on you. You can be like, *Fine, this is the situation. I have to stay here.* If you're being sad, then your life will be pretty much fucked up and you'll end up eating antidepressants. But if you just look at it and you think, *Okay, fine. I have to deal with this*, you can do it. It's a matter of telling yourself, *I can do it. It doesn't matter how hard it is.*

Sometimes if you have a dream that you're focusing on, something that you really want to do, that helps. And I guess if you have some people left behind that really need you, it also helps. Because you always think of those people, and you will work hard . . . If not you end up depressed, or end up in mental hospital. And you'll be like, *If I end up in mental hospital, who will help these people that I left behind?*

We had rice and chicken every day. It's called SERCO: Service of Rice and Chicken Only. The officers said they get really cheap rice in Malaysia. I don't know where they get the chicken.

It was good. People just think life is really okay if you're getting somewhere to sleep and food to eat. But if you are free and you've got nothing to eat, that is more appreciate-able. The air is the food when you're free, you can walk from place to place and you're getting this air.

I knew every corner

My psychologist Christine was a beacon of hope in the sea. She would take us outside the camp. Show us around, try to buy fruit for us so we can eat near the ocean. She would do everything to help us forget these awful thoughts. But you know what, our sadness was just like a coat. Like, you're wearing this coat, and you take it off when you're going out of the camp, and when you come inside the camp, you have a coat of sadness. She tried her best.

There's this bird called the Christmas frigatebird, they are only found at Christmas Island. She would stop the car, and let us watch the frigatebirds drinking the water. They would go up, up, up near the sky, and then again dive, and then go to the water and drink like that. And we would be like, 'We wanna stay here for half an hour.' She had other clients but she would be like, 'Okay, fine. I will do it for you guys.' We would stay there, watching the birds. She made tea for us. We drink the tea, we relax.

I remember once there was a lot of rain, and then all these red crabs came out, kind of big crabs. You can't run over them, it's like a crime in Christmas Island. And then Christine told me, 'Get out of the car and please move the crabs,' so I took this stick because I've experienced, back home, getting goats out of the way. They didn't move until you hit them.

She cooked for us. Pasta and banana. Banana is a kind of famous Somali thing that we eat with everything—spaghetti, rice. It was so fun. After eight months it was the first time that we ate actual cooked food, sitting in a living room, living like a normal person again. Just hanging out with normal people. I liked it. But it was so hard: I couldn't touch the knife 'cause I was afraid of the knife. Every time I got panic attacks, I just thought a Serco officer was looking at me. I was hearing some voices. Like sometimes even now, when I'm at home by myself and I'm cooking, I hear some voices. Like, an officer talking to me, telling me, 'You're not allowed to do that.' And I will look around and just see I'm at home, in my house.

By the time I was out of Christmas Island I knew Christmas Island like the village I was born. I knew every corner, and I was in immigration detention! My psychologist used to drive us everywhere on Christmas Island. There's this restaurant called the Gourmetaria or something like that, and I remember the first time we ate chips. She bought chips for us, and we were just facing the sea, and the rain came. In CC it rained, but the rain in CC is like acid. But the rain in that place was like, oh my god, I could feel the rain on my body. I could feel the water going inside my skin, you know? There was all this wind. You could smell it. It was just totally different.

My psychologist tried her best.

I felt like I was a journalist

I always dreamed of becoming a journalist. I remember when I was back home I used to take the water bottle and pretend I was reporting from Baghdad. I would be like, 'Hani Abdile, CNN, Baghdad.' In CC, they couldn't let me go outside to do journalism but what I thought is, *Okay, fine, in immigration you are my parents*. I left my real parents in Somalia but I don't know when I am going to see them. So I put in a request. I said, 'I wanna write a newsletter which will be only about this centre.'

My newsletter was called *CC Weekly*. CC was the camp that I used to live in, and I only got to release the newsletter on Fridays. And that's how *CC Weekly* started. I took the idea to the Serco program manager, and I told him about what I wanted, and he said, 'Go ahead.' But I needed extra internet.

I needed a lot of things, I needed a printer. So I told my case manager. At that time I had really cool case manager. I think she was aged between 24, 26. She said, 'You know what, I can't give you a hundred per cent permission to use more internet hours, because we have to be fair with everyone else in the centre. But if the officers in the internet let you use it, then go ahead, I won't say no.'

Then, guess who was the internet officer? Tim Hay. Tim Hay was like this cool, cool officer. He used to wear a cowboy hat. He was the second person that I interviewed for *CC Weekly*. Tim, he had an interesting personality. He was just carefree, he was just like, 'This is not my property. You need internet, use it. The computers are here to be used, not to be watched.' Simple. So I used it. Georgia was there, she was the night manager. Georgia is the best human ever. She lives in Newcastle now and I met with her there. It was so good, going and hanging out with Georgia. We went for food in Newcastle, we went to a music festival and it was so good to see her with no Serco clothes. Looked much better.

I used to put in my newsletter: how many people were sent to Nauru, how delicious the food is, who has a headache. I used to research English courses online and if I found one I put it in the newsletter. I did research. I used to listen to the news a lot, so that I could try to capture whatever the government is actually doing.

It just screws your head. You read something, then you finish and you write something, you put a script together, and you say, *This will be good for Friday.* You put all your time in research, and you have one hour internet everyday, and you get really good information, and you write it down. And the next morning the policies change, and you have to change the article. And you just feel like, *Why are they doing this?* It was too confusing. It was like Melbourne weather.

I also used to get a lot of encouragement quotes from the internet. I used to interview the officers, and ask their hobbies, what do they like to do. And I used to have 'Refugee of the Week'. People were keen to be interviewed by me, which helped give me courage to do it again and again. *CC Weekly* lasted for six weeks. I did it for six Fridays and it used to be very interesting. I felt like I was a journalist.

Remember the day they introduced the policy that they were gonna take people to Cambodia?* That's the day *CC Weekly* stopped. I just thought, *Cambodia, it has a history of war. They got a lot of poverty.* So, what I thought was, *These people, already, they're suffering because of poverty, and they wanna take asylum seekers there?* When you take asylum seekers to Cambodia, you have to give them a better life. And of course Australia will give these people a better life because they gonna give them certain income until they find jobs. Of course the people in Cambodia will get angry. So that's what I wrote about.

So, they just thought that was no good. Because they didn't wanna hear the truth. And I think the truth is small, you know, bitter. Nobody ever wants to hear the truth. At the end, the Serco manager, the big big boss, she said it was propaganda.

Nauru and Manus Island became my nightmare

One caseworker always said, 'Go home, 'cause people in Australia, they don't want you,' and all these things. It was kind of like, breaking your hopes, you know? I stayed there

---

* In September 2014, Australia and Cambodia signed an agreement for the voluntary relocation of refugees from Nauru to Cambodia. As part of the deal, Australia agreed to pay an additional $40 million in development assistance, plus up to $15 million for logistical costs. At the time of publication, six people had accepted resettlement in Cambodia, four of whom had since returned to their home countries.

for eleven months. I was trying to be patient. I was waiting for the day I would be out of this place. But I would never be out, and Nauru and Manus Island became my nightmare.

So, I'd met my mental health nurse and she'd tell me, 'If you're tired, maybe you can go back to your home country.'

And I had this feeling like, *My life is totally over now, I don't know what I'm doing.* All I could feel is that I wanna kill myself, that's all I feel like. I don't wanna do this thing but it keeps telling me to do. I wanna do it. But I don't wanna do it. But I wanna do it.

My room turned into my grave. I could see my bed and I could see someone putting soil on top of it.

Later on, my friend Bahar—she's an Iranian girl—she came, shouting, 'Taifa, she's so upset, she went to her room!' I ran to the room, because she's my friend, but by the time I entered the room, everywhere was like, blood. She was trying to kill herself. So I started calling the officers. I was feeling like, *Oh my god, what is going on in my life?*

Me and her, we were two people who always talked to each other, whenever . . . When I saw her sad, I gave her hope and she became better. When she saw me sad, she gave me hope . . . For us, our home is somewhere we can't be returned to. We used to think, 'We are young girls. We need a better future.'

The officers came. They kept her on constant watch, so an officer was watching her 24 hours. It doesn't matter if the officer is male or female.

It just was like, 'Oh my god, what's happening? Why this is happening to me?' I went and sat near the basketball court, watching the moon and I'm like, *Moon, you are there for me I know.* Just only one night my life changed.

I tried to kill myself but I couldn't. Because it was something that I couldn't do. Part of me wanted to leave the world and part of me still wanted to stay. I started praying, and I said,

Oh god, did I come to this country just to end myself with my hands? I tried actually, I tried to harm myself, I tried to kill myself. And then I saw the officer—she came to my room, and she could see what I was doing. She saw papers, 'cause I wrote a letter to my family. And I wrote a letter to Immigration. I wrote a letter to Serco. And when she read the letter she recognised I wanted to do something, and she called, 'Code black'. When someone wanna kill themselves they call 'Code black'. They took me to the medical centre and the nurse checked on me. Then they put me on constant watch.

It's like you're running from elephants, but you're running into a lion. The mental health officers, they are not helping. Immigration, they are not helping. But Serco, they were the only ones there for me. Always the people who worked in the centre, in CC, they were the people who made me feel like, 'It doesn't matter, we are here to help you.'

A week later, I was feeling much better. I felt like I was normal again, because I felt like I was really guilty. I broke the rules. First of all, I did something against my religion. Because my religion doesn't let me kill myself, it's a big sin. I broke the confidence toward my friends. I felt like now I didn't have any support.

One night before I sleep, I wrote this poem:

> Day and night will pass
> An ocean of stills
> An ocean of fears
> An ocean of sadness surrounds me
> My room turns into my grave
> Only my pillow knows what happens
>   after I lie down
> Into thought
> A silent tear will roll
> Until tiredness locks me out of the room.

I was just writing all this and then I took the poem, I cut it out of the book, folded it, put under my pillow and slept. I slept, like, a really deep sleep. I had all these dreams. And then around nine o'clock, someone was knocking at my room. It was an officer, and I opened the door and I was like, 'What, officer?' She was like, 'Immigration.' I was like, 'Tell them, "Fuck you, I'm not going!"' She's like, 'No, you have to go to Immigration right now. Go!' She was one of those officers where I felt like they were so kind to me, they were always there to support me. And so I was like, 'Okay, I'm coming.'

And then I went to the office, I sat, and I told my case manager, 'If you tell me bad news today you will see fire.' And poor guy, he was a new case manager. And he was like, 'Hi, my name is . . .' whatever—I don't even remember his name and I don't wanna remember. He's like, 'My name's whatever and I'm your case manager,' and I'm like, 'I don't care. So what is the thing?' And he's like, 'Today I'm gonna send you . . .' and I was like, 'Where are you gonna send me?' and he's like, 'But before I tell you, your two friends have to come.' He meant Taifa and Amina, my friends.

I could feel it, this was something different. Everyone was smiling. The officers, their faces were full of happiness. They were like normal, you know? It was just something different! I could look at the officer and see in their eyes, it was written, 'Good luck, Hani!'

Then my friends, they came, and he was like, 'Okay, I'm gonna tell you. You guys are being transferred to medical in Darwin.' I saw these pink bags, so I knew they were sending me to the mainland. Because if they're sending you to Manus Island or Nauru they give you blue bags. So I was happy. It was only fifteen minutes before the plane took off! So I went back to my room, and packed my stuff.

I think Christmas Island was my first home. It doesn't

matter when, but one day I will go and stay there. I want to go back and spend time in CC. And just go and see it, because it's my home actually, that's where I started my life. I think that's where most of my tears dropped, you know what I mean? I think the island is beautiful but people make it look bad.

You see the people who used to torture you

When I got out of detention I was so afraid to cross the road, 'cause we'd been told that if you cross the road wrongly you go back to detention. Every time I would be like, 'Officer, I want someone to go with me.' I couldn't use the metal things in my house, because every time I wanna use them I was thinking, *Maybe Serco is looking at me.*

When I came to Sydney I realised freedom is not walking free. It means to be free mentally and physically. My brain was still locked until three months later, then I realised, *Oh my god, now you are outside*. I made friends, and it was better. Community detention is like normal living, you can go and buy what you want. There's a shop and the carers would go shopping and you can go and choose whatever you want to eat. We had a car in case of needing the hospital or emergency services. It was good, it was just amazing.

We were six girls in the house. We had lovely carers. I really loved them. Leaving community detention was hard, because I was dependent on people. I kept forgetting my shopping, I couldn't do anything by myself. I wasn't cooking, 'cause I had got used to coming home and the food was ready. Now I have become more independent and I live with very good housemates. They are really good people.

When I was on holiday in Melbourne we had an event where I was performing poetry and there were people from Manus Island, Papua New Guinea, who performed, and they said, 'Papua New Guinea is a good country. And we don't like to detain people.' They said, 'You guys hate us because you have a bad experience with us,' but they said it's not like that. Maybe every government, it doesn't matter where they are, they always create hatred in the world.

When I went to Melbourne I went to see Goodie, the first Serco officer that welcomed us when I first came to Christmas Island. It was different, seeing her—she's still got the same smile, she's still the same person.

There was also this lady that I met when I was in Christmas Island, and she was actually so bloody bad to me. After Sarah Hanson-Young[*] came to Christmas Island to tell us, 'Just don't worry. One day you will be out of here,' she came afterwards and she was like, 'No, that was just lying and you guys will never settle here,' and she made me really cry. I was so sad about it. Then later, one day I was walking in Central Station in Sydney and then I bumped into her and I was like, 'Oh, I'm so sorry!' and then I looked up and I saw the lady and she's like, 'Darling! You're here!' and I just said, 'Remember you said, "You will never settle in Australia?" but I'm here!' She wanted us to go for coffee, but I didn't want to. I was like, 'No.'

It was really kind of strange, seeing the person. You see the people who used to torture you somehow, and you just look back and you'll be like, 'It doesn't matter.'

I made good coffee

I did a barista course at TAFE, where my school was sponsoring us, and then after we finished the course TAFE suggested we should find a job so we could practise our coffee skills.

---

[*] Sarah Hanson-Young is a member of the Senate for the Australian Greens. She was the Greens' immigration spokesperson until mid-2016.

One of our teachers, a schoolteacher, he discovered Parliament on King in Newtown, which is a coffee shop that employs refugees, and he told the school counselling. I went to Parliament on King and the owner Ravi just said, 'Can you make me a coffee?' So I did a latte for him, and he liked it. But for the next few days, he used to throw my coffees away. I made coffee and he would put it in the sink. But he was good—he was testing my knowledge—and he kept doing it until I made a good coffee. Now I love making coffees, and spending time in the hospitality industry. 'Cause before I didn't think that I was confident enough to work in the hospitality industry. Everything is so busy. Working with Ravi actually makes me feel really confident.

I feel the people who I met in Parliament on King and the owner Ravi are people who believe in who I am, who respect that I am a human being, and that I must be treated well. I feel like it's my homeland, like my mother's place—I feel welcomed.

Ravi and I went sailing the other day. It was so fun. We went down to Botany Bay and Ravi was teaching me how to sail. It was good, 'cause I had this feeling that the first time I came out of a boat I was taken to a detention centre. But now it was a different feeling because when I came out of the boat I was going to my house.

The funny thing is, they didn't care

Benjamin

Benjamin was taken to Nauru in 2013, with his family. He told the first part of this story on Christmas Day 2014. He is still on Nauru.

You just have to cope with it

We were in OPC3* for a year and three weeks. In that time lots of things happened between us and Wilsons, the security guards running the camp, especially with my father because everyone trusted him. So if problems happened, people would tell my father and my father would try to help. But after a couple of months the Wilsons tried to somehow punish us as a family, you know, for just simple things. One day my father was in the line for food and the Wilson didn't let him go inside—he sent another family in rather than us. My father tried to just talk to them but suddenly they called

---

* Offshore Processing Centre compound number 3 is the family compound in the Nauru detention facility.

the police. Police came and they sent my father straight to custody.

My father had a stroke when he was in custody. He's a little better now, after four or five months, but he's still really not able to use the left side of his body very well.

Because of the stroke, they sent my father alone to Darwin. They gave us a time to visit just before he left. There was a neck brace around his neck and he was in a wheelchair. I could just see him for fifteen minutes and then they took him away and sent him to Darwin. I was eighteen at that time and my sisters were all minors. There wasn't a guardian for us, but they let us be inside a camp. My sisters, they all got lots of problems. They couldn't sleep at night. Me either.

I went to the psychologist and I told her, 'I've got these types of problems,' and she said, 'You just have to cope with it. You cannot go to where your father is. You just have to wait until he comes back.' I warned them that if they didn't give me any answer—at least tell me how my father is—I would suicide, and she laughed at me and said, 'Go, do what you want to do.' And so I cut my wrists and my hand, because I couldn't control it anymore. It was too much for me. And the funny thing is, they didn't care. They said, 'If you keep trying to do this we will send you to the custody too.'

My sisters came and they saw lots of blood coming out of my body and they called Wilson.

When my father heard that I cut myself, he did his own protest. He sat in the wheelchair and he didn't eat, he didn't move, he didn't drink anything.

I tried to tell them it was against the rules

After this, things happened to my father too. When he first went to Darwin he was in the family camp. He was a single male but he was in the family camp. I had a friend over there in the family camp who was looking after him. I was little bit okay because I knew my friend was helping, but after my father's protest they sent him to the single camp. In the single camp he was totally alone. There was nobody to help him. When I heard this I tried to talk to Immigration about it and tell them that this was not fair, what they're doing to my father, that my father needs someone to help him. But they didn't answer me, they just forgot about it.

After two months they sent my father back here, to Nauru. He was still the same. In that time they didn't do any medical checks for him. He was just wasting his time over there. My case manager came and said, 'Your father is back in Nauru.' I was so shocked and a little bit happy too because I thought that maybe he's okay. I went to OPC1* with my sisters to see him. I was sitting there with my sisters, talking with them, and suddenly one of the cultural advisors came—his name was Darryl—and he told me, 'Your father has to go back to the gaol.' I asked him, 'Why?' I tried to tell them it was against the rules—if someone is not medically well, you don't put them in custody—but they didn't care. I said, 'If you want to take my father you have to take me too because I need to look after him.'

My father was in custody for three days and they just let me be with him only for one night. After that we went to OPC1. We were there for months. They kept sending my father to court for what had happened, just for a simple argument. We just kept going to the court, every day, and at the end of it they found that my father was not guilty and they sent us back to OPC3.

For now I don't have any plan for my future because I am still feeling that I am captured. I'm still feeling that I'm not a

---

* Offshore Processing Centre compound number 1 comprises accommodation as well as a medical centre and immigration processing buildings.

human. I'm still thinking about what's happened in the past. I can't think about what I am now, and what I'll do in the future.

I just need to get my freedom first, then I'll try to find my way somehow.

Nearly two years later, in October 2016, Benjamin continued his story.

We have beautiful futures

I'm still here.

I came here when I was eighteen and now I'm nearly 22 years old. I wasted all of the best time in my entire life, the time that I was about to make my future happen, the time that I promised myself I would study hard and become the best. But I couldn't, because of the Australian government.

Five months ago, my neighbour, his name was Omid, he burnt himself right in front of my eyes. We have beautiful dreams, we have beautiful futures, but everything has been ruined. We are all exhausted.

That day, my neighbour Omid, he burned himself in front of me and I still cannot forget it. Omid was a good person. I still feel unhappy, I still feel stressed about him. I still punish myself, *Why didn't I make him stop?* But I didn't know that he was gonna do it, and he did it in front of me. He burned himself. I tried to go and put the fire out on his body, but I couldn't do it and he died. And I still punish myself because I think that if I was a bit smarter I could have saved him.

When the UNHCR people came to our settlement to talk to refugees, Omid and his wife were the first ones they met. I don't know what happened but I just saw that Omid and his wife went to their house and after like five to ten minutes Omid came back and he was soaked in petrol and he was shouting, 'I'm tired and we are all tired and I cannot take it anymore.'

He was actually complaining to the government of Australia, 'It's enough. Whatever we have suffered in all these years, it is enough, for we are innocent people. We're not terrorists. We are innocent people and we were just seeking freedom.'

And then he just turned the lighter on and set himself on fire. I ran to him and tried to put him out with blankets but I . . . he was still conscious when we took him to hospital. He was there, he was having so much pain. The hospital here is a very, very bad hospital. When this kind of incident happens, the Australian government asks for an ambulance aeroplane to come to Nauru immediately, but for Omid it took like twelve hours or more than that. He was suffering from the pain and no one could help him. The ambulance came late and he died. After he got back to Australia, the Australian government didn't even pay for the body to be transferred to Iran. Omid's family paid for that.

He burned himself to show it around the world, to big countries, that there is no hope, there is no happiness, there is no life here.

This is not a place that I can live

The payments that we receive from the Australian government are very low. We get just two hundred dollars each per fortnight from Connect Settlement Services,[*] which is not enough for all of us, you know. Living here is very expensive. The food and

---

[*] Connect Settlement Services was contracted to provide welfare support, and health, education and employment services for refugees and asylum seekers on Nauru. In September 2016, the company stated it would not tender for further contracts. Its contract ended in December 2016.

everything is all imported from Australia. You have to spend all your money just buying your food.

We are still having stress about water. When we were in the camp we were having problems with showering—we only had a right to shower for three minutes—and now we are outside we still have those problems. Just today they told us that there's a shortage of water so you have to be careful with it. We were protesting and they sent me to court for unlawful assembly, which I don't understand. I should have a right to make a peaceful protest so I can tell the world that this is not a place that I can live. We are desperately seeking other powerful countries to help us and release us from this inhuman policy. This is the most painful part of my story—when you realise no one cares.

I wanted to study. I put myself into danger coming to Australia. My main requirement was having freedom—freedom of speech, a society where people respect human rights. My plan was to study hard. I had finished my diploma of pure maths and physics, but I wanted to study more . . . maybe civil engineering or electrical engineering. But with all these punishments in these three years I became so lazy I cannot even read a book right now.

I always try to forget the bad incidents that happened to me before, so I just go to the gym. Try to lose some energy so I can relax. It's not a very good gym, but at least it is something. This is the best vocation you can have: going to the gym and coming back home.

I always try to be charming

My dad is much better . . . he is physically good now. But mentally he's worse than before. Most of the time he is at home and not doing anything, because there is nothing to do. He feels guilty because he is thinking, 'I have ruined my children's future.'

There is a very, very cold relationship in every family here. I mean, you get frustrated very quickly. You cannot talk fairly and make good decisions, because your mind has been punished a lot. Our life is like this, you know? We are unhappy so everything goes in a bad way. For example, I always try to keep my family motivated. I always say, like, 'I'm one hundred per cent sure that in 2017 we are gonna get out of this island.' I always say this. Every month I'll say that next month there will be good news from the Immigration department of Australia. I always try to motivate them, but they always say, 'No, it's an illusion.'

I'll try to do something, but it always turns out that I make it worse—because I have hope. They say, 'No, you lied to us.' My sisters always say, 'You lied to us last year. You told us that we were gonna go out of here in 2015, but we are still here and it's 2016.' These kinds of things . . .

We talk about Immigration, we talk about what's gonna happen, we read all the media. We try to make our own observations from there. It always turns out that we discuss it for two hours and we finish in a very unhappy mood. I have to say, we have those conversations every day. [*Laughs.*]

Sometimes time goes very quickly, but sometimes, it really kills you. Like when we reach the end of the year, because we expect something *magical*, like at Christmas . . . that Santa brings a gift. We wait to see if maybe Mr Peter Dutton* will announce something that we have wanted to hear for all these years. But it never happens. [*Laughs.*]

I usually don't show my pain or my frustration to my family. I try to keep it to myself. Whenever I go inside our

---

* Peter Dutton became the Minister for Immigration and Border Protection on 23 December 2014.

room, I always try to be charming. This is what I do, I always try to keep the energy up, because I don't like to upset them. I am upset, but I never show it.

If I want to be honest, the only thing that I enjoy is going to gym and coming back home. But my family doesn't enjoy that. My sisters want to go to a decent shopping mall, buy some good food, buy some good clothes. Or maybe they want to go to a cinema, or a zoo. But the only entertainment that we have here is just drinking alcohol. Forget what's happening and just get drunk for a night.

I have good friends here, even Nauruan friends. The Nauruans I hang out with, they really understand our situation and most of them have been studying in Fiji and Australia. They are qualified people and they respect humanity. When you hang out with them, you enjoy it, because they don't get insulted if you say something about the governments of Nauru or Australia. These two governments have created all these traumas. The people are innocent, you know?

The problem with my refugee friends is we can't really tolerate each other anymore. I mean, we live here without excitement. We see each other every day, talk about the same old things. We get tired of each other. I'm not saying this in a bad way, but this is a human being—you feel discouraged. Seriously, we don't have anything to say to each other anymore! We know everything, whatever happened from when he's born until now. It's like time has been stopped.

It will be like I'm reborn

My situation has changed. I've learnt how to be strong and keep myself motivated, so I'm not doing any self-harming and suicide. Sometimes the Australian government makes me worse. For example, when Peter Dutton says refugees are uneducated, or Scott Morrison* says we need to live here forever so Australia's borders are safe and sound. I just try to heal my pain so I don't get really out of control. I have learnt that even if I . . . did something crazy to myself, nothing will change. I just have to make myself healthy, so if I get out of here I could try to show the Australian government that I'm not a bad person, I'm actually a very useful person, and a very successful person. And I'm surely gonna do that.

I have read books about what successful people have done in their lives. For example, Mahatma Gandhi, Barack Obama, and also, Larry Page, founder of Google, and all of those people. So many people I cannot count them [*laughing*]. I've read their books, I've learnt from them—with all the struggles they had, they could still manage their lives and become successful.

I'm sure that one day I'm going to get out of here and reach my main goal, which is freedom. Yeah, I imagine I will enter a country where there are more opportunities, so I can improve myself, I can improve my education. I will start my new life—it will be like I'm reborn. It'll be a very big event. I'm sure it's going to happen and it will be soon. It will be very soon.

---

* Scott Morrison was the Minister for Immigration and Border Protection from 18 September 2013 to 23 December 2014.

I felt I had magical power

Donna

Donna Sherwani came to Australia as a child with her family by boat from Kurdistan. She was only thirteen when they arrived in Australia in 2000. Along with her family, Donna was detained first in Darwin and then at Port Hedland Detention Centre. She is trained as a lawyer and recently completed a masters of international relations at Melbourne University.

Everybody's story is different

Apart from the obvious need to survive, to get a better education and so on, everybody's story is different. We are Kurds from Iraq. There was a rumour that Saddam was going to use chemical gas again on the Kurdish people so a lot of people started fearing for their lives again. We took the rumour seriously and when the opportunity arrived we just used all the money we had—not that there was much—and my whole family and I went to Iran, then Malaysia, then Indonesia. I was twelve when we left Iraq, but I turned thirteen in Surabaya.

I am the oldest. When we left Iraq, there were only three of us siblings. My mother was pregnant with my little brother on the way and he was born when we got to Australia. The boat trip was seven days and seven nights.

We had misconceptions about where we were going and what we were heading towards. People were saying, 'Oh, if you go to Australia, you will be given sheep, a farm, and you have to raise cows and do farming,' and things like that. I remember my parents saying on the boat, 'Oh, doesn't matter, as long as we are safe and we can feed our families, because we are running away from terror.' That's what I remember them saying. My sister and I were really sad—we were saying, 'We don't want to go to farms. If we're running away, we want to go to places where there are buildings and it's clean and there are streets.'

Not a lot of children were aware of what was going on, but I was always aware. I was aware of all the political stuff—of our standing, of the fact that we were Kurdish, that we left Iraq and that we were approaching Australia.

A clinic

We eventually ended up on these shores. It was November 2000. First, we were intercepted by the Australian navy around Darwin. As soon as we got into Darwin, we were taken to a detention centre where we spent a couple of days. They cleaned us, injected us with all kinds of things. I remember a woman saying, 'Oh, this is for measles or malaria, anti-this or anti-that.' Nobody knew anything. It was just like, 'Okay, next.' We were almost stamped.

I became accustomed to being herded into halls with a lot of people. In Darwin, there was a lot of argy-bargy going on. At some point we were put into a huge hall, like a basketball court, where we were all lined up and we were all crying and they were asking us questions. That huge hall was the scariest thing, I think we slept there overnight and the next day we had to register our names on forms and things like that. My father was speaking in Arabic and he got everybody's birthdays and things wrong. Not mine though. Everyone was so nervous because of the pressure and trauma.

The detention centre in Darwin was much cleaner in comparison to Port Hedland detention centre. It was much whiter and smaller. It was like a clinic, to be honest. There was a sand patch where I remember playing volleyball with some of the men. We were there for a couple of days. It wasn't a long time.

I didn't feel like we were being detained. I thought of it like a welcoming thing—they were helping us out and we were up for better days. I had absolutely no idea we were going to go to another detention centre. In fact we were very confused. I'm not sure if my parents knew, to be honest.

We came to this ugly place

I was very happy every time we were told we were going to another place. I got hyped up, even if the next place was worse than the last. I was just happy to move places—it felt like progress. They took us on a plane. I thought, *We are being treated well, otherwise they would have just sent us by another boat somewhere or something like that.* So I thought it was a good sign. I sat by the window looking at green fields and just feeling very excited, not knowing where the hell I was going to.

I only realised things when we got on a bus and my eyes met the hot, sandy plains in Western Australia. That's what I remember. In my mind I was thinking, *What is this country Australia?* Because it was like the 1960s or 1970s, not that I had lived in that time. Some of the buildings were worse than in Iraq. I was like, *What is going on? This is an ugly place! We came here?* I felt like, we risked our lives, my mum and sister nearly drowned, we left everything behind and wasted all this energy and money and we came to this ugly place? I realised on the bus we were going to a detention centre. That's all I saw: country towns and detention centres and steel bars and halls.

I was looking through the window and crying inside. I will never ever forget that moment. I saw barbed wires and the walls of the detention centre. It was very hot.

A really, really handsome Australian actor

There was a small TV in the corner of our room at Port Hedland detention centre. There were no chairs or anything so I would look up at this TV in the corner near the ceiling. Every time this show started up, I'd stand there for 30 minutes, just watching like that.

There was a really, really handsome Australian actor. He was with this girl, his girlfriend. She had dreads and was always riding her bike and I was like, *Wow!*

I dreamt about him, fantasised about him.

The girl was wearing shorts, and I used to say to myself, *Whenever I get out I'm going to wear shorts for the first time in my life*. And then I used to be like, *I'm going to have a blond boyfriend too. I don't care if my mum doesn't allow it, I'm going to have a blond boyfriend*. I imagine writing to him today as a joke, 'By the way, when I was in detention centre, I used to have a crush on you!' The only problem is I still cannot find the name of the TV series.

I would also dream of the streets. When I was a child, I always wanted a bike and then I saw her riding her bike on these Australian streets. I was like, *Whoa, could this be*

Australia? I knew what Australia looked like on the map but that was the first time I saw Australia in my entire life—through the TV screen.

You can feel like you're enemies

People were very, very mean. Everybody was doing things for themselves. It was like an every-man-for-himself kind of thing.

Like, if you said hello to a girl and her mother saw that, she would spank that child and say, 'Don't say hello to so-and-so's daughter again, I told you not to say hello to anybody.' Things like that make you heartbroken. You would decide to just be quiet and not speak to anyone. Then sometimes random people would speak to you. It was confusing. Once I had a conversation with two Sri Lankan guys who were strangers. They were in the playground and were very nice and we talked about where we were from. I spoke a little English since I had a phrasebook that I was using on the boat. That was the only time I managed to have a conversation with people at the detention centre, but I kept thinking, *Shouldn't we unite, since we survived?*

In that situation, especially if, culturally, you are not used to speaking to one another about your feelings, it is very difficult. Everybody just keeps things to themselves. There is no exception, man to wife, or woman to woman, no. In fact, because of that silence, you can feel like you're enemies with everyone, even your family. That's not to say that families won't protect one another, but you have some sort of thorns between you.

It was as if everyone blamed the other people in the detention centre for their problems. Like they were thinking, *I fled my country but why are you here too? Why are you taking my place?*

There was almost like a competition about who had been there the longest. At that time, our family was the most recent. My mum would ask questions about how long people had been in detention. People would tell us and my mum would ask, 'Are you sure? I mean, if you've been here for three and a half years, then we should just give up looking forward to getting out.' I remember thinking that this was worse than having been through war.

People were also kind of jealous of other people who had their family with them. It's like they felt self-righteous. They all hated our family for some reason. They were like, *You sit down, don't even have any hope,* like that. I was like, *What is this? Three more years in this shit? With a TV that small?*

There was a rawness from the things we were all fleeing. When you've had war, when you've had people against people, and then you end up in the same gaol, there are cultural clashes between people. It is almost absurd. Imagine people of different walks of life—different religious, political and cultural backgrounds—face to face with each other, not knowing what to say, what to do. The silence is sometimes unbearable. Supposedly we're all fleeing for our lives but still Kurdish people would think, *Why are the Arabs or the Iranians fleeing?* And the Arabs would think, *Why are these people fleeing?* And so on and so forth. This is the internal war that you have to grapple with.

I would feel the limits around me

I realised that Port Hedland Detention Centre wasn't small—it was like a freakin' community, and it was even scarier.

We all called it gaol. I would fall asleep, and wake up the next day, so hopeless and even more helpless. I almost missed the streets of Kurdistan, running around the rubble. I even missed the ugliness. As soon as I'd exit the main hall or the dormitory I would feel the limits around me. I could see the walls, barbed wire. I knew I couldn't get out of there. But I still dreamt of freedom.

One time there was a woman who was helping people. I thought, *Oh wow, this person is an angel.* I remember chasing a man and asking him questions so that I could communicate with that lady. I thought, in my mind, that I could get my family out by speaking to her. I remember waiting for this man to come back to me, to see if she was available to speak with me, just a thirteen-year-old girl. I wanted to surprise my family and say, 'Guess what! We're going out because of me!' It was my dream then.

I would think, *Oh Donna, you dreamed of going abroad*, and here I was abroad but in gaol. I used to remember my cousin who told me be careful what you wish for. I actually thought that the reason we made it to Australia was because of me. I always felt I had some sort of intuitive magical power—that if I wanted anything the universe would grant me it. So when I was in the detention centre I blamed it on myself. I thought, *I made the wrong wish and now everybody is going to suffer because of me.*

Everything just broke down in my heart. I couldn't point to one thing and say, 'My heart is broken because of this.' I wasn't sure why we were detained. I don't think other people understood either, to be honest. We thought that Australia would accept us because we were fleeing. To get through this time, I would rely on my imagination. I always used to make stories up in my mind, like, that a hero was coming to save me. If I could imagine that someone was coming to save me, I always had hope.

'Jingle Bells'

They had long tables in the dining area and we all lined up to go in. Then on a cold white table, they put the food in front of us. During the dinner times, oh my god, I hated my mum because we always had to give her our fruit. I missed fruit so much. Mum was pregnant and she craved citrus—lemons and oranges. Every time we had any oranges my father would take all our fruit off our plates because he couldn't get anything extra for mum.

One time, somebody asked for more food. I remember it vividly. There was almost a war inside that place. So that night they didn't give us any food. Because mum was pregnant, my father begged someone for food for my mum and he got some. Us children were all looking at my mum, thinking, *She gets food but what about us?*

I think we had classes every day for a couple of hours. It wasn't compulsory but I remember my mum telling us, 'Go to the classes and learn the ABC!' My mum is obsessed with education; she's always like, 'Oh, everybody must learn. All of you must become number one.' And she didn't care what we studied, she just said study, study, study. So we three, my siblings and I, would go. But there weren't a lot of kids there because some other people's kids wouldn't go. Adults came as well, we were all in the same class.

My English teachers taught us 'Jingle Bells'. It was in November, so it must have been because Christmas was coming on. At the time, I didn't know what a Christmas carol was. We were learning dialogues back in Iraq, like 'Hello Mr Brown, how do you do?' Things like that. But at the detention centre I don't remember learning about such things. Now, when I hear 'Jingle Bells' every Christmas I feel ambivalent about it.

The thing is, my siblings don't remember anything from detention. My sister doesn't remember anything at all. I'm like, 'How can you not remember this?' She goes, 'I honestly cannot.' She says she wishes she could remember. But I remember a lot of things vividly that I can't even describe.

Three weeks

We were in Port Hedland for nearly three weeks, but the thing is, we're not sure how or why we were let out. It didn't make sense. One afternoon someone came into the room and they were like, 'Sherwani family, everybody out. You're leaving.' Was it because of us children, or because my mother was pregnant? Was it because my father was nice to somebody? It was a weird happiness. I felt scared at the same time. I was like, *What if we go somewhere else?*

When they said you're going out, I kept thinking, *That's so unfair!* I remember it almost like in a movie, when the actor has a thought and bubbles go up into the air. I was like, *But so-and-so's family has been here for three and a half years. It doesn't make sense. Why are we going out after three weeks?*

When I left I was crying on the bus. I left with a heavy heart, especially for the people who had to stay in detention. I was very confused, but nevertheless I was very happy. It was the first happiest day of my life. From those nearly thirteen years of my life I don't have any other happy memories like that.

We never ever talk about such matters

We were taken by bus to Perth. I remember there was aircon on the bus. We just knew that we were leaving and we had absolutely no idea where we were going next. A couple of hours later we ended up somewhere else and met a woman from a church organisation. She took us to a house in Midland. It was a massive, very old house.

The church brought us food: bread, cereal, spices, different kinds of meat, and all that. My mother cooked a lot of things. It was as if we had never eaten. I put jam on everything. I even put jam on meat! I like the sweets. Chocolate, oh my god! We just ate and ate and ate, all of us. We wondered, *Why is Australia so kind to us all of a sudden?*

We always talk about that time. We're like, 'Do you remember when we put on so much weight because in one week we ate everything?' But we as a family never sat down to talk about detention, until recently. My parents still don't talk about it. We never ever talk about such matters.

My face is plastered to the window

Jamila

Jamila Jafari was five years old when she fled Afghanistan with her mother and her younger brother. She thought it was an adventure to find her father. Now twenty, she lives in Perth and studies at university.

The day that we were leaving

I was born in Afghanistan just before the Taliban came about. The Taliban, they wanted to take over. My family and I, we're Shia Hazara—the Taliban hate the Hazaras—and we supported a resistance political party. So, culturally, religiously and politically, we were on the other end of the spectrum. That made us a big target.

In 1999, Dad had to run off because it wasn't safe for him. And then, after a while, it wasn't safe for my mother, my brother and me either. I asked Mum what was going on, where were we going, and she said, 'We have to leave.'

I remember the day that we were leaving. Everyone around us was crying: my aunty, my grandmother, even my mum, and I didn't understand why. I assumed we were going on an adventure to find Dad.

I had a little doll that I absolutely adored. It was my only toy—that I remember having, anyways. I asked if we could take my doll with me, because the doll was with me everywhere I went. Mum said no. The way that she told me, I knew I had to listen. So I gave the doll to my aunty, who I also adored. I told her to look after it. We get in the back of the van—my mum, my little brother and I—and the van starts driving off, and I see my aunty, my grandmother and my grandfather standing there crying, and my aunty has my doll in her hand. Her figure gets smaller and smaller as we drive off. We turn the corner, she disappears and all I could think about was my doll. I'm sorry, it's so many years ago, I don't know why I get so emotional.

We made our way to Indonesia and we were extremely lucky to meet some really lovely families who were also refugees fleeing Afghanistan. There was a Hazara couple and they had three boys. There was also another lady; she had a son and a partner with her. The parents were a massive support network for my mum. The older boys were like brothers, always looking out for us. They were that shining light in all of that darkness, you know?

Adventures are supposed to be fun

So we got on the boat, and there were 435 people on it. It was a wooden fishing boat. I remember being at sea. They were really rough seas so we were always jolting to the side, but I didn't mind that much because every time I got a little worried or I wasn't sure what was happening, I'd ask my mum what was going on and she'd tell us, 'We're looking for Dad.' So I was like, 'Cool, that's fine. Wherever Dad is, I'll be safe with Dad.' You know, adventures are supposed to be fun and exciting, so I didn't mind.

The boat was really old and unstable, so the engine broke down a few times. And every time there was wailing and crying from the women and the children, there were people reading out prayers. Just imagine being in this extremely unstable vessel. You look on all four sides and all you can see is the blue sky, the blue sea and nothing else. The Australian navy intercepted us once we reached Australian waters on the thirteenth day.

We were taken to Christmas Island and transferred to Darwin, and then transferred down to Woomera.* And, man, I don't think there are enough words in the English language to accurately depict how horrible Woomera was. Just, thinking about it, really . . . I'm trying not to be weak.

They stared me down

First we were taken to the compound where the new arrivals were put, so we couldn't contact the people who had been there for a while. I remember, I would look at everything and it was just . . . the desert, basically, all around us. They had dongas—demountable buildings—all lined up, and in each donga there was just enough room for two bunk beds and a tiny passageway. It was so tiny. It had a small window out the back with bars on it and just behind the row of dongas was a fence with barbed wire. It was so disgusting and stuffy. It was no place for any human to have to be in. You're either in that tiny donga, or you're outside, but all you see outside is just fences around you. They were both equally as bad. You

---

* The Woomera detention centre was located about 450 kilometres north of Adelaide. It opened in November 1999 and closed in April 2003 following a number of high-profile riots and protests, including a breakout in 2002.

just had to put up with it, you know? There was no other option. There was no green area you could go to, to escape all of this confinement.

My mum, one day she told me: 'Go outside. Play outside.' I went round the back, behind our donga. There were about two metres between the back of our donga and the fence. I was skipping about and I noticed these vehicles on the other side of the fence. Like, rows of vehicles. I've stopped because I'm curious to see what's going on. The car doors open and I see these people dressed in black: black shoes, black pants, black shirt, black hat. They step out, they're staunch, and their figures are really dominating. I remember being so intimidated. I was doing nothing wrong, I was just skipping about. It was . . . crippling. I don't really know how to put it into words but their presence was so scary that it made me want to crawl up into a ball. They stared me down and I burst into tears. I was frozen. I couldn't move. I didn't know what was going on! This image, it's always been in my mind, ever since that encounter.

All this time Mum said, 'We're finding Dad.' I think the adventure stopped—I stopped thinking of it as an adventure—when we got to Woomera.

The word 'freedom'

We had the initial interview, and it was in a lovely, clean, air-conditioned building—really different from the dongas. There was a desk, an interviewer, an interpreter and a chair. Mum sat on the chair as she was being interviewed, and my brother and I had to sit on the floor. I think they gave us a piece of paper and a few coloured pencils to occupy us with. And, I mean, it should have been something enjoyable to do but what was I supposed to draw? Razor wire all around me? That's all I'd seen ever since I'd arrived here.

So, once you've been initially interviewed, they transfer you over to make room for the other new arrivals. The other donga we were moved to was much bigger and it had a small living area, a corridor and three bedrooms on each side. Each bedroom had two bunk beds. So we took one of the rooms there, there were other Hazara families in the other rooms. And these other Hazara families, they were, I think, the epitome of what detention does to children. Of the psychological effects detention has. The lady, she had quite a few children. She had two older boys: one was thirteen and the other was twelve. She had lots of girls as well. When I think of detention, what I saw with them are a big part of the memories I have.

Woomera was the most notorious detention centre in Australia. There were lots of protests and riots and that sort of thing while we were in Woomera. I saw adults and children with their lips sewn, bruised and all this stuff. The thirteen year old and the twelve year old, they both sewed their lips. The mother too.

During one of the riots on 26 January, I was standing there and there was arguing going on. There was screaming, people screaming out, 'Freedom! Freedom!' It was the middle of the desert during the really hot season and the conditions were just unbearable. I remember the thirteen year old, he had some kind of blade. He'd written the word 'freedom', he cut that into his skin, his left forearm—I'm sorry this is so graphic—his skin's ripped open, his blood's dripping, and he's screaming out, 'We want freedom!'

I could never remove that image from my head. It's so vivid. And his voice is . . . it's shaking, there's so much pain in his voice. A thirteen year old! Doing that to himself! And all the other adults, older children, protesting and screaming out, 'Freedom, freedom, freedom.' When I think of my childhood, that is one of the main words that I remember, like it's been engraved in me, and I have never . . . I wish I could . . . I wish I could remove those images from my head. But I can't. It's impossible.

After the boy cuts himself, the next thing I hear are people screaming and crying out because a man has climbed right to the top of the fence and then he just jumps off. He lands on a coil of razor wire and people are shrieking, they're crying out. Everyone is so surprised. As he lands, his weight causes the coil to bounce, so he bounces a few times, like a heartbeat. His arms are all cut up because of the razor and he's bleeding. There's a documentary about him, called *The Man Who Jumped*. He didn't die, but the conditions in the detention centre drove him off the edge, literally. You wouldn't do that if you were completely sane, you know?

And those boys, they were so damaged, honestly. They did a lot of hectic things but I just admired them so much for their fearlessness, their boldness and their bravery. It's not an easy task to sew your lips together, to go on a hunger strike, to then resort to cutting into your own flesh. You couldn't help but admire them for having those personality traits in the face of such hopeless times. I think there were other people who felt the same way about them, even people older than them.

Red earth

We arrived at Woomera and had our first interview before 9/11 happened, and were waiting for the results. Then, we heard about 9/11. I remember people saying, 'Afghanistan has attacked tall buildings in America.' There was a lot of fear. Whatever the treatment of refugees and asylum seekers and boat people was, 9/11 completely changed it. They put a freeze on all visa applications; they were refusing to process anybody.

People were throwing mattresses out onto the ground in the detention centres—and it was just earth basically, no grass, no pavement—and lying there in the 50-degree-Celsius heat, in protest, not even drinking water; people with their lips sewn, lying there, lifeless bodies. Everywhere you turned you'd see people lying, protesting.

One day, I was outside and everywhere I looked was red earth, dry and flat. I'm trying to imagine how the real Australia would look. I picture rolling hills, lush green vegetation and I'm trying to figure out how far away it would be and how long it would take us to reach the real Australia, even though we were in Australia. They had tracked Dad down: he was in Australia. So by this stage, I knew Dad was here, and I was trying to picture him in the green, rolling-hill scenery, and I'm just wishing so badly to be with him.

There was a stretch of road along the fence. I put my fingers through the fence and I'm looking out. A car zooms past and I'm trying to imagine how it would be not to have my world stop at this fence. This was it—this was the barrier and I understood that. It's this fence that's stopping me from getting to my dad, from getting to the rolling green hills.

I remember some of the employees working at the detention centre. There was this donga that was like an educational centre. We were taken in there and it was absolutely lovely. It was so bright and colourful, it was air-conditioned and there were desks and bits and pieces of paper. There was this really, really lovely guy. He must have been in his forties, fifties. He came in and sat on the ground and he was doing all these silly things to make us kids laugh. It was about one hour of just laughing. In comparison to the guards and all the other employees there, he was just so lovely. The next day we were so looking forward to going back in there. But he didn't turn up again.

The sky looked pretty for once

One morning, it must have been six o'clock, I was sleeping and Mum woke me up. She was like, 'Get up, they've called our names over the PA system.' The atmosphere of that day, in comparison to all the other days we'd been there, it was just so different from the onset. The moment I woke up, I just felt so different and so alive. Even the sky looked pretty for once and the weather was nice and cool.

So, we walked down to the office and they told us, 'Your visa's arrived.' And it was honestly the best day ever, the environment felt unreal. They were taking us out the next day, so we had that one day to pack what little belongings we had. It was always a really happy occasion for the person who got their visa, but also sad for the remaining detainees.

There was a tradition in the camp where, every time someone got their visa, as they walked out, the remaining detainees would spill out water at their feet. It was like a good luck thing. And the day that it happened to me, I was so happy and so excited and all I could think about was, 'I'm finally going to see my dad!' And it felt like an adventure again. I felt happy again.

And I see him

So we said our goodbyes to all our friends who had become like family. From Woomera they drove us down to Adelaide. From there, someone had arranged for us to get on another interstate bus to travel to Sydney where Dad was. I don't remember the journey but I remember the end, when the bus was starting to slow down—I think it was somewhere in the CBD—and I hear a lot of noise outside the bus, and people start to open up their curtains. I see these massive, tall buildings and I'm intrigued. It was like nothing I had ever seen before. There are all sorts of people, all shapes and sizes and colours, and everyone looks so busy. Everyone's walking really fast, trying to get to the places they're heading off to. Amongst this crowd, this busy, busy crowd, there's only one figure that catches my eye. And I see him, he's dressed in a T-shirt and trousers and belt; T-shirt tucked in, in early 2000s fashion. And he has a moustache and short black hair and Hazaragi eyes and he's power-walking like he's a man on a mission! The bus stops, the man walks to the front door of the bus and I've recognised him by now. My face is plastered to the window, and so are my hands as I scream out, 'Babai!'

It's the first memory I have of my dad. Obviously, he was around when I was born and stuff, but I don't remember that. So, it was like . . . a new birth, like seeing the world for the first time.

We got off the bus, we hugged and we were just so happy! We had smiles plastered on our faces. We got into a taxi and drove out of the city, over to Auburn, which is where he was living at the time. Turned out Dad had taken the same journey as us.

The next day Dad took us out to the shops. We didn't have toys, and I still missed my doll so much. He took us to this toy store, and it looked like heaven! I chose a Polly Pocket set. Do you remember those?

And, you know, growing up we did have a lot of toys and stuff like that, but it was never the same as my doll that I had to leave behind. The first time I finally got in touch with my grandparents and my aunty, I asked my aunty, 'Where's my doll? Have you still got her? Have you been brushing her hair, washing her face in the mornings?' I always remembered her and mentioned her. When I was about ten or eleven years old I brought her up in conversation again, and Mum was like, 'You need to stop thinking about her. She's gone. You're not getting her back. She probably doesn't look the same anymore. Because, you know, it's been a few years—toys wear out.'

But it was that separation that really got to me as a kid. And, even though I had all these toys, all these new dolls, it was like my parents were trying to compensate for what I had lost. But it was never the same.

Keep my lips zipped

The real difficulty after getting out of Woomera was the temporary visas. They're horrible and I don't see any logic in them. If you deem someone to be in genuine fear of persecution and stuff like that, and you grant them that refugee status, then why keep torturing them for a further three years?

The years that we spent on temporary visas were really hard. It was a massive uncertainty. Dad's three years finished up before ours, obviously, because he had been here before us. Around that time, when he was filling out his forms, going in for interviews and stuff, I remember being so scared. I remember praying my little heart out because I didn't want to leave my teachers or my school. Initially Dad was rejected, and it felt like the end of the world. But he appealed, and when he was granted permanent residency, it was automatic for us as well.

Growing up, I always felt different, I always looked different. And it didn't feel entirely like home, to be honest. For a few years, I didn't feel like I belonged. And because I had been bullied for my scarf, my religion and stuff like that, I always tried to be as 'Australian' as possible. But there was always something about me that was different to the rest of the crowd, and that made me a target. So, when I learnt English,

I made the big mistake of abandoning my Hazaragi language. I wanted to be the same as everybody else. Looking back now, I wish I had put in more effort into speaking Hazaragi, because now I can't speak it that well. I realise that now, and I have this deep regret in me.

For a very long time I suppressed everything, and I was never willing to tell anybody I was a refugee because I thought I was illegal, that I was a 'queue-jumper', that I didn't deserve to be here because I'd done something wrong. I remember news snippets and the then-prime minister John Howard. When I think of him, this one speech is what comes to mind: 'We decide who comes to this country and the circumstances in which they come!' The whole room is cheering for him, and that really gets to me. The strong way that he said that—it was convincing even to me! I thought I was a queue-jumper—like when you're standing there in line at the school canteen and kids jump in, in front of their friends, it was annoying. And then I'd think, 'Hang on, but that's what the prime minister says I'm doing.' It built up this massive guilt inside of me, and I didn't know how to get rid of it. The only thing I could do was to suppress it. Keep my lips zipped. Not tell anyone. Because if that kid pushing in line angered me, then I thought that the whole country had every right to be angry at me for supposedly pushing in line, for supposedly being illegal.

The first time I told one of my non-Hazara friends was in year 9. This was when asylum seekers and refugees were back in the news a lot. I was like, 'How do I say this to her?' We were absolute best friends, we were joking, laughing, and I was like, 'Haha, I'm a boat person!' I was so petrified of her reaction, I was like, 'What did I just say? This is the end, she's not going to want to be friends with me, I'm going to be alienated from the entire group.' But she was like, 'Really?

That's cool.' And she moved on. This massive weight from my shoulders was lifted.

That was a point in my life where I started doing my own research and I came to realise that, 'Hey, what my family did was not illegal. We are not queue-jumpers because there's no such thing as a queue in regards to being a refugee.' I think it changed my perspective of my own existence in this country, and I felt more at home. I accepted myself.

She said, 'You can be my son'

Taqi

Taqi Alizada's family are from Afghanistan. Taqi fled Pakistan as an unaccompanied fifteen year old. He spent eighteen months in Indonesia before arriving in Australia, where he completed high school at Dandenong High School. He is now waiting for his Australian citizenship so he can bring his family here.

A lot of things came into my mind

A couple of years ago I didn't know much about anything. I was kind of stupid, I was too young. I didn't know what life would be like. And the idea of waiting in detention—I always thought waiting is waiting, don't worry about it. But now I care, I am more adult, and I have experienced a lot of problems.

I suffer from depression and stress always. But at the end of the day I feel good because I can be smarter than others my age because I have lots of experiences of those things. I suffer from those things but I feel kind of lucky.

I can speak six or seven languages. They are Urdu, Hindi, Indonesian and our language, Hazaragi, and Arabic and Malay. Malay and Indonesian are pretty similar.

Most Australians my age, when they see my card balance, they are always shocked: 'How you get so much money? How do you still have it? Are you still saving?' They can't save; they have five dollars and then it's gone on fish and chips.

Yeah, I am good at saving. People always tell me that I have savings, that I know how to deal with other people. They always like my socialising; they say, 'You always cooperate with all kinds of people. Like, if it's a junkie you cooperate, if it's a professor you cooperate with them, if it's, like, middle-class people you can cooperate.' This is because of that kind of experience.

When I was in Indonesia I got a phone call saying that my father was missing. And then a couple of months later my family left a message on Facebook saying I should call. I made a time to go onto the internet, and they said, 'The good news is your dad is at home. The bad news is he got tortured, he's in very bad health condition.'

At that moment I was so helpless. I thought, if he has been tortured who knows if he is going to live or not. And then a lot of things came into my mind, and I was so depressed for a couple of months. I lost a lot of friends. Everyone thought that I was on drugs or something, because sometimes I was shaking, I lost a lot of weight. Then he died. He passed away four years ago.

I left home

So, it was 5 March 2011. Most of my friends had left Pakistan and told stories of what happened to them afterwards. And as I saw there was no future in Pakistan I told my mum that

I wanted to go. But my dad, he knew the way I'd go, by boat, and the struggle, and things, and he said, 'No.' I had arguments with my mum, then my dad, and even my older brother. At first no one agreed with me going. And then later on all of them agreed.

I left home around twelve o'clock. It was a pretty sad moment. My mum, she did not know that I would be smuggled by boat and these things until then, so she cried, and my older sister cried, and I was pretty upset. I left the home. I saw some of my friends on the way, and I told them I had a boxing competition in Peshawar and everyone believed it. I did not want to tell anyone that I was going to Australia. I was fifteen.

With the help of a smuggler, Taqi travelled with a small group of fellow under-age asylum seekers, first to Malaysia, then to Indonesia.

WOW Hotel

It was first time that I had travelled in an aeroplane, legally or illegally. There was a plan for us to stay in a hotel for the night and the next morning go to Jakarta. Some people saw us—as foreign people we looked suspicious—so when we departed from that hotel there was a policeman and he stopped us straight away, saying: 'Australia, Australia, Australia'. He took us to the police station and we stayed there for a night. And then after a night they said, 'We will take you to the WOW Hotel, a five-star hotel,' blah, blah, blah. We didn't believe them. We were refugees. We were criminals. Why would they take us to a hotel?

But it was Immigration's place. We were locked in there for 45 days, four people in one room. It was a five-star hotel, but there was only the one bed and we were four. The door was always locked. If you wanted to ring your family you had to pay the guards. They would take our mobile, give our family a missed call, then our family would ring us. Just for that, we paid five dollars.

Those 45 days were the hardest in my life. It's like it took 45 months. We always looked at the watch, and it was always the same. Tick tick, still the same, still the same.

When we washed our clothes we had to hang them to dry because there wasn't a dryer. One day we washed our clothes and wanted to hang them outside on the balcony, so I was knocking on the door. No one came, and I was knocking louder, and bit more louder and then a guard came and hit me. Slapped me, couple of slaps. My friend came to try and stop him and he hit him too. The guard said, 'This not Afghanistan, this is Indonesia.'

The guards could do anything they wanted. There was no way to complain, no requests, their supervisor or manager never came. The guards were way older. When we paid for the telephone, they would collect the money and then bring girls at night-time, and drinks. One night I was sleeping, and I think Marwin came in, one of the guards, and he said, 'Wake up, wake up,' and I woke up and he took me to the balcony, and there were three girls and two other guards, Anwar and Abdullah.

So there were drinks, and I think they were going to have party. So I sat there and I said, 'Hi,' to the girls and we started talking but I couldn't speak Indonesian and they couldn't speak English. And then I said I wanted to go to sleep. And I don't know what they did that night, or what happened, or why they asked me go out there. I have no idea. But usually every Friday, every time they got money, we would see some bottles of beer or wine or alcohol on the balcony. They made parties with our money, just from letting us use their mobile to give a missed call to our families.

A big saloon

After that I found a smuggler from there, and the smuggler said, 'You're going to pay Immigration staff to transfer you.' He said I should pay them US$3000, then they would transfer me from there to Jakarta.

So I paid them, and they transferred me from WOW Hotel to Jakarta. My other friend, who didn't pay that much money, they transferred to Tanjung Pinang detention centre. From Jakarta, they transferred us to Bogor,* where there is a shelter for people under eighteen, and I was there for sixteen to seventeen months.

The first time I came to the shelter there were a couple of Afghan guys our age, so I was pretty happy. Our bedroom was kind of a big saloon, and then there was a double bunk bed—we had to sleep on that. There were fourteen or fifteen boys—it was pretty noisy, you couldn't sleep well.

We were allowed to leave the shelter but we had to be back by ten o'clock. If you were going to be a bit late you could ring them, and then they would be fine. And if you wanted to stay somewhere at night-time, you could fill a form and give details and then they would let you stay. If you didn't come back for two nights your payment from UNHCR would be stopped.†

---

* Bogor is a city around 60 kilometres south of Jakarta.
† UNHCR is responsible for the care of unaccompanied minor asylum seekers in Indonesia. Together with its implementing partner, Church World Service (CWS), UNHCR runs a small number of shelters for unaccompanied minors in Indonesia, including this one in Bogor.

In the shelter I saw a couple of boys who had girlfriends. So I asked them what was going on, how to get a girlfriend. And the boys would say, 'Just ask *nomor*'—which means number—'and they will understand.' And so sometimes the girls would ask us, '*Nomor?*' and we give them our phone number. And they might say, 'Hi,' or send messages in Indonesian. We'd show the security guard and he would explain, and help us reply. And so, through talking to girls and having girlfriends, I learnt Indonesian.

She said, 'You have very nice eyes'

On the first day after they transferred us to the shelter, my case manager came to the shelter and said, 'Welcome.' She could speak a bit of Persian. She said, 'You have very nice eyes, nice colour.' At that time I was the youngest guy in the shelter and I felt much more comfortable and much safer when I saw older women, like my mum's age, or older than that, so I felt comfortable and safe with my case manager, and that's why I was honest with her and whenever she came to visit I would always try to sit next to her.

There was another Afghan at the shelter and he said to her, 'You can adopt Taqi. Taqi needs you, you can help him.' So this is what happened. She told me she could adopt me, as she had only one daughter, and she said, 'You can be my son.' And I said, 'Why not.'

Yes, I got my refugee status. Australia have a policy that they don't want any minors because it kind of complicates things for them. And so, when I realised they do not accept minors from Indonesia, I got on a boat.

The water was pretty rough. We couldn't go back, we couldn't go forward. There was one family on the boat always screaming and shouting, 'I want to go back, take us to some island, I don't want to die with my kids.' The second day we finished our food and water. On the fourth day everyone lost their hope. We didn't know where we were going to end up. I was lying on the deck of the boat and I could see one sultana, and I was so lazy, I didn't have the energy to get up and get it. But there was a 60-year-old man who did jump up to get the sultana. One thing I learned was, never hesitate. Three days, three nights, no food, no water. We were trying to find any other ship or boat, to ask them for food or water. On, I think it was the third or fourth day, there was a big ship coming by and we tried to get to them, but they must have thought we were thieves or trying to get their money or cause trouble, because they skipped. The fifth day, we saw something that looked like a ship, and we came closer and closer and it was Christmas Island. And we thought, *Thank god.*

I was on the news

Then as we came close to the land there was a navy ship. Straight away we told them we were asylum seekers looking for safety. Then they captured us and gave us water and milk and said we couldn't go to the detention centre until tomorrow morning.

And so in the morning they took us to the navy boat. And when I was on the boat I had one wish: that I would get on the news. So I was trying to sit at the front so that when they took picture I would be seen. And it actually happened, I was on the news.

Eighteen of us were minors and they sent us to Charlie camp that night. We were in Charlie camp for a month. At Charlie everyone has their own bedroom, and there were

THEY CANNOT TAKE THE SKY

Serco officers always around us. They were scared something was going to happen. They were always around us.

The food was always rice, with some meat and some salad. They give us one piece of fruit. And they called us by our number, never by our name.

After Charlie, they transferred us to Leonora detention centre* for two months. Charlie was kind of a boring place. To call family we had to wait for hours and hours, and sometimes by the time the telephone box was free it was nine or ten at night and we had to go to bed. It was pretty hard. But when we came to Leonora it was fun. We had a couple of pool tables, we had schools, we had outside excursions. We would go to the mountains, have a drink and some fresh air and then come back, just for a walk.

At Leonora, there was one teacher, and he said, 'You should write a complaint letter. They should not call you by number. You are not a criminal, you are just an asylum seeker.' I had never thought about it before that, but once my teacher said this I was always aware they should not call me by number.

I never thought I would do those things

Leonora is a big centre. There was—I can't remember—I think more than two hundred containers that we lived inside there. Mine was number 185, right in the corner, at the edge of the detention centre. I was scared at night-time, always scared, always thinking that there was something moving in my bedroom. For the majority of the two months I was having bad dreams. I was feeling there was something in my

---

* The Leonora detention centre operated from 2010 to 2014. It was located about 800 kilometres northeast of Perth in Western Australia.

bedroom. I made a complaint and they said, 'There is nothing going on in there, you will be fine.' But still the nightmares were the same.

Where my container was it was always windy, and I was scared this wind was going to do something. The nightmare was usually like someone was holding my hand, trying to get me, and there was always someone trying to open my fridge, and I would have a feeling that there was someone and then wake up, and nothing.

I spoke to boys who had been in detention for almost a year. I was scared that if that happened to me, I would lose myself. I was scared of that. There was one guy who had been there six months and I was scared of him. I don't know whether it's true or not, but the boys said that he had been in Indonesia for a long time and Immigration thought he was helping smugglers and that was why he had been in detention so long. And I was so scared, because I had also been in Indonesia for a long time, and I had told them I could speak Indonesian.

There was one guy who often tried to suicide. And there were always all these Serco officers with him after, whenever he tried to suicide. And there were also a couple of other people who had mental disorders. *No*, I thought, *no matter what happens I will not hurt myself.* I sometimes get depressed and stressed, but I never thought I would do those things.

Yeah, I also remember—I will never forget—that every Sunday at nine o'clock, the Indonesian lady who wanted to adopt me would call me, and I would always have a chat with her for an hour, which also reduced stress. She would always send me an email asking how I was, and what was going on, every day. And I still have them—my emails, most of them are from her, for three years, every day. Her emails made me feel like I should be someone.

And after two months in Leonora, I got transferred to Dandenong. Melbourne was freezing at that time, it was September or something. It was 2012. Two immigration staff came and picked us up from the airport. In the car, radio FM was playing, and the announcer said 'G'day mate,' so I knew it must be Australia, and that made me so happy.

In December 2014, I went to Pakistan to visit my family, and even though I was with family, in the place where I grew up, I still missed bloody Dandenong. If I go for a couple of days out of Dandenong I miss Dandenong, I don't know why.

I dream about him

The most important thing I want is to have a successful life, bring my family here, do something for the community, and be useful for them. To have a good job, a happy life, a lot of money in the bank, a nice car, a nice house, a job that I will never lose, permanent forever.

I really care about my youngest brother, I love him the most. I want to bring him here. Because he is young he can be something if we can bring him here and teach him. Right now he is eight. The day he was born, one of my wishes was that I would take him to school—that on his first day of school I would drop him off and pick him up from school. My wish never happened, but I still have a wish to do it here—to take him to school, or uni, or take him to his first job. That is my wish.

My father tried to find a safe place where we could stay, but my father got tortured, and passed away because of that torture. Usually I dream about him. I think about the lost possibilities, I think about that. He is always on my mind. I always think that he's asking for help, always imagine him asking for help. I don't know what kind of help. Maybe it's help for my family, doing anything to get them out.

It was a strange, alien land

Aran

Aran Mylvaganam fled Sri Lanka and came to Australia as an unaccompanied minor at the age of thirteen. He lives in Dandenong with his family and he is the spokesperson for Tamil Refugee Council.

I'll become a father

Possibly any time, from now to another three weeks, I'll become a father.

I come from a very conservative family. I wasn't brought up the right way, I would say, in the sense that the village I grew up in was quite backwards in its approach towards women. I want to make sure that my child lives free and lives in a society where she is aware of all these issues around her. I want her to know the struggle women have in society.

The world that she is going to come into is completely different from the world that I have come from. She probably won't be facing bombs and having to live away from her parents and staying among strangers at a young age, but nevertheless she will have her own struggles. I will give her the support to fight that struggle, you know.

These are my memories. In 1994, my uncle was very sick and I remember my grandfather went to visit him and he was hit by a motorbike and died. The reason I'm sharing that story is, that day there was an attack in our village by the Sri Lankan navy. My grandfather's best friend also died. It was a Friday.

I'm from a coastal village in northern Sri Lanka called Nagarkovil. Most of the villagers were fishermen. Our village never had any modern technology. We had no electricity, we had no telephones, we had no television. We relied on firewood to cook, it was all ancient stuff that we were using. We had no fridge. The way we would preserve food was by putting salt on it. The reason for this was there was a total embargo, the Sri Lankan government didn't allow electricity for Tamil areas. If we wanted to listen to music, we would put a bike on a stand, someone would ride it, and we would connect it to a motor and listen to the radio, right? That's how we listened to the news and everything. The village life, even while the war was around us, it was a beautiful life. I still love it. I still miss it, I still haven't gotten over it. I still want to enjoy that, you know? One day I am hoping that I can revisit that lifestyle, that place, and experience my childhood again.

Funeral after funeral in every house

Whenever there was an attack by the navy we ran to the temple. I was a very religious boy. I'm an atheist nowadays, but back then I was a very religious person and I had a very special relationship with Lord Muruga. My dad and my grandfather and my uncle and me—we were all named after Lord Muruga. And we would go and hide at the Lord Muruga temple when the navy attacked us. This was our lifestyle.

I had a very close relationship with my schoolmates. Our school was an open school, we studied, like in the Ancient Greek times, under the trees. It was an open area and every class had to take care of their classroom. So we had a broom for our class and I was the one taking care of the broom. So while a lot of bad things were happening around us, it was a happy environment.

On Friday, 22 September 1995, at Nagarkovil school, we all were studying. Up until lunchtime, we were happy, we were playing. Soon after the lunch break, they came and dropped seven bombs. They dropped the first bomb near the school. These were 750 students in plain white uniforms, you know? They dropped the first bomb and I remember a friend of mine, he started screaming and running out and then we all followed him. And we all started running out into the open, people were in the open and that's when I ran to the tamarind tree and I was hiding.

Right next to the school was the huge tamarind tree and then next to it was my house. My mum, she was calling our names. There was absolute chaos. People were screaming and my mum was calling our names. I ran towards my mum and she took me to the front verandah of the house and we were all sitting there and still the plane was rounding. And at that point my second eldest brother, he was running towards the gate, he was running towards us, and at that point they dropped . . . they dropped a few bombs over that tamarind tree, and all I can remember is smoke. There were a lot of children hiding under the tamarind tree, and all I can remember is smoke.

And we got up and we all ran away from the bomb and went and hid in the Lord Muruga temple. And as we were running towards the temple I saw one girl fall down, but we had no time to check on her, we just ran away from the bomb, thinking there was going to be another attack. When we came back, once the plane had left, the whole village was in total chaos. Everybody . . . we were just hearing screams everywhere. And when we came back we found my brother, he was chopped in half. He was crying for water, you know. And then I found a friend of mine hanging on the tamarind tree, and all his intestines and everything had come out. I remember my cousins died; one was a six-year-old girl, she was found in pieces. It is a day that I will never forget, and it is the day that continues to drive me to seek justice, the experience that has shaped my future.

My brother didn't die straight away, he was taken to the hospital. That evening it was funeral after funeral in every house. Then there was another funeral for my brother in the village and that was the first time I really saw my dad cry. He was a very hard man, you know, a tough guy. Seeing him crying like a little baby . . . it was . . . it was very emotional. But I couldn't cry at that time.

After that, we still chose to stay in the village. That was the choice of pretty much everyone. Nobody wanted to leave, because people didn't know what else to do. But a month later they attacked the village again.

We were sleeping in the mud

My dad decided to take my older brother and get him smuggled out of the country somewhere. Some of my relatives had gone to Europe as workers before, when the war started. The idea was to get my brother joined with them in London. While our dad was away we had another attack. This time they targeted the fish market. Soon after that, we just took whatever we could carry and we left on foot. I remember sleeping near the Kilali Lagoon for days. We were part of five hundred thousand people who were fleeing Jaffna on foot. We were sleeping in the mud. I still remember my cousin, who was only about seven—she was calling the gods' names, all these names, and that has remained with me for a long time, because here was a really young child begging for god to save her.

We went to the other side of the Kilali River, to a large area controlled by the Tamil Tigers. In the refugee camp there were hundreds of families. We were given food by the Tamil Tigers and then they built us cottages nearby in the village. It had become normal by that time, but we were living in constant fear. Because of the war, Dad was stuck away from the refugee camp, outside the Tamil Tiger–controlled area. We heard my brother was stuck in Sierra Leone—he was gaoled in Sierra Leone, and he was only sixteen. From end of 1995 until 1997 we were in the refugee camp. Then my uncle decided that it would be safer to get all the young kids out of the country. I was thirteen.

We needed to get a permit to go through the Tamil Tiger–controlled area, and once we got through the Sri Lankan military checkpoint we had to use fake identities. It was all with the help of my uncle. Our intention was to go to European countries, you know? I was one of the last to leave and while I was in the capital city we heard the news that my brother had managed to get out of Sierra Leone and find his way to Australia, so this is how my route was changed. Back then in the 1990s, nobody wanted to go to Australia. It was a strange, alien land.

'Where is your visa?'

An agent was helping us—I call them agents not people smugglers. Obviously there are people who just want to make money out of people's misery, and it's always going to happen, just like the insurance companies, who make money out of people's misery. But this person who helped me out, she herself was a victim of the war and she was genuinely helping people to get out of the country. With her help I got on a plane. I came on a plane, not by boat. I was alone. At the Malaysian airport I was met by a woman who gave me a boarding pass. I got onto the Qantas aeroplane. I remember that day very well. I hated the airline magazines they had, because the smell was really bad, it made me get dizzy. The crew were white people. You know, they would have been some of the first white people I had seen. They gave me a blanket and I stole that blanket. I seriously did that, thinking that it was worth a lot of money.

I got off the plane at Sydney Airport, went to the visa checking area and I stood in a queue. I got to the counter and the guy said, 'Where is your visa?' And I couldn't hear any other words except visa. I was just smiling at him and they realised that I was probably a refugee. They took me into a room and asked me questions. It was terrifying.

Everything was completely strange, even the technology. I had never seen telephones, computers, all these things. [*Laughs.*] I was seeing it for the first time and it was very terrifying. I really thought, *Why did I leave my country and come here?* I was crying. At Sydney Airport they interviewed me and they asked me a lot of questions. They gave me chocolates before they asked me questions.

Then they took me to a lift and I thought, *Shit, this is it—something is going to happen to me*, because I had never been in a lift, never even knew lifts existed. They took me into a lift and I'm like, *Am I going to be beaten up?* We had heard stories of refugees having their hair shaved and getting beaten up really badly in countries like Singapore and other places. All of a sudden the lift door opened and they took me into a caged van and I found there were other refugees as well, waiting in the caged van, and together we were taken to Villawood Immigration Detention Centre.

I was put in a room on my own, with a single bed and an attached bathroom. High security. The door was locked at night-time. So the first night I was in tears. I'm like, *How can you lock me in?* I was scared of staying on my own, because I was always scared of ghosts, particularly after the death of the school kids. I was banging on the door, I was crying, I was calling out for my mum and dad and my siblings. I felt like that would be the end of me, you know? They eventually let me out, after more than an hour. In the common living area there were guards watching cricket. I didn't know cricket as a game existed back then, but later I realised they had been watching cricket. They were watching a cricket match between South Africa and Australia—this was in March 1997—and I stayed with them. I was completely in tears, tired, and I slept on the rug.

I loved Fanta, back then

After that I got used to staying in the room, so they locked me in and they would come and open it early in the morning. There was breakfast, lunch and dinner. I had never had cereal before, never in my life! Definitely, no, it is not filling at all. We have rice and curry for breakfast. [*Laughs.*] Yeah, so the food I didn't like, but nowadays I would probably pay lots of money to have that food.

My brother contacted me two days later. The first time I heard his voice I was very happy. He had been away from all of us for about two years. By this time he was in Maribyrnong detention centre and he was just about to be released to Dandenong where they had housing for refugees. My brother organised a Tamil lawyer, who helped us out. I had a few interviews and the interviewer would ask questions about why I had fled Sri Lanka. It was quite a relaxed interview—it wasn't an interview like these days, where they look for mistakes. The interviewer understood the situation we were fleeing from.

Would I prefer Villawood, or Sri Lanka? Obviously Villawood. Everybody would choose Villawood. The memories of what I faced in my country never went away. While I was in the detention centre there were so many days I would have nightmares.

The guards would come and open my door about eight o'clock for breakfast time and then I would go out. They had one of those arcade fighting games, you know? You had to put money into it though. Sometimes I would go early in the morning to see if anybody had left any credits behind so I could play for free. They had a vending machine where you could get Fanta and Coke and all that. And for me, that was my world. I loved Fanta, back then.

The pool table was free to play, and I would be one of the first to get to the pool table and play with all the men. There was an Indonesian guy—who was probably a bad guy, you know—who was the first one to teach me swear words in English. He taught me how to play pool and I became really good at it back then.

We could also watch TV. Sometimes Tamils from the outside would bring old VHS tapes and we would watch Tamil movies. I had never watched TV in Sri Lanka, ever, so the first time I watched a Tamil movie in my life was in Villawood detention centre. It was called *Arunachalam*. I remember it well: the hero was adopted, and one day he had issues with the family, and he left them, only to realise he was the son of a multi-billionaire. There was a challenge his dad left behind, which was he had to spend 30 crores, which was 300 million rupees, within 30 days. I wish I had that problem. He accepts that challenge—not to get the money, but to make sure that the money goes to look after the poor. It's a very funny story. That was my first movie.

I remember there was a guy from Pakistan who was facing deportation and he was on hunger strike. And I myself had been on a fast a couple of times. Most of the refugees back then were getting out within a month, so when you were not being released, you'd become frustrated, although it was short compared to these days. And so I would not turn up to the meals. I remember one time I probably missed about four meals: breakfast, lunch, dinner and then the breakfast again. I was taken into this room where they gave me banana and bread and I had to end fasting, after them begging me. But that was the norm in the detention centre.

Occasionally you would have fights over who used what. I was actually beaten up quite a few times by old men—not really bad, they would slap me and hit me on the head and all that. Because I talked back, you know? I remember, there was a chubby white guy, probably a European, and I can still remember his face. This particular time this guy beat me up it was over an argument over who could use the pool table. I talk back, and older men don't like that when you talk back.

There were guards inside, but they weren't everywhere. I was a little kid. I remember an Iranian girl and a Middle Eastern man had gone into the toilet together. That was quite funny, everybody was talking about it. And occasionally all these adults would get together and watch SBS. Back then, you know, SBS had a naughty after-hour thing, which I had to hide away from. For me at that age, it was like, *What the hell is that?*

I spent a couple of months in Villawood Immigration Detention Centre. I knew my release was coming because I was taken to medical check-up. Then they came and asked me where I wanted to go. I wanted to be with my brother but I also wanted to be in Sydney because that is where I had made a lot of friends in the centre. But my brother was adamant and eventually we ended up choosing Melbourne. I didn't know what to expect. When I got off the plane I saw my brother and he kissed me and I was really embarrassed because he was kissing me in front of everyone. Yeah, it was a really happy feeling. And then they took me to the car and I started feeling like vomiting from carsickness. I started my life in Dandenong.

I was looking for someone to love me

A couple of weeks after I came to Dandenong, I went to language school and I was on my way back when there was a helicopter and as soon as I saw it I panicked and threw myself under a tree. That is what you are meant to do in Sri Lanka. And I waited under the tree until the helicopter went, and I was in tears, and I walked home. That is something that I still remember. I still had a lot of trauma, there was no treatment for it. No, no counselling services at all.

My brother worked in factories and he would get whatever job came his way. And being a young kid himself, he didn't know how to look after me. I was looking for someone to love me, someone to look after me, you know? And I didn't get the right love. I'd get hit by my brother a lot as well. I mean . . . poor guy, he had a lot on his plate, so I don't blame him. And also he comes from a society where you have to respect the older brother, do whatever he says. And I was not going to buy that. He would just shut me up by hitting me, and sometimes it was in front of a large group of people, not in private, and he would embarrass me in front of many people.

My mum was still in a refugee camp so we could only write to her, but there were some relatives we were able to call who were overseas, some who were in Colombo. We would have really large mobile phone bills, because we were not able to control ourselves, we would call relatives.

In two years, we moved into about five houses, all in Dandenong. The Sutherland Road house was quite funny: we would play music, really loud music, annoying the neighbours, and people would occasionally call the police, and then we had to apologise. It was my brother and me and two other guys. Also, sometimes we wouldn't have enough money to pay the rent and the landlord would chase us. One day, I remember the landlord got in the back of the house and caught us hiding under the bed. He was Italian. He would sit in the house until we went and borrowed money from someone and gave it to him.

My brother was working to support us and send money back to our family in Sri Lanka as well. Eventually we decided to abandon all the other guys and stay together by ourselves because my brother felt that we were landing ourselves in trouble. Also, by this time I had become mentally unwell. I was studying in language school and then high school. I became quite lonely, I was isolated from the Tamil community. I was admitted to Dandenong Hospital and taken to Monash Medical Centre for serious depression. I was seventeen. There was one guy there— me and him shared a room together—and his nose would bleed all the time. For me it was quite scary seeing that blood.

My parents were in Colombo. My school principal and the year 9 coordinator, a local politician and a few others all got together and worked out a plan to bring my parents to Australia. I was in hospital for more than a month. They had a farewell party for me when I left.

When my parents came . . . I still have the photos of that moment. We were at the airport. My mum came and hugged me. It was a strange feeling, actually. When I left Sri Lanka I had been very close to my parents. I was in love with my younger brother and my sister as well—we would go and do so many things together. Now, three and a half years later, there was so much separation between us. I loved the fact that my mum was there to cook for me, but I don't think I've ever been so close to them as before, even to this day. I think my experience in the community here separated me from my family forever. I was not close to my older brother either after that, like the way we had been.

Did you hear about it?

I got into Monash University, to study science and arts. My depression never really got away from me. I lived a really lonely life. There were many days I would come home and sit on the sofa and cry, you know.

While I was at university the Howard government was trying to introduce voluntary student unionism. I got involved in that campaign and then started throwing myself into various different campaigns. It was my dream to get involved with Tamil activism. I started presenting two Tamil community radio shows. In 2009, we started seeing so many refugees coming into Australia, so I decided to start the Tamil Refugee Council. Every time Australian politicians came up with silly claims about Sri Lanka, we would be out there putting out a press release criticising them. I was a regular visitor to the Tamil refugees in Maribyrnong detention centre, as well as at Broadmeadows. Some weeks I would go there every single day. On some occasions refugees would treat me as if I was one of the refugees in the centre.

The death of Leo Seemanpillai was a big thing for us. He was a Tamil refugee who self-immolated and died in Geelong last year. Did you hear about it? He self-immolated, in fear of getting deported. I was in Wonthaggi, speaking at a forum in support of refugees, and as soon as I heard that Leo was in serious trouble I left the forum and went to The Alfred Hospital. You know how sometimes, when you're in the middle of a crisis, your whole body goes numb? You're in a state of shock? That's how it was for me when I was in that hospital. Like I couldn't feel what was happening around me.

The doctor told me, 'Look, Leo is not going to make it.' I thought he wasn't trying hard enough to save Leo's life. So I was begging with him, you know . . . and then sometime later I called Leo's father, in Tamil Nadu, and told him that Leo was dead. That evening we filled out the forms for organ donation. We had to get his parents to read certain documents. We were awake all night and at about 9.15 a.m. we went to Leo's room and we said our final goodbye.

I wish I had married a long time ago

My wife is related to Leo. She's Tamil, from Sri Lanka. That was the first time we met. After Leo self-immolated, Lavanya was the one in the refugee camp in Tamil Nadu acting as an interpreter all night for Leo to donate his organs.

After that she was my contact in terms of what was happening in the refugee camps in Tamil Nadu, so she was constantly staying in touch with me over the phone. Around that time we decided to get engaged and start the spousal application. It wasn't a proper love marriage and it wasn't an arranged marriage either. I asked Lavanya. She said, 'Oh, I have to talk to my mother.' And then I had to talk to her mother, who said, 'Oh, we have to talk to the church.'

Six months later we got married. She is an achiever; she is an extraordinary person. She was born in a refugee camp and has lived as a refugee all her life. Having her with me is adding strength to everything that I'm doing. I wish I had married a long time ago. I don't believe in marriage because it is very much tied to the persecution of women throughout history, particularly in my culture. But I do believe that having a companion in life is a good thing. When you have a really hard, long day there is someone to talk to, which hadn't been the case before I met my wife.

Have I come out of depression altogether? Probably not. I don't know if you ever can. What is keeping me going is the sense of justice. I have experienced some terrible things. But people who have been responsible still hold high positions, and I would like to see some sort of justice for what our people have gone through.

There's always a level of depression in all of us . . . and . . . I do think that my past . . . my past experiences still haunt me. When I drive, for example, sometimes I think about it. You . . . you . . . want to ask questions: why did it happen, you know? I get really angry: why did this happen? Why couldn't we have avoided it? But then, as I get to know more and more about other people's suffering, I think my . . . my own suffering becomes one of many sufferings. But it's still in there.

Voices

On leaving, arriving and a song about the homeland

SOLMAZ came to Australia with her son

So, I'm Solmaz. My mind is not tidy enough to know where I want to begin best.

My life growing up was a very difficult one. Maybe even torturous. At a very young age, I was forced to marry someone. It was part of the culture of my family in the ethnicity I grew up in. We lived in the outskirts of Tehran. It is quite customary for people to marry their daughters off at a very young age. If there is a good suitor who proposes, they let their daughter marry them immediately. It's not like it was an option. It was something that most people did the same way. So I got married as a teenager and had a child and that was my life.

JOHN GULZARI fled Afghanistan in 1999

I came from central region of Afghanistan, a region called Hazarajat, and that basically means the land of Hazaras.

We have only a few singers. There's a guy by the name of Dawood Sarkhosh, a famous Hazara singer, currently seeking asylum in Europe as a refugee. He released this song in 1997, a song about the homeland, about the sorrow of our people. Our people have been refugees our whole life, neglected in Afghanistan. I brought the tape with me. On my way from Jakarta to one of the islands called Lombok I told the driver to play that one, and he asked why, and I said, 'Before I drown I would like to listen to this music for one last time.'

I still have the tape now. Whenever I listen to this song, it takes me back to when my country was very peaceful, and the memories with friends and family before this seeking refuge, before the destruction of my country. It takes me back to those places where I used to live, it takes me back to my homeland where we had a peaceful life, my family, next of kin, tribesmen, relatives. And the time that I enjoyed with my mother and father and siblings. Some of them cannot come back.

ALI HAIDARY arrived on Christmas Island in 2009, and later his family, including his daughter RAHILA, joined him in Australia

Ali: When my daughter was born, I didn't see the difference between a boy and a girl. So I didn't care what clothes she would wear when she was a child. We didn't actually teach her that she was a girl. But when the Taliban came, I heard that they were against these things—that they were against education for girls, particularly. But by that time I think my daughter didn't understand that she shouldn't go to school because she's a girl, so she dressed up in boy's clothes, then just went to school.

Rahila: I was a bit cheeky, I would say, and naughty maybe. [*Laughs.*] I was really confident and had that self-esteem. I really didn't like that my cousins would get to dress up, leave home and go to the madrasa, the religious class, but I couldn't go. I had to stay home alone and there would be no one to play with. Sometimes I'd put on my cousin's clothes just for fun, but this time it wasn't for fun—I just wanted to experience being a boy and going to madrasa. Dad didn't know. I think I just wanted to learn.

There was the teacher and all the boys sitting around the room and they were just reading the books, and I sat close to my cousins. They were like, 'Why did you come? Why did you come?' There were people whispering around and laughing, and the next minute the teacher realised there was a girl in the classroom. Okay. All that yelling and anger. The teacher said to me, 'Go home. You're not supposed to be here.' I think someone else might have seen, like the Pashtuns, the members of the Taliban. They considered me as a grown-up girl, at the age of six. I didn't understand the consequences.

Ali: The people that were sent from the Taliban just came to me while I was watering the plants. They warned me that if . . . if she did it again they were going to kill her. She had to leave. I was sure that if my daughter stayed she would do something else. I always wanted my daughter to be educated and to go to school, but I had never thought that they . . . they would be so cruel. I was . . . Inside, I was still proud of my daughter. It was just the situation that I couldn't handle.

Rahila: I know that night was really hard for my family, particularly my mum. She wouldn't cry, but I know that she didn't sleep the whole night. I could hear her, uh, like, I had that feeling that she was hurt.

The day I had to leave, first thing in the morning I just woke up before everyone else. There was this favourite place of mine at the riverside, I could feel the sun rise there. I had built a really tiny sort of house, with the branches of the tree and I would just go there and sit and watch the river. But that morning I couldn't see a lot because it was still dark. I just went there and I knew that I wouldn't be able to feel this river tomorrow. You know the . . . waves, the water, that sound, I just loved that. I still love it. If I have a preference to go to a place, I'm like, 'Is there a river somewhere or a waterfall I could see?'

And then . . . then I couldn't actually stay there for long. I could hear my dad, he was calling, 'Where is Rahila?' The car was already there and I had to leave.

MOHSEN is a twenty-year-old refugee from Afghanistan

I didn't want to go on the boat, but everyone was jumping in. I said to the guy who I came with, 'What are they doing? Where are they going?' He said, 'We are going in the boat. We are going to Australia.' All I was thinking was, *Why this boat?*

It was the worst journey of my life. From the first night the boat had a hole. Then as we were going the small hole was getting bigger. It was raining—very bad. There was water and food for the first and second day. The food was for ten people but there were 80 people in the boat.

I was just thinking about my family. I was not worried about what would happen to myself, I didn't care about dying, but I did worry about what would happen to my family. I was thinking about my mum. If the Taliban kill me she gets my body in a bag. If I die on these seas she will never have peace.

Everyone lost their hope. Because of having no food and no water, some of them were like dead bodies. We emptied the seawater with buckets; when I felt weak I used cups. I haven't told my dad about the boat journey. If I tell my dad about that journey he is not going to feel good. He will think he sent his son to die.

———

MAYA left her country with her mother and siblings

People ask me, 'Do you regret coming to Australia?' I don't regret it, because I see the people who are still left behind in Indonesia now, with no future. It was worth it. It's not something I'm happy that I did, because in my whole life this is the only not legal thing I have done, and I am ready to take the consequences. But I consider the reasons why I made it. And I'm not here to hurt anybody.

So, the boat journey . . . I will never forget. I'm trying to move on, but more and more I realise it's something I need to live with. It's the bravest thing I have ever done in my life. I wouldn't think there is something worse I could do than taking a boat without knowing how to swim, and in the hands of people you shouldn't trust.

Well, the boat journey . . . how can I explain? I hate it. I swear to God. I hate talking about the boat.

———

SOLMAZ

My son, the two of us left the country together. We tried four times to take a boat. The first time the police came and we had to run away. Then another attempt, another attempt. The third time, they took us all on the boat. We thought we were leaving but then we realised that actually they gave all of us to the police. When the police intercepted us, they kept us on the water the whole night so that we didn't run away. They kept circling us on the water. It started raining and we all got soaked. In the morning they put us all on a truck and they took us to this huge hall—I'm not sure if it was a hotel or what it was. There was some food. They kept all of us there while they were doing some forms or other things.

I saw that things were quiet, so I told my son to run away. He ran first and I went after him but the police noticed and they stopped me. My son actually had my mobile phone.

Then the police took us to a detention centre. After a while my son called a friend's mobile and he said, 'Mum, what should I do? Do you want me to come back?' And I said, 'No, you go. Establish yourself somewhere so I know that you're secure. I'll find a way to come.'

Three days later I was standing by a window at ground level. It was the kind that only goes up a little bit, you crank it open and it sort of tips open. Because I was skinny, I could use a special technique to throw myself out. I looked around and it was quiet so I threw myself out and ran away.

I went to the street and found a taxi. We had stayed at a hiding place for a few months before and I knew the name of the place and I had learned the area. I told the taxi driver where I wanted to go. He took me to the station and told me to get a bus from there to the place.

We knew that we couldn't go back. We knew we were going to have to find some other way, but we never even thought about going back to our home—that was not an option.

THEY CANNOT TAKE THE SKY

JAWID arrived aged nineteen after years avoiding Taliban violence

One thing I do remember, we arrived very close to the beach at Christmas Island and we saw that there were some families on the beach, they were swimming there next to the jetty. So I thought they might show some reaction, but to them it seemed very normal. They were not even paying attention to us that much. That is something that I always picture of Christmas Island, the families swimming there on the beach.

OSAMA DARAGI fled Iraq, arriving in Australia by plane

In Turkey, I met a guy—he sold fake passports, Iraqi passports and visas. They changed the picture, they put my picture in and then I booked a ticket for Australia. It wasn't my choice to go to Australia, but the guy said, 'With this passport you can travel to Australia, easy.' I didn't know anything about Australia.

I ripped up the passport in the plane and I threw it in the bathroom. And then I got off the aeroplane with nothing—no ID, nothing.

I was so scared, shocked, I didn't know anything. My English, it was so bad. And then when I arrived at the airport, I walked around for more than four hours, just to hide myself, because I don't know anything. I just hid myself there, like in the toilet, for a couple of hours. Then I went where there were some couches, I sat there, and one officer he asked me, 'Do you have any passport, ID?'

I was so scared, I couldn't even feel my lips, all my body

was shaking. When they started to do the interview with me, I was crying and the officer he said, 'Don't be scared. In Australia we're gonna save your life.' They gave me biscuits and juice, water. They were so nice.

It was more than five hours. And at the end they said, 'We're going to send you to a relaxing place. They're gonna give you clothes and food and a special room.' And in my mind I thought they were going to send me to a hotel. I didn't know anything about the detention centres.

Then two officers from Serco arrived at the airport. When we arrived at the detention centre, I saw the big gate, cameras everywhere, and I thought, *Oh my god, this is really a gaol*. They took everything off me—my clothes, my shoes, everything. They gave me a new shirt, new shorts. Then I went inside and I saw it was a gaol. I was at Maribyrnong detention centre.

MOHSEN

We saw two navy ships coming. I thought, *I don't care what is going to happen, I don't care about police, at least we will be alive.* They quickly moved us to their ship and we got sent to Christmas Island. When we got there everyone was very welcoming. I felt good. They were nice people, welcoming and happy. Then, after some time they took us to the detention centre. I noticed the boys around me looked very sad. You know when you talk with somebody and you can't feel comfortable, you're talking with them but they can't talk back? It was like this. I was staring into dead eyes with no soul behind them.

THEY CANNOT TAKE THE SKY

SARA was a translator and interpreter in Iran, living with her husband and sons

When we arrived at the detention centre it was like heaven. I felt I was in a very safe place. This is the reason I'm saying the camp was not that bad—I'm comparing my life to that of a dead person.

The camp was very clean. The services were good. The whole place was open but, for example, if you wanted to eat there were certain times you could go to the restaurant. If you wanted the internet there were certain times you could use the internet. There was only one shop. During each week they gave us some points. These points were like having money. If you went to each one of the classes like craft class or English class, they gave you two points. You could go to the shop and buy toothpaste, chocolate, nuts, notebooks, pens, bags or makeup.

JOHN GULZARI

We were put, one by one, onto the bus and taken to this RAAF base in Broome. It was so isolated. Around there was a jungle and inside was a razor wire, and then once we went inside there was another razor wire and a processing centre, where they took our photos and fingerprints. I was feeling a sigh of relief. I remember the first day when people were taking the photo, they were saying, 'Why are you smiling?' And I said, 'Thank god I'm safe.'

MAYA

For me, Christmas Island was heaven. [*Laughs.*] I didn't care where they put me, I didn't care where they took me, I just wanted to sleep. That's all I wanted: to take a shower, sleep. The soap they gave me to wash I finished that night, that second! It's supposed to last a few days.

We arrived at night-time. They . . . they took my brother from us. My brother was tired, we were tired. We couldn't argue, we couldn't talk about why or when. We thought they were gonna take him somewhere, and bring him back. But they just took him. He was scared, we were scared. So we just took a shower, slept.

In the morning, someone shouted, 'Breakfast!' For a few days we didn't sleep, and this girl was shouting for breakfast. For maybe a month, every time I woke up, I woke up dizzy. I needed to sit, then stand up. Then I talked to the doctors. They said, 'It's because you stayed a long time in the sea, so, still your feet need to get used to the ground.' I said, 'If that's it, okay. I thought I'm pregnant from the sea!' [*Laughs.*] It was like, every time, feeling dizzy, dizzy.

My brother was at the single compound for only boys, somewhere else in Christmas Island. We didn't understand where he was. He didn't understand where we were. So we told one of the caseworkers . . . we wrote a lot of questions. So, one time they called us, they said there was a phone call. And I swear I remember that day. We got the phone call, we talked, we heard his voice. It was the most relieving moment because at least we knew they weren't lying. He was okay. Because I wasn't trusting anybody at that time. Oh god, it was . . . my sister kept crying. We were not brothers and sisters who are emotionally together, you know? We were mostly throwing shoes at each other. 'Don't hug me, please. Don't talk to me. Please.' That kind of thing. We only felt we missed him that time, and he was worrying about us so much. The first question he asked was, 'Are you girls okay? Are they hurting you?'

ZARA was smuggled out of her country with her daughter ATHENA, who was then seven years old

Athena: The worst thing at Christmas Island were the toilets. They were really bad. We had to share them with everyone else. There were four toilets for the ladies and four toilets for the men. Bleugh. The shower and the toilets were together. It was smelly! We waited for the cleaners to clean the toilet, and then we would always go in for a shower. That's the best way to just do it. That was Aqua? That was the first camp . . . No, that was the second.

Zara: The first one was worse.

Athena: Oh yeah, that one was bad, too. The first one was like a medical place where we got checked up. Like it was a huge tent kind of thing. And then there was like bunk beds. Me and Mum didn't sleep on the bottom bunk.

Zara: She was scared of mice . . .

Athena: Rats! It was terrible. So we slept at the top of the bunk. There were 60 people in there or so. With the *rats* . . .

Zara: Also, it was very hot at night-time. And mosquitoes. I couldn't sleep. I was scared that mosquitoes were biting Athena.

Athena: There were crabs at Christmas Island.

Zara: Yeah. So many crabs. Everywhere.

Athena: There were like bridges over them, basically. All the wooden walking things they had to build, or else we would step on the crabs. Once we saw this huge crab—

Zara: Like rainbow coloured—

Athena: It was mostly greyish purple-y, though. And then there were other colours mixed in it. It was huge. It was the biggest crab I've ever seen. And I've seen a lot of crabs. [*Laughs.*]

HAL-HAL writes, sings and dances; she arrived in Australia in 2013

When they put us in Christmas Island detention they were saying, 'This place is for family, this place is for singles.' Friends who came with me, they were separated from parts of their family. They have rules, like such crazy rules. You can't stay up after eight or nine at night, and then they have many different camps. First you have to go to this camp, and then you transfer to another, then you transfer to third, some people to a fourth. I remember I told them that I wanted to go in a room with one of my friends but they put me with someone strange, and they put one of my friends with a different person and then when we told them that we wanted to change they said, 'You can't, your name is on this room,' like, no negotiation.

And some people stay there longer. We were feeling very depressed because people who came after us transferred before us. And we were saying, 'Why don't they do that to us? Like, what's the reason?' And we were very scared. We said maybe it was because we were wearing head scarves, or because we're dark skinned. Absolutely, a lot of people came after us but they transferred before, but all of them were white. They came from places like the Middle East, Lebanon, Iran. Plus, if you want to ask a Serco something—if you need something for your room or food—they will help people with white skin more than dark skin.

ALI REZA grew up on the border of Pakistan and Afghanistan and travelled to Australia alone

I was a minor, so they took me to the minors' detention where there were plenty more minors. We stayed two people to a room. We didn't see any adults or the family that arrived with us, because they had been separated from us. For a month we were just unsettled.

There were thirteen of us left from our boat, the rest were transferred to detention centres in Australia. But the authorities no longer believed we were minors; they told us we were eighteen years old. So they did interviews again. I said, 'If you want to make my birthday a different time and me a different age, this is not a big deal for me, up to you guys.' I knew that was under the control of the government, so I had to do whatever they wanted. They made us new dates of birth and ages and they transferred all of us to the adult camp.

ALI and RAHILA HAIDARY

Ali: The first night, when they brought all the phones and told us to call our families, no one called, because we were thinking, *They're going to record our voices, and they won't let us stay in Australia.* But then in the second week, I called my family. Still some people wouldn't call, but I just couldn't wait. I couldn't remember the phone number, so I called one of my friends and told him to tell my family that I was on Christmas Island.

Rahila: Oh . . . so . . . before he called, that friend of his, one day he came and said, 'A boat sank in the sea on the way to Australia and I assume that your dad was on that boat.' I remember my mum breaking down at that moment. And like . . . you can't tolerate . . . you can't just . . . and then, after few days that man came again and said, 'Your dad has called me and he's on Christmas Island.' But by then we were thinking that, *Oh this man must be crazy*, but we gave him the number for a mobile we had in the house. And then one day it was ringing and I picked up the phone and it was a shaky voice and I couldn't recognise my dad's voice at the start. But then he was calling me his daughter—*bachay* in Hazaragi—and . . . I kept saying, 'How are you, Dad? How are you, Dad?'

I didn't know where Christmas Island was. But I had a map of the world on my wall. It was actually on the map. And then the next minute I was just going crazy. I was yelling and I was shouting around the house and Mum was just like, 'What happened to you?' And I was like, 'Mum, Dad called us and he's safe. He's on Christmas Island.' And I can't forget my mum's face, glowing. Her eyes . . . I think she needed that. Her whole body needed that, needed to know that Dad was safe. And that small smile on her face was just so beautiful.

THEY CANNOT TAKE THE SKY

REZA YARAHMADI arrived on Christmas Island in 2009; after being released, he began campaigning for detainee rights

You could see people crying when they were talking to their families—crying talking to their kids, crying talking to their friends, or hearing a relative or friend had been caught by police in Indonesia, or that their relative had passed away.

When I spoke to my family I wouldn't tell them—I could not tell them—about detention life. But there were other people who told their families, and my mother and sisters heard about it. When I got out of detention I talked to my mum, and she said, 'You have to love your sisters, because that four months you were in detention they had no food, no sleep. They were crying, stressed about what is going to happen to you in that gaol.' And I said, 'Why? It was good place,' and they said, 'No, you were not telling us but we heard from other people the place was horrible.' But I told my family, 'At least I am safe.'

JAWID

After one month we were transferred to the main detention centre. It was a very new experience for us. We were very happy to go there, to see so many people there. There were around one thousand detainees at the time. Hearing stories. Then we spoke to other Afghans who were in the main detention centre. Some people had been there more than a year, some for eighteen months, some for two years. And when I heard those stories, I was very worried. So many years and you still won't know how long you will be here? I was still remaining optimistic that hopefully this wouldn't happen to me. But it was worrying at the same time. *If that happens to me, how can you survive here for two years? If it does happen how can you last?*

PART II

I wore a black shirt to my ceremony

Ali

Ali Bakhtiarvandi arrived in Australia by boat in 2000, aged 34. He was detained until 2004 in three different detention centres. He is now an Australian citizen.

I'm addicted to cups of tea

I'm working at the chemical factory in Ballarat. I have a big order at the moment I have to finish. It is ten hours a day; I am working two hours' overtime because I have to finish that order as soon as possible.

I had chemical work in my background. I was working in petrochemicals, back in Iran. That's why I like this job and I think it's been over ten years that I've been doing it. I'm a formulator and also machinery operator. We're making herbicide and different products for farmers. Some of the products are a little bit hard to make. As I said, it's a really good job. Most of the people in Ballarat they don't like to work there because we have to use a full face mask and for the first few days when you start working there, because of the face mask, it's hard to breathe. But we are used to it.

It's hard to see myself getting tired physically but lots of times I get tired mentally. Mentally means when I see the politics in Australia—it's not working and it's playing games with people, and I get really tired. I would love to see something nice after thirty-something years working as a human rights activist. It's really hard to see. Another thing also: the news in the world, the Gaza and Iraq situations. Civilians killed for nothing. Crazy people. It's a broken heart I have, you know? Seeing those pictures on TV and also hearing it everywhere, it stops me being happy at all. But it does not stop me being a political activist. Still, I'm happy to continue this until the end. I was a political activist in Iran from 1979. I'm worried to say more than that because I don't want to make any problem for my family. This is really risky and dangerous. I am safe here in this country.

Life in Ballarat is, I can say, it's beautiful. I've been living there since 2004. It is a really lovely, nice community. The place I'm living, it's a double-storey unit and I'm living by myself. I have another five neighbours. Sometimes if my neighbours are not around I can practice music, because I play two traditional Iranian instruments. I listen to music, listen to the news most of the time, and try to have as normal a life as I can. In one small sentence I can say I have no problem in Ballarat with anything.

As soon as I get back from work the first thing I do is make a cup of tea because I'm addicted to cups of tea. And then I start answering the telephone or making calls with refugees and talking to them about their situation. Most of the refugees I'm involved with at the moment are in the community and they have been waiting a long time for their applications to be processed. I talk to them and, using my experience back from 2000 to 2004, tell them what they should do to cope with this situation a little bit easier. I try to do as much as I can because I've gone through the horrible immigration system. I can understand it's really, really hard.

They are treating us like really dangerous people

I arrived in Australia on 5 June 2000. We arrived at Ashmore Reef. Then we came to Darwin and from there they took us to Port Hedland detention centre. We were 36 people, including women and children and also a pregnant woman. All from Iraq and Iran.

The people smuggler said, 'You're going to Australia. You will be there in eight hours.' We were on the way three days and two nights from Kupang to Ashmore Reef. Also, the people smuggler said, 'As soon as you get to Australia you will be arrested by the United Nations and you will be in isolation for 45 days. Then you're going to be released to the community with your visa and you will start your new life.' That is the only information we had.

The treatment from the first minute we got to Port Hedland detention made every single person think differently. *Oh, this is not right, because they are treating us like really dangerous people. Why we are here? The door is locked. There is no TV, no telephone. How we can tell our family we are in Australia and we are safe and we are alive? And how long are we going to be here like that?*

For the first month we were in the isolation block. Fully isolated from the rest of the compound. No nothing. The only people we could see were from the Immigration department and also the security company called ACM.*

---

* Australasian Correctional Management was a subsidiary of the US security company Wackenhut. It was awarded a contract to run all Australian immigration detention centres from 1998 to 2003.

Thirty-six people, everybody living in same place. We were using the toilet and shower system together—women, children and men. They have doors, but it wasn't separate. The Iraqi family started complaining about it, because of Islamic Law and also because it wasn't right for women and men to be using the same bathroom or shower. Then they let the women have the single shower outside the block. We had ten minutes' fresh air in the morning and fifteen minutes' after lunch. That meant less than half an hour a day.

People in Port Hedland live in houses next to the detention centre, but we didn't know that. The compound had over eight hundred people in it, and we didn't know anything about it. When we were living in that block, people in the compound had a demonstration and they smashed the fence and went to the street and were arrested by police. They took them to Perth gaol. And we didn't know anything about it.

One day we went for fresh air time outside. We received a tennis ball. People from the compound, they hit the tennis ball with the cricket bat. We looked at it, there was a white paper inside. We thought, *Oh, they sent a message*. The message was in Persian and it said, 'You come to horrible country. We are here for more than a year.'

Anyway, after one month, they started to call people for a first interview. My first interview started after eleven o'clock at night. I went to a different area in that detention area; they took me in a car. To be honest, I didn't know what the interview was for. I had no idea. There was a woman from Immigration and another woman as an interpreter. The interpreter said to me, 'She is from the Immigration department. She is going to ask you some questions, but before she starts do you have any questions?'

I said to her in Persian, 'I'm sorry, I don't know what you mean, because I have been interrogated by intelligence services and usually they put handcuffs on my hands, and use the black material to cover my eyes as well. The only interview I know, it's that.' She translated that to the Immigration woman and she said, 'No, just tell him we are two women here and this is your process and something we have to do.' She asked me some questions. It finished by twelve o'clock.

Ten or fifteen days later, they called me to see a lawyer. I went to the room again. He said, 'I'm your lawyer. We're going to talk about your problem, about why you came to Australia. This is going to be private between me and you.'

I was believing. I talked to him for more than an hour. But the statement he made for my case was only three paragraphs. I still have it. After more than an hour: three paragraphs. We didn't know anything. He gave it to me. I signed it. He gave me a copy. But still I couldn't read it, you know. And when he said, 'I'm a lawyer,' I was trusting he was a person who was working for me, not working for the Immigration department.

A few days later a man came and he said, 'I'm your case officer.' He was from Perth Immigration department, and I was shocked when I saw him. He wore a T-shirt and was full of tattoos on his body. Someone said he was member of dog racing in Perth, something like that. Before he started, he showed me that in his file he had every paper I had shared with my lawyer. I couldn't say anything, because I had no information and I didn't want to make my process hard. Anyway, he talked to me for almost two hours, I think. Then I was taken to the compound for first time. Everybody, when their process finished, they went to the compound.

There were too many people there. Women, children, you know. Different nationalities. From Kosovo, from Bosnia, from Russia, from Vietnam, China, Iran, Iraq, Afghanistan. Everywhere was full of people, and there wasn't room. We had five double-storey blocks called A block, B, C, D and G.

And all of them were full. We asked the ACM supervisor and she said, 'I don't know. Go find somewhere for yourself.'

An Iraqi–Iranian man—who was really nice man and accused of being a people smuggler, they deported him finally to Iraq in 2004—said, 'If they are not giving you a room, come to the family area and I'm going to make my son's room empty for you.' It was called the family area but everybody was living there together: single women, single men, families.

In the compound there was a Telstra phone, but we had no money. At that time it cost a ten-dollar Telstra phone card for seven minutes' talk to Iran.

A few days later, some people came and said, 'Your name is on the whiteboard for an interview with the federal police.' In that time, people said that whoever goes to talk to the federal police are released a few days later. It means they get a visa, and you're going to get your visa too.

An old man from the federal police came to talk to me, again talking about my case, three hours of interview. Three days later I was rejected by the Immigration department. I think it was September.

I came here for my freedom

Then I said to the Immigration department, 'I didn't come here to stay locked up. I came here for my freedom. If you cannot let me to go out as a free person, I would like to see someone from the United Nations, because I'm not a criminal.' They said, 'No, nobody is allowed to see you.'

So that's it. I stopped eating. The first ten days actually were a little bit hard because I never had an experience like that in my life, except sometimes in war time back in Iran—because of the horrible war situation we sometimes didn't have food to eat, but just for one day, two days, maximum three days. That

'I used to have flashbacks a lot. I realised that I was shaking all the time, I couldn't catch my breath. I had anxiety all the time, all the time': Neda.

'I remember there was one water tap in the middle of the desert, surrounded by barbed wire': Munjed Al Muderis.

'I believe if I am silent, I am a dead person, I am gone. What I believe is: we are all human beings. If they abuse you, one day, they will come and abuse me. So we have to stop them': Reza Yarahmadi.

'The most horrible thing in the detention centre was the different tricks they used to deport people. The night was worst time, because they usually start to deport people at night. Sometimes in the daytime they told someone they had a doctor's appointment, and then that person disappeared': Ali Bakhtiarvandi.

'On my way from Jakarta to one of the islands called Lombok I told the driver to play that one, and he asked why, and I said, "Before I drown I would like to listen to this music for one last time"': John Gulzari.

'One thing I realised in the detention centre was that I never saw a guard who did not smoke. I used to ask them, "Does everyone in Australia smoke?" and they used to say, "No, we smoke because we have a tough job"': Jawid.

'Back then in the 1990s, nobody wanted to go to Australia. It was a strange, alien land': Aran Mylvaganam.

'When my daughter was born, I didn't see the difference between a boy and a girl': Ali Haidary. 'I was a bit cheeky, I would say, and naughty maybe': Rahila Haidary.

'I always felt I had some sort of intuitive magical power—that if I wanted anything the universe would grant me it. So when I was in the detention centre I blamed it on myself': Donna Sherwani.

'I remember the day that we were leaving. Everyone around us was crying: my aunty, my grandmother, even my mum, and I didn't understand why. I assumed we were going on an adventure to find Dad': Jamila Jafari.

'The sky is like a friend for a prisoner, because around you everything is metal fences, but the sky, they cannot take the sky': Behrouz Boochani.

'When I got to Christmas Island, everything was different. The first thing I could see was crabs and chickens, 'cause they got a lot of crabs and chickens and refugees': Hani Abdile.

'Maybe after this prison I will end up in another prison, or I will have a better life. I don't know what will happen. But from what I can see now, I'm still having a dark future': Abdul Aziz Muhamat.

'I'd like to study instead of doing nothing. I want to study for my future. If you want to change something you have to learn. Education is light': Omar Mohammed Jack.

'If we finish it—if we kill ourselves—we might go to a place that is not a good place. And there might not be a reset button. So, we have to finish this journey, we have to continue': Amir Taghinia.

'When I was released into the community I felt there was a huge change in my body. All that time I had been unable to do anything and all of a sudden I had so much freedom. I was able to feel that my body had consciousness': Peter.

time, no—just water. I was feeling really sick, honestly. My blood sugar was really low, my blood pressure really low, and I lost weight, from 67 to 53 kilograms. But I said, 'I'm sorry, if you ordered some food from outside, from the best restaurant in Port Hedland, I would say, "No." I'm Iranian, I didn't come here for my stomach, I came here for my freedom. I didn't have a food problem in my country. No. I don't want you to do anything for me like that. Just leave me alone.'

Day eighteen, one of the security guards came and said, 'The nurse wants to see you.' As soon as they put me in her room, they said, 'You are not going back to the compound until you start eating.'

They took me to a very small room, with a video camera in the corner. There was no window. All the walls and also the floor was covered with very hard sponge, like a mattress but very hard. No bed, no pillow, no blanket, and air-conditioning on 24 hours, and the light on 24 hours. There wasn't any switch inside the room to turn the light off or on. A small window in the door, you know, for the security guard to see me inside, what I'm doing. They took my clothes away. They gave me a white surgical gown. They didn't give me another one to change into. One month I was wearing that, without a T-shirt, without pants, without underpants, without anything.

One month I was in isolation. On my hunger strike day 46, someone from immigration or the medical centre in detention came with a piece of paper and they said, 'Mr Ruddock sent us an email or fax'—something like that—'and he said, "If you don't start to eat in the next 48 hours a doctor can force you." Could you please start eating?' I said, 'I'm sorry, no.' And by that time I didn't have feeling to move, you know. They used a wheelchair to take me to the bathroom or sometimes outside.

On day 48 they opened the door. I was lying on the floor. There were five or six big security guards. I was feeling sick, and shocked as well. What do you want to do to the person who hasn't eaten anything for a long, long time? Two of them held my legs while I was on the floor. Two of them held my hands, this was four of them. The supervisor, she put my head between her knees. Another officer with a video camera was filming it. The nurse and doctor tried to use tube from my nose to my stomach. And the doctor injected some liquid thing.

That was really, really torture, because it wasn't easy to breathe with something going from your nose to your stomach, while they didn't put you to sleep using anaesthetic injection. I couldn't breathe. I didn't have any energy or power to move, because I was sick and held by big security guards. There was nothing I could do that time. And they went. They shut the door and they went.

At night-time, they came, opened the door, and said, 'Your food.' I said, 'No, put it outside. I don't want it, I don't want it.' I was there for another few days. Then they said, 'We're going to take you to Juliet Block. And we are not going to release you until you start eating.' I was there also for one week. They brought one of the detainees there for some different reason, and he said, 'Look, it's not going to work. People are waiting for you inside the compound, you have to go and join them in doing something together.'

I was really tired. Really tired mentally, because I hadn't seen anybody, my friends, for a long time, and the treatment of the security company and Immigration also made me more sick. I started eating. They released me from isolation.

Night was the worst time

Then later, still in 2000, a lady from Immigration department came from Canberra. She said, 'I have a special mission to see you and talk to you.' I thought, *Oh, I've become a very important person, to have someone coming from Canberra to see me!* She said, 'I came to let you know you have to go back to your country. There is no way you can stay here. Even if you are in detention for ten years, we're not going to give you a visa.'

I said, 'Could you tell me why?' She said, 'Yeah. Just, listen, the Australian government and the Australian people, they don't like people like you. We don't like political people. That's why we're not going to give you a visa.' I said, 'Okay, could you give me a favour? I'm not that person who signs to go back voluntarily. If you use an injection and deport me back to my country I would appreciate it. If you do this, as soon as I get to Iran, something will happen to me, and that's the Immigration department's responsibility, and you are under the big question mark. I'm not going to stop you.' She was shocked.

When I was rejected by the Immigration department, the paper said they didn't believe my case. But she said, 'We believe you. You are a political activist and we don't like it.' That is two different things. Which one I should believe?

Every second of detention centre time is horrible. While I was in Port Hedland, I could see people walking, because the detention centre is very close to the sea, you know? From the second floor you can see the water, and sometimes you could see people walking around. I was always thinking, *Will I be allowed to walk that way, one day? As a free person?* It's hard to think like that.

But the most horrible thing in the detention centre was the different tricks they used to deport people. The night was the worst time, because they usually start to deport people at night. Sometimes in the daytime they told someone they had a doctor's appointment, and then that person disappeared. Then a security guard came to take his or her stuff. When we had to go to the medical centre, we told each other, 'I'm going.

If I don't come back after fifteen minutes, it means something happened. Tell everyone.' We tried to look after each other like that.

You cannot throw stones or rocks at the system

During that time we started painting T-shirts as a protest inside the detention centre. They gave us T-shirts, all the same colour, good for painting and making a demonstration: we wrote on them 'Freedom' and 'Free refugees'. Usually that was my job to do that.

We made another demonstration inside and it became violent between detainees and the security company. It was 2001. In all the time I was in the detention centre people smashed windows, smashed the fence, threw rocks or stones or something like that. But I never did anything like that, or swore at anybody, in all the time there. No, because I always believe we haven't any problem with the fences or the staff in the kitchen or the restaurant or the medical rooms. We have a problem with the system, and you cannot throw stones or rocks at the system. Fighting with the system is different.

But my name was on the list of leaders of troublemakers in Port Hedland detention centre. They took me back to the same isolation room. I was there for three days, I think, then they came in the morning and opened the door, took me outside to the van and took me to Port Hedland airport. No shoes, no sandals, no thongs. With tracksuit pants and one T-shirt. They never tell you anything. And when we get close I saw the police surrounding the airport in full gear. For few seconds I was thinking there might be some important person coming, because I had heard about BHP company in Port Hedland and I thought it might be them. Then I find out those police were there because of me and my other friends.

I thought, *Oh, I have become a really dangerous terrorist in Australia,* for the police to spend lots of money like that, to surround the Port Hedland airport.

We didn't know what was happening. Look, the immigration system in Australia is exactly like the CIA system in America. You cannot find out what they are doing. They took my friends to a bigger aeroplane and took me with another two to a very small aeroplane and we left Port Hedland to go to Perth. I didn't know where Perth was, or even what it was. Out the window it was all desert. When we got there, another van came, they put handcuffs on my friends' hands and took them to Perth detention centre. The security guards with me, they took me out and said, 'Do you want to go to the toilet? Are you thirsty? Do you want to eat something?' They tried to be a little bit kind and respectful.

They said, 'We are going somewhere,' and this took us five or six hours. It was from Perth to Melbourne, but I didn't know. It was night-time and, oh, geez, I saw the lights. *This is a huge city! What is this? Where is this city?* We came out and some security guards were waiting for us. I ask the lady, 'What is this city's name?' She said, 'Don't worry about it.'

They took me to Maribyrnong detention centre. They opened the isolation room and when I went inside I saw my other two friends there, the ones who had gone in the bigger aeroplane. They didn't want us to be together in a small aeroplane, that's why they made us separate.

I said, 'Do you know what this detention centre is?' They said this is Melbourne detention, Maribyrnong. Before they came to Port Hedland, they were in Maribyrnong. They were seamen. They jumped from an Islamic Republic Iranian ship in Port Melbourne and they didn't go back.

They gave us a separate room. It was very small room, with two double bunks. The first night was really scary, because I came from a big cage in Port Hedland to very small cage, with lots of different people. The number of refugees was very low. Most of the people, their visa was expired and they were working illegally. Some others were released from gaol because of drugs or something like that, and were awaiting deportation. They were usually from Asia: China and Vietnam. When I say scary, not because of those people. Everybody there was really friendly. Scary because I didn't know what's going on in this small area they call a detention centre. It was very hard to even breathe.

Who is gonna be that person?

Next morning an officer came, and he said, 'You have a visitor.' I said, 'What do you mean by visitor?' The first thing that came to my head was that this was a trick from the Immigration department to take me out of this area and it might be something to do with deportation.

Because you know, it was a fully strange thing to me. I didn't know anybody in Australia, except Immigration department people and security company people. Somebody came to visit me and he or she knows my name? Who is gonna be that person? My other two friends were also called for the same visit. They said, 'We have to go. If they want to deport us, we are not sure we can stop them.'

My heart started beating a little bit normally when I got to the visit area. I saw a lady, she introduced herself as Pamela Curr.* I can say I trusted her straight away. It was my first face-to-face meeting with one of the Australian people and I saw she was a really kind person. She said, 'I found your name in

---

* Pamela Curr is an advocate for refugee and detention rights, including for many years with the Asylum Seeker Resource Centre in Melbourne, which was founded in mid-2001.

The Age newspaper. It said they sent you here after the problem inside Port Hedland centre. I'm here to do as much as I can and help you if you need lawyer.' Before we met her, we thought this country was really racist, because the security company and Immigration department people would say, 'Look, Australian people don't like you. Australian people don't like you to be free. Australian people are scared of you.' And we believed it because we had no connection between ourselves and Australians. Meeting her changed my mind about Australian people.

We had lots of visitors in a very short time. Three times every day: morning, afternoon and night. And that gave us more energy, more power to be strong as before, because we saw we have the support of the Australian people against this situation. I saw even old people coming in very cold weather in Melbourne, staying in the queue outside for 45 minutes to visit us, plus driving from their suburbs. I'm sure, unless I get Alzheimer's, I will never forget the Australian people I saw when I was in detention and also when I was released. Sometimes, because they knew we were feeling really sad, they tried to make us laugh. They were full of kindness. It's not really easy to talk about it, because it was huge. I thought, I met a bunch of angels in Australia, you know, visiting three times a day. It made the heavy situation inside the camp a little bit lighter on our shoulders.

Still we had problems inside with the security company, with the Immigration department. In Maribyrnong detention centre while I was there none of the bedrooms had doors. It was open. And there was no switch to turn the light on or off. The security company turned the light off every night any time they wanted. Sometimes the light was on until two o'clock in the morning and sometimes ten o'clock.

Both detention centres were gaols. Built from gold or made with tents and razor wire around it, there was no difference for me. Gaol is gaol. For myself, the difference between Port Hedland and Maribyrnong was finding out there are lovely people living in this country. And another thing was that it was easy for us to give reports to people about what is going on inside. There is a factory next to the detention centre and my room was very close to that factory fence. People came to the factory site and we talked to them from the window in my bedroom. Security couldn't do anything about it because that wasn't illegal.

I got a camera. I took photos of inside—the living room, bedroom, bathroom, everything—and I gave it to one of my visitors. It looked very dirty, very old. They put the photos on the Refugee Action Collective website. As soon as they did this, Immigration and the ACM company changed lots of things, like new furniture, new curtains—they made everything look fantastic.

I'm not going to wear handcuffs

I had a problem with my tooth. I went to see the nurse. She treated us really horribly. She said, 'I will send you to see a dentist outside detention.'

They called me for my appointment. The nurse said, 'The Immigration department said you have to put handcuffs on to go outside.' I said, 'No, I'm sorry. I am not a criminal and I'm not going to wear handcuffs.' I went back to the compound. That situation took me three months. My lawyer talked to Immigration and Immigration said that is ACM's choice. ACM said, 'It is Immigration's choice, we cannot do anything about it.' They were actually playing a game, you know. My right face was very swollen and really bad. Under my eyes it was the colour of eggplant skin—really dark purple blue. It was like someone had punched me. I couldn't eat very well and the medication started not working.

After three months, I went to the dentist in handcuffs. I was sitting in the dentists' foyer and some people were there, looking at me really strangely. *Who is that person? Under his eye is really dark. They put handcuffs on him. Four really big security guards with him. He might be a really dangerous person.* If I was one of them, I was going to think like that.

The dentist pulled out five teeth in less than fifteen minutes, while handcuffs were on my hands. When I came back to detention one of the security guards said to me, 'If I was you, I would never let them put handcuffs on my hands, because that wasn't right.' I said, 'It took me three months, I cannot sleep, I cannot eat, I cannot talk—I didn't have a choice!'

I saw a woman come for me

In early 2002, after thirteen or fourteen months in Maribyrnong detention centre, one night I had many visitors. Visiting time finished at nine o'clock. I was busy saying goodbye to my visitors one by one. I saw a woman come for me and she was crying. She said, 'I heard about your hunger strike and I was wondering if I could visit you.' I said, 'I don't want visitors to come here and cry for us. I want everybody to be happy, because that makes me stronger, you know.' She said, 'I promise not to cry.' She started coming to visit three times a day. She was living in Footscray, five minutes' drive from the detention centre.

And after a while, one night she came and said, 'I want to talk privately. I found out how you can be released from detention.'

I said, 'I'm not sure you can do anything about it, because I have one barrister and few lawyers working for my case,'

'I found out if we get married you can be released.'

'Thank you very much, see you later.' Honestly.

'Where are you going?' she said.

I said, 'Look, my political life is really important to me and it's never led me to play games with anybody's life for my freedom. I have five sisters. If I do anything like that with anybody's life, I have to let someone do the same thing with my sister's life, and it's not possible for me to let anybody to do this. But thank you very much, that was kind and I'm sure I will be released one day. It's not that hard for me.'

Anyway she continued to come to visit. One day she said, 'I talked to my family and I really want to marry you.'

'I'm too old to play games,' I said.

'No, really.'

I said, 'Okay.' I don't know actually if I was happy. She was a really kind person. People in detention, they pushed me to do it as well, because everyone liked her. I couldn't think properly—*Is this right or wrong?*—because my head was full of problems from the years in Port Hedland and Maribyrnong.

We let the Immigration department know we were engaged. One Wednesday morning, a security guard came and called me to my doctor. But they put me in the isolation room and a few minutes later an Immigration manager came. She said, 'I received a fax from Canberra. You have to go to Port Hedland, because we don't have enough beds in this detention centre.' I said, 'I counted last night and 24 beds were empty.' She said, 'No, I'm sorry. I received a fax and you have to go. You are not allowed to go back. You are leaving for the airport from here.'

At the same time, my fiancée came to visit and reception said, 'He is not here. We don't know where he is.'

To be honest I think they got tired, because visitors were making meetings with the Immigration department about lots of problems inside. We had no blankets in cold weather and the heating system was not working. Visitors had to bring blankets for most of the people inside, especially in the family area for women and children. They wanted me to go to Port Hedland because they thought it would make their problem less.

I was really upset. They took me to Port Hedland and to the isolation block, again. At nine o'clock somebody gave me a phone card and I used the public phone inside the isolation block to call my fiancée and say, 'Look, I am in Port Hedland detention centre.' I said, 'Don't worry about it. I am here, I am safe. I am not happy, but it is what it is.' The next day they released me to the compound. Everything was the same, except the number of people, now less than two hundred people. But still I had some friends there, families and also singles. Now it was different because visitors came from Sydney and Melbourne and Brisbane as a group—maybe one hundred people, sitting around the detention centre fence outside and talking to people all the time.

We got married on the 29 November 2002 inside Port Hedland detention centre. It was in an interview room close to the isolation room I had been inside for the hunger strike. I was just in normal clothes, without any friends. Just me and my fiancée and two witnesses from outside who were friends with her. I wasn't happy at all, because getting married inside gaol, you know, it wasn't right to me.

That day they let us to go to a restaurant in Port Hedland with a security guard in uniform. Can you imagine? Everyone in the restaurant was looking at us really, really strangely. To be honest I didn't enjoy the day. I was just acting like I was happy because I didn't want my wife to be sad.

A few days later my wife said, 'I'm going back to Melbourne and I'm coming to say goodbye tomorrow.' Early in the morning one of the detainees went crazy. He went onto the roof naked. Then some of my friends said, 'You have a phone call.' I picked up the telephone and my wife said, 'I came to visit and they said something happened and visiting is cancelled.' She asked them, 'Please, just let me say goodbye to him face to face.' They said no.

I remember the smoke

A while later we called for a meeting. We talked about organising a hunger strike and calling the media in the next few days. Other people's view was different to mine. In a very short time people decided to smash all the fences inside, because every block was separated by fences and razor wire from another one. That was for emergencies, to make it easy for the security company to lock gates to stop people joining any problem. As usual, I was one of the people against this. After living in Melbourne, I had more idea that this was all made by Australian taxpayer money and if we make them pay more money, it's going to change their view against us. People didn't listen, so they smashed the fences. Then they jumped to the double-storey isolation block and started a fire there. Immigration says it cost ten million dollars. I remember the smoke came out from that building for almost 48 hours.

When something like that happened, the security company went out of the compound for their safety and left it in detainees' hands. Lots of police came. They locked the gate again and for 24 hours we couldn't visit each other in different blocks. Then they started searching people's rooms. Someone jumped into my room at six o'clock in the morning. 'Don't move! Don't move!' I was really shocked. They pushed me to the wall and searched my body. They put handcuffs on me, plastic ones this time. They took me to South Hedland police station with some other people and put us into the police cell.

They were arresting people who were accused of making that fire.

I couldn't have done it because at that time I was using a crutch to walk. I had a problem with my right foot. I had that crutch when they sent me back to Port Hedland detention and I had been using it for nine months. The people who made the fire were jumping from a two- or three-metre fence with razor wire. How I can go there, make a fire and come back?

The conditions inside were horrible. There were more than twelve people. The federal police said, 'Your name was given to us by Immigration.' Immigration said, 'Federal police gave us your name. That's why you are here.' It seemed like we were a soccer ball, you know, passed between Immigration and the federal police. We said, 'We are not going to eat anything until we find out why we are here.'

After three days inside was really hot, humid. We decided to drink a cup of tea. They said, 'No, no hot drink for you. It's illegal inside the gaol.' I received a parcel from one of my supporters in Melbourne. They brought it from detention to the police station gaol. It was cigarettes, Lipton tea, soap and shampoo. Exactly everything we needed at that time. I said to people, 'Don't worry about it. There is shampoo—we can have a shower. There are cigarettes—we can smoke. There is Lipton tea and that's fine. We are not going to be worried about anything else. If we are together, we can have a good time.' We made cups of tea with the hot water from the shower.

After more than a week they released us, except one person who tried to kill himself inside the cell. They took us back to detention. I went to my room and I couldn't believe it was my room. In the middle, like a mountain, were all my clothes, everything. Like someone had come to search for the gold or whatever you have.

THEY CANNOT TAKE THE SKY

We're having a party tonight

Camp was quiet. It was late 2003, nearly 2004. One day, the activity officer, she said to me, 'Do you want to go with other Iranians to the shopping centre? Just for fun?' I said, 'That would be good. I can go there and buy a present for my wife.' Usually they never let us be farther than 50 centimetres from them, but she said, 'Look, I'm very tired. I'm going to sit here. This is the money. Go do whatever you want and come back here. I'm going to trust you.' My friend said to her, 'Okay, I have to tell you something. I really want to buy alcohol and because you said I'm going to trust you, I have to tell you this.' She said, 'I didn't hear anything. Do whatever you want. Just be careful, because when we go back they might search you or the stuff you bought.' He bought a carton of Coca-Cola, took all the Coca-Cola out. Then he bought a carton of beer and changed the carton. He bought two bottles of whiskey, one under my belt, one under his belt.

When we came back to detention, we tried to be very friendly with the security guard. He said, 'Oh, you bought soft drink?' We said, 'Yeah, we're having a party tonight!' We came inside the compound and went to the room. We had air-conditioning lines on the top of the wall in each room. We opened it and put the drink in there to be cooled. We had a fridge as well in our room, but it wasn't something we could leave in the fridge. I never touched it, you know, but other people had a good time.

Around then one of Immigration officers called me and said, 'You have to sign the paper to go back to your country. You have 28 days to think about it, otherwise you're going to be deported.' I said, 'Thank you very much and my answer is: do whatever you can, because I'm not going to sign this paper. I don't even want it left here.'

The 28 days passed, a second time, a third time, and then they said to me, 'If you want to go to Baxter detention centre we can organise for you to go there.' I had already heard from Pamela Curr in Melbourne they were going to shut down Port Hedland detention centre in less than a month. I said to him, 'I would love to go to Baxter.' We had a connection with people there by mobile phone and they said, 'The situation there is really bad. It's like a real gaol.' I wanted to see it, feel it myself, because you have to be in the same situation as people, otherwise it's hard to understand what the atmosphere is like inside.

Are we going to walk on the street?

I packed my stuff. I opened the back of my tape recorder and radio and I put my mobile phone in. I said, 'I'm ready any time you want. Just let me say goodbye to my friends.' They said, 'That's okay. We're going tomorrow.'

I went to Baxter. It was late night when I got there, after eleven o'clock. They checked all my stuff and they didn't find the mobile phone. I thought, *I'm going to have a problem opening the back of the tape recorder.* One of my old friends from 2000 was already there, so I said to him, 'How can I find a knife or something because I need to open the back of this?' He said, 'Don't worry, I'll give you a screwdriver.' Inside Baxter detention centre, a screwdriver! Less than ten minutes after I was inside I had my mobile phone out of the tape recorder.

In Baxter, there were different compounds with big grass areas in each. You cannot see anything outside, except the sky. Everywhere was full of security cameras and there was a special room for security guards inside the compound. To be honest, compared with Port Hedland and Maribyrnong, Baxter was a five-star hotel to me, because it was really clean. To go to visit the centre you have to go through four electric doors.

I promised my wife to be quiet. It was hard, but also I was physically and mentally really, really tired. I was broken from inside. Honestly, I was really broken. And I thought I had done all I could for my freedom and everyone else's. There was nothing else I could do. We were always thinking, *What's going on in the future? Are we going to be deported, or are we going to walk on the street?* From Port Hedland we could see people, but not from Baxter. But it was hard to find any answers for the questions that came to our heads.

For that freedom I had paid a big price

I was in Baxter for three to four months. In August 2004 they took me to Darwin for an unrelated court case. I was at a hotel in Darwin with one of my detainee friends, Reza. We met each other in Port Hedland in 2000. We were from the same state in Iran, but we didn't know each other there.

The security guards were friendly. They said, 'If you like, you can have a swim at the hotel swimming pool, or if you wouldn't like to, you can stay here, smoke and enjoy your time.' One of them, his mobile phone was ringing and when he answered, he said, 'Someone wants to talk to you.' It was my wife. She said, 'Did you hear the news?' And then she said, 'Amanda Vanstone* gave you a visa.'

You know, I wasn't happy at all. That news didn't even make me have a very small smile on my face. For some reason I was really sad. Because, first, for that freedom I had paid a big price: almost four and a half years of my life I cannot get back. Second, if it's true, how I can forget all the friends I have in detention centre, and what is going on with them?

---

* Amanda Vanstone was Minister for Immigration and Multicultural Affairs from 2003 until 2007 in the Howard government.

We went to the city and ordered lunch. Again, one of the security guards' mobile phone started ringing. It was a call from the Immigration department, so he gave the telephone to me. The person said, 'Congratulations. You've got your visa.' He wished me well and whatever. When the conversation finished, the security guards said, 'Congratulations. We are very happy for you. You are a free man now.' Believe it or not, since I heard it from my wife, I hadn't said anything to my friend who was with me because I didn't want him to get sad. I said to him, 'I'm sorry.' It was really hard for me to talk, you know, to say anything. When we finished lunch, we came out onto the street, looking at the shops, and security said to me, 'You are free. You can go anywhere you want.' I said, 'No, that's fine, and anyway, I have to be with you because I don't know anywhere in Darwin.'

We went to the hotel. They said, 'We're going to make a barbecue party tonight for you.' How can you go from being a person who is considered dangerous for four and a half years to a person they make a barbecue party for because he's got a visa?

A woman from the federal police came the next morning and took me to a very beautiful hotel. I got my visa and my wife came to Darwin. We stayed there at the hotel for a few days and then went to Ballarat. I've stayed in Ballarat since August 2004. I started working in the Ballarat chemical factory in November 2004, and I'm working there until now.

You lose your life, you cannot make it again

One year after I was released from the detention centre I received a bill from the Immigration department: $227,049.10 for the time I spent in the detention centre. I believe less than ten people from 2000 until that time got a bill. I started fighting with this situation. It means you are released, you've got your visa, but still they are going to make you upset, to send the message to other people not to come to Australia because there is huge detention time waiting for you, a huge bill waiting for you.

I took the case to parliament with the help from Catherine King, member for Ballarat in Canberra. I had paid between seven thousand and eight thousand dollars and then I received a letter from the finance department saying I didn't have to pay any more.

When I had my citizenship ceremony in 2009, I wasn't happy because it was nine days after my sister died back in Iran, aged 57. I had filled in the application for citizenship four times and each time Immigration sent it back, saying, 'You didn't fill this, you didn't fill that.' I was really upset. I called one of them myself and I said, 'I'm going to take a week off from the factory and I'm going to chain myself to the Immigration department.' We sent the application for the last time and I didn't receive anything until I received a letter from Immigration department saying, 'Mr Bakhtiarvandi, you missed your citizenship ceremony at Ballarat Art Gallery.'

I called the number on the paper and she said, 'You missed it because you didn't turn up on the day you had your ceremony.' I said, 'Do you think I'm Jesus or a prophet who knows everything without anybody letting me know? I didn't receive anything from the Immigration department so how can I go there? Why does everything like that happen only to me?'

I wore a black shirt to my ceremony. There were some Liberal members of state parliament and the local council and some other people there. They said congratulations. I said, 'Don't think I'm a happy person to be here for this piece of paper you call citizenship. For this piece of paper I spent nine years of my life. Four and a half years in the detention centre, then carrying a huge bill on my shoulders, and now nine days ago I lost my sister.' Some of my friends, including my ex-wife, were there and they said, 'Don't say anything. Don't worry about it.' I said, 'No, they have to know that if you play games with people's lives it's really dangerous. If you lose money, you can make money. If you lose your life, you cannot make it again.'

Music is the biggest thing that can make me relaxed

My wife and me, we lived together for while, but we both had problems and it didn't work. She is a fantastic girl, still I like her. I had problems because I spent very stressful time in detention centre. To be scared of deportation every single night for four and a half years, I'm not sure anybody can say it's easy to forget. It's not easy. I think it's causing more problems for me because I'm involved with refugees and I can hear their problems. The effect of this is too much. To be honest, I have less time for myself to have a normal life. I like to be really busy but most of my time, apart from my work, it's going with politics and being a refugee supporter. I'm not complaining, because really I don't want to see anybody going through the system.

Hopefully this situation is going to end and it will give me more time for music, because music is the biggest thing that can make me relaxed. The last time I had a concert in Ballarat, people afterwards were complaining to the committee of the festival, saying, 'Why, when we have someone like him in Ballarat, have we never heard anything about him and his music? Why are you not using him more than this?' That was really nice to hear and I was actually very happy. We didn't make money for ourselves; we raised money for refugee support and it was very good.

I still love the mountains more than anywhere else

Neda

Neda lives in Melbourne and has begun studying for a PhD in health sciences. She arrived in Australia in 2010.

A big wall between us

I'm from Iran, from a big city. I grew up in a very loving and supportive family. I think it's very important for your early childhood and your teenage years to have a very supportive family because if you learn the basics of how to go through life, if you understand it, it will keep you going for the rest of your life. My father and I, we were very good friends—actually he was one of my best friends. He used to take me to the mountains. We used to go every weekend and walk, like, bushwalking. He used to tell me moral stories that had hidden messages in them—that you should never give up—and he believed in me so much. He always discussed everything with me and he asked my opinion about everything he was doing in his life. Even though I was very young I had a sense of value, that my father valued my opinion. He gave me that sense of strength, that sense to be strong even when things get very hard, and to believe, to see the light at the end of the tunnel. I still love the mountains more than anywhere else.

We were very close, but I never showed him my weakness because he used to tell me all the time, 'I believe in you and you are a very strong woman.' When I had a very hard time I tried to hide it from my family. Even when I was leaving my country, I didn't tell my family.

Aside from my family, who I love, there was a hostile environment in Iran for women—there is a lot of discrimination in laws and practices especially. I realised that aged about ten or eleven. I realised that I was different to boys, I have to wear hijab, I'm not allowed to do what boys can do. It was like a big wall between us. Your rights are based on your gender.

Every voice would be suffocated into silence. They push you down and it's something that you cannot accept. Women have got limited rights in their marriage, in their guardianship of their children. There are a lot of issues, especially for people who belong to minority groups: they have limited rights for education or public healthcare. I went to university. It's not hard to get into university but the hard part is to get a job, because it's a male-dominated society. If you don't have the same attitude as those who are in power, you've got no chance to get into any kind of job.

I made that promise

I was working for my father, who was in the building industry. At first I wasn't very active politically. My father was supporting me to be equal with men but he used to tell me, 'Don't get involved too much with political issues in this country.' He was very afraid that I would get in trouble. My brothers did not agree with these discriminatory laws and injustices which were practised in my country. My youngest brother, we were very close together and we knew everything about each other. Once, he called me to his room and he said he believed what was going on in this country was just completely wrong, in regards to human rights and women's rights, and he said, 'We're going to do something about it.' I said, 'We are normal people. We've got no power. We can't do anything.' He said, 'If we believe that we can do it, we will do it together.'

So it was time I decided that we should not be quiet, we should stand against this government's injustices. There was a protest march a couple of days after they released the 2009 election results. I was filming the protest. Before I realised it, I was at the head of the march with a camera in hand, and I quickly realised that the situation was fast becoming incredibly treacherous. A group of police came from everywhere, from every direction. So we had to escape. They were beating everyone in front of them, they were shooting people. They didn't care who was in front of them—women, teenagers, girls, anybody. Some of the people who were in that protest, I never heard from again.

I think after the protest I became a completely different person. I got involved with the other protests that came after the elections. One time when I was filming I was taken to a government facility for questioning by the secret police. After a period of time I was released from that facility but my older brother got in touch with me to say that the government agents and secret police came to my father, to my family home, and they were looking for me. I was just trying not to be home, staying with my aunties, staying with my friends. But then I lost my youngest brother.

After the protest he had injuries, brain injuries. He used to take a lot of medication. One day, in the morning I went for a walk along the river. I was really worried about him because he was really sick and he was depressed about our situation. When I went back home, I thought he was sleeping but it was eleven o'clock. Then I realised he was not. He had passed away.

Then I was summoned to the station, to the court. I immediately knew what would be the outcome if I handed myself to the authorities. I knew that I had to leave. It was the single most difficult decision in my life, to leave my beloved mother and father and all my loved ones behind. It was a very difficult decision, but there were no options available. The situation, it was like a prison for me. Maybe the prison's bars are invisible to everybody but it has exactly the same conditions as gaol.

I just . . . I couldn't go to sleep at night. It was a very hard situation. You don't know where are you going, there is not any tangible plan on the table. You just put your clothes in a bag. It was six o'clock in the morning. I went to my brother's apartment. I told him to quietly come down the stairs and I would be waiting in the car. He got into the car and I just told him, 'I'm in big trouble and it's something that I can't take a chance on—if I stay here, I might be in the prison by this afternoon.' I didn't know when they were going to come because it's what they do, they just come through your door and take you away. My brother recommended that he contact somebody that he knew in the airport. He said, you know, 'At least we can organise it.' Because if you want to leave the country as a single woman, you can, but they have to check everything and ask you a lot of questions and if you are a married woman you can't leave the country without your husband's permission. It's a very tight, strict situation.

I went to say goodbye to my brother who had passed away. When I went to the cemetery, to his grave, I just promised him that if I survived on the ocean, if I could get myself to a safe country, I would do everything that I could for those like him. For many others who are in gaol, for other women such as myself. I don't believe in this religious government, but still I believe in God. I made that promise to him in front of God.

I could survive that ocean

When we saw Christmas Island from the distance it was a beautiful, green island. It was a very good feeling to stand on firm ground. When you are on a boat for two weeks, every day you are moving, side to side. I was very happy that I wasn't on the water anymore because I was seasick all the time. I was very happy that I could survive that ocean.

The first thing they did was an interview and health check and after that they put us in different rooms and blocks. They gave us food and clothes and after that they said, 'You have to wait for your interview.' There is not much to do while you are in the detention centre. The guards won't tell you anything about what is going to happen. They just try to keep the environment calm and provide you with food or your requirements but nothing more. It's still like, you're locked up, you know? It's funny that afterwards it doesn't seem to be much to other people, but it seems a lot to you when you're in the detention centre. Every day is very long because you are all the time thinking of when you are going to get out. It becomes kind of psychological. At least when you are in the prison, you know, for example, when the date is that you have to stay there until. The difference between a prison and the detention centre was its uncertainty. It's not knowing anything about your future—the stress, anxiety. You don't know what will happen.

The daily routine was mainly going to the dining room, having meals and taking part in some activities. We had really limited things to occupy ourselves with. But it took probably only two hours of your day. Sometimes we used to play volleyball with other residents, those kind of things, but it was mainly just sitting all the time. There was a fair degree of bickering and arguments taking place between the residents because of this situation.

We had some happy times in detention centre, for example, when we were celebrating people's birthdays. We had very limited ingredients, such as bread, butter and jam. And actually, these were the simple moments when we could be very happy. Just for short periods of time we could forget about our conditions. I was keeping myself busy a lot by learning English, because my English was limited to just introducing myself. We didn't have a teacher. Everything that I could find in the facility, I would just get it. I had a small dictionary with me so I just tried to read it. For example, I would read one page and it would take me maybe two days!

The majority of the staff were very friendly and courteous but the issue was that it was very difficult to be in an environment where someone else is in control of your daily life. It was a strange feeling for myself and I think for the others as well. Everyone was in a high level of stress and anxiety in that environment. You couldn't ever plan for the future ahead. I can still remember that there were times where you would fall into a deep, dark hole, because your life was in limbo and you were surrounded by the constant uncertainty in your life.

When you are in detention centre you are just afraid of doing anything. When I was in my country, the government was observing everybody's move, so we still had that in our mind, that we still were very afraid of everything. If someone asked me my name, I just panicked! You know? I tried to keep a distance with people because I was stressed for myself and I started to psychologically suffer. Sometimes I ate a lot and sometimes I stop eating for a few days. And then they would put an officer in front of my room to check on me. It was just very, very stressful.

I made some friends while I was in the detention centre and we still remain very good friends to this day. One day, I went to the medical centre and there were two sisters sitting there and one of them had a little girl. They thought I was an interpreter because I wasn't wearing the clothes that we received in the detention centre and I was speaking to the nurse a little English. So they came to me and asked, 'Could you please talk to this nurse and tell us what we require,' and that was the start of our friendship.

They were the two main people. I think making friends was very important, to just take you out of that situation a little bit, because you could speak to each other and have company and take the pressure off you for a while.

The next world

After about three months I did my first interview on Christmas Island. The interview was very hard because you have to go through all the details, which really is very stressful. They ask you questions that are very sensitive. It took about five hours for my interview, and when I came out of the room I just collapsed, and they took me to the medical centre. I was sick for about a month. One thing about Christmas Island is that you are very fortunate if you don't get sick. Because if you get sick, the medical care is not very effective. One night I had a lot of pain in my body, so I went to the medical centre and asked the nurse to help me because I was suffering a lot. He gave me an injection. I experienced a severe reaction to that medication and I truly thought that I was dying. I couldn't catch my breath. I can only remember that a group of medical staff gathered around me, talking feverishly. After that, when I opened my eyes, everything was different, completely different. A different room, a different environment. I truly thought that I had died and that I had passed into the next world. There was a beautiful woman who came to me and spoke to me in Farsi, my native language. As soon as she told me that her name was Rouha, I thought that I had definitely died because her name in Farsi meant 'an angel'! She was telling me, 'You are beautiful,' and I thought that she probably wanted to make me feel comfortable so I said, 'Thank you. Can you please tell me where I am?' She explained to me that I had been airlifted to Perth to be in the hands of medical staff and a good medical facility. I was very, very anxious and after a while I had a panic attack again. I started to get panic attacks very often.

I was taken to the family detention centre in Perth, which was far nicer than the previous place I had been staying. It was a family detention centre and people with medical issues, health conditions were also taken to that centre. There was another woman who had miscarried on Christmas Island. There was a woman who had had her arms broken. It was a small centre close to the airport.

In Perth, the staff were very friendly and very welcoming, so that made a lot of difference. They used to take us for excursions, so we could see people in real life around us. On Christmas Island the only thing that you can see is bars—bars and officers. Nothing else is going on. In Perth, they used to take us to the park to see children playing. I watched the kids playing and the people going about their lives. I lived for the day where I too might walk freely like those people I watched.

In one way I had peace of mind. I am very happy to be in a country where you've got freedom, but at the same time, every night when I went to bed I'm thinking of people who are suffering and I'm feeling kind of ashamed that I left everybody, everything, behind. But the thing is, it's always in my mind to someday, somehow, get a platform to be a voice for those who are in my country.

There were people, who came from Red Cross I think, who used to teach us about Australian culture and the way of living in Australia, about different states and where the main communities and migrants are. Just to give us a big picture of Australian culture and demographic issues. There were Aboriginal people came to tell us the story of themselves. It was very interesting because I had no idea of what's happened in this country.

There was a guy who taught English as a volunteer. He taught English to anybody who wanted to learn. He also was a visitor of a family who lost their daughter in the sea. So he used to come and say hello to them often. Everybody came when he used to visit that family. All of us gathered together and had coffee and biscuits. It was the nicest time that we had because when you are in the detention centre you feel very lonely. When we had visitors it was somebody who's caring about you, somebody who's thinking of you, so it was a very special time for us. He helped me so very much to get an understanding of the language. So after my release from the detention centre I stayed in touch with him, by email and phone. After he taught me for a few months I got to the point that I entered university, and he helped me so much in my study too.

The first day when I walked out of the detention centre, it was just the best day in my life. It was beautiful. I just remember I was smelling the flowers and touching the trees. It was a wonderful feeling. It will always remain with me, for the duration of my life. It was good, the first couple of days—I was just going out and I wanted to feel the freedom. But the thing was, I was really sick and I hadn't realise it much before, because I had been so worried to just do my process and to get everything right. I think about two months later I got my permanent residency. It was that time that I realised how the journey had affected me. All these new anxieties added to the anxiety that I had experienced in my country. I used to have flashbacks a lot. I realised that I was shaking all the time, I couldn't catch my breath. I had anxiety all the time, all the time.

I won a major battle in my life

I found Perth very quiet and I didn't know many Persians. I knew that there was a big Persian community in Melbourne, so I thought I could probably make some friends or have a network. So I decided to move to Melbourne. First I went to Sydney—I knew a family in Sydney—and I found it was very busy. I don't know, I was very anxious. I thought I might go to Tasmania. I was in Hobart for two or three months, I just couldn't settle down. Finally I went to Melbourne. When I found accommodation, I was sharing the house with three other girls, Aussie girls! Sometimes when I was speaking English they were just looking at me with blank expressions. Probably I didn't know what I was saying! I couldn't make my point, so it was a bit funny.

I didn't have enough confidence to come out and sit in the lounge room and talk to them. It was funny, because when it was Christmas time I thought that something had happened. Two weeks before Christmas all the girls had disappeared, and the house was so quiet and I went to the streets and nobody was on the streets and I thought, *Oh my god, what's going on here!* You know? I was just going mad, I didn't know what to do. Even now, after a few years here in Australia in the community, Christmas time is the most difficult time of my year.

It was always my intention to learn the language to a good level and also to get some education at university. It wasn't only because I liked studying, it was also because as I came this way to Australia I had a chance to meet the other people who were less fortunate than myself, and that changed my path. My background was in mathematics and accounting. So I was trying to get into some kind of study to be able to help those who are less fortunate than myself. I did my degree in health. To be honest with you, the first year I was completely terrified. I can still remember when I went to the library I was just watching other people, because I couldn't even type the keyboards quickly, I was very slow. When I turned my head and looked at other people, they were just typing so quick and everybody was laughing and they were discussing things and I was so terrified I couldn't even go and discuss the subjects with the other students. I remember for the first semester of my study I never laughed.

Studying in a foreign language, it sure presented me with some difficulties, but at the same time I was suffering from severe insomnia and post-traumatic stress. There were times where I truly thought I was going to die, because I didn't know how to do an essay. I had very poor sleep for a long time and my body just crashed. I was a full-time student. I was just dragging myself to the library and sometimes the security guard would approach me because I was walking like a drunk, or I was just very unwell. I was in the library for maybe fifteen hours but I was productive for maybe five hours. It was a very difficult time.

I decided to change everything because I met a very nice girl from Cairns. I started to see that she was a top student and I was just watching her, what made her a good student. I realised that first of all she was very happy. She was very happy, she was very active and she got involved in everything.

So I decided to change the way that I was studying. Yes, I tried to be happy—I still couldn't be very happy but I tried really hard. And I started to talk to people and got involved. And you couldn't imagine it, my mark increased from 56 to 88. That was the second semester, and by third semester it came to 94. So it was very big progress for myself and I was very happy about that.

Oh, my graduation day was a highlight of my life! Not only had I completed my study but I won a major battle in my life, about if I can get over all these difficulties and sickness and my conditions. It was a very big day for me, I was so happy. When I was called on the stage to get my degree I peered into the crowd to see my teacher, who flew from Perth to come to my graduation. When I was looking at him, he had tears in his eyes. It was a very nice feeling to see that somebody else is caring for you.

I've been very fortunate since I came to Australia. I've met very nice people here who have been supportive, who love me so much, so I always appreciate that. But I think nobody wants to leave their country. Nobody wants to leave their culture, their family. When I came to Australia I almost lost everything. I lost my family, I lost my language, I lost my culture. I lost the land where I was born. I think having people from your culture makes the situation a lot more bearable for you. The great majority of them are asylum seekers and refugees. Some of them I met on Christmas Island. We get together on the weekend, we have barbecues. I used to teach them English. We used to go bushwalking, those kind of things. But also, when one of us has got a problem we discuss it—what you have to do, where you have to go, who you have to contact. So it's kind of like your family. It's something that I don't want to lose.

I had a cause, and I was fighting for it

Wahid

Wahid was arrested for protesting against the government in his country. He never expected to seek asylum. He is now a permanent resident and lives in Melbourne with his wife— they met after his release from immigration detention.

One of the beautiful moments of my life

When I was, like, 25 years old I got an opportunity to work in software development, and then I became managing director for this company. I wanted to change my career into something that would be expandable, so I became a business consultant, and I was doing this until I went to Australia. I consider myself as having had a blessed childhood. I grew up in a family with two parents and two sisters and one brother. I'm happy that I got the opportunity to be raised by them. We would be considered as a middle-class family. Both my parents were working.

When I was young, during the holidays I used to go with my uncle to coffee shops—like, old-style coffee shops. He used to go on a daily basis and stay hours with his friends in that place, and I used to go with him and come back to my grandparents' place around two or three in the morning. I was like five or six years old, but I was having fun. They would play chess, dominoes and smoke, stuff like that. I remember they would spread sand on the floor, so it would be easier to clean the ashes from cigarettes at the end of the day. That's one thing I remember. And loud TV, loud voices from the games. I was very popular in this place. I still meet people who knew me when I was four years old, and they still remember me and remember the old days.

I participated in protests calling for revolution. Well, that was one of the beautiful moments of my life, to be there. It was just, like, a feeling that all sorts of people are gathering for one cause. Regardless of ideology, regardless of backgrounds, regardless of age. You would see a lot of sacrifice for each other. Like, someone would just push in front of someone else to take a bullet for him. I saw this. There was basically no food because police were closing the streets, so people would just share a loaf of bread together.

We'd been attacked a million times by the police force and by the thugs hired by the government, but we stayed there—just defended ourselves and stayed.

I was arrested. I was detained for about six or eight weeks. That was a horrible experience for me. The torture and trauma were systematic in all ways, like physical, mental, other stuff. But at that time I had the feeling that what I'd done was the right thing. I had a cause, and I was fighting for it.

Nobody knows

I came to Australia. I put my claim for asylum and they took me to Villawood. The whole front was just a wire fence—very ugly and scary because it seemed like a very high security area. We would go through one gate, and then they would lock the gate behind us and they open another gate. You had no information at all about what's gonna happen to you. You don't know if this place is just like a prison, or if it's just like a detention centre. At that time I didn't know the difference. They said, 'Okay, that's your stuff, you go into this room.' The flooring was very old tiles, like forties style. And it was painted maybe three decades ago. Lots of spiderwebs inside. Fluorescent light. *Alright, how long am I gonna be here for? God knows when. Alright, what's gonna happen with my immigration thing? Nobody knows.*

All my mind was thinking at that moment, was, *Are they going to send me back?* The idea of going back to my country was terrifying, because I knew that as soon as I landed at the airport I would be detained, and sent straight away to gaol. That meant I would be going through all the torture and trauma again—but even worse, like a hundred times worse.

I was trying to not go crazy

They have this idea that everyone eats curry. I would say maybe 70 per cent of the food would be curry. Chicken curry, beef curry, lamb curry, but it has to be curry. That's detention centre culture—they think that overseas people, we eat curry. I remember one officer, he was Australian but originally from India. He was complaining to me, 'I'm Indian and they're cooking too much curry, I don't even eat that much curry.'

I started to know some friends through the learning area. I knew that they had made a small mosque where they do the prayers, so I started to get to know some people there. Yeah, actually, after knowing people it became easier. Because I spent like ten days without knowing anyone.

Every detainee, they give him 25 initial points to spend on the shop. They would request you to participate in activities, and every detainee would get, like, two points per activity. This rule was made to get people to participate. I knew a few people that wouldn't even leave the room at all, not even to eat. Everyone got messed-up brains because of what was happening around them. I saw some friends hanging themselves with bedsheets. They made a rope and hung themselves. Or cutting their veins. Stuff like that. These things should be avoided. Doesn't have to be happening.

I was trying to not go crazy there, so I participated in some activities. They had English conversation classes, in which everyone would gather in the library and talk about different topics. It was a tiny room with a couple of lounges. That was my favourite because it's very healthy to speak your mind, and also to accept other people's opinions. You don't have to agree with them, but to accept differences.

Usually you will have a roommate. And, not all the time will you be happy with your roommate. Well, my roommate didn't care about his personal hygiene. So the room was smelling really bad, because it didn't have any windows. You had to turn the aircon on, obviously, because it was a confined room. But what's gonna happen if you're running the aircon while the room is stinky? The smell is just going to be rolling over. Like, it was horrible. I put in many requests to be moved out of my room. Anywhere . . . These kind of requests usually just go into the rubbish. I knew that one spot was empty, in one room. So instead of writing another request, I took my stuff and I went to the other room.

In detention, I never made trouble with anyone. Never had a problem with any other detainee, or an officer. I'm not an aggressive person. If I wanted to ask for something, I asked for it. If I saw that something was wrong, I requested it to be corrected, and I put the reason behind it, and the logic. I'm not going to fight. My father, back in the sixties and the seventies, he was a social leader in my city. I learnt from him how to give my argument without being fanatical about my opinion. He is the one who made me love politics since I was young. I saw everyone around us respecting him as a good man, with good manners and morals. We had a big library in our house. So I grew up loving books, loving to read, and I could go to him any time and discuss any issue. He wouldn't try to enforce his opinion but he would just say what he knew, and his view.

In Villawood, for a long time there were no socks. And that was during the winter. I had socks, but I would speak for others. And the others were told, when they went to request clothes, 'Let someone from outside bring you socks.' Some people in detention, they don't want to make their visitors think they are taking advantage of them by saying, 'Bring me this, bring me that,' you know? So some people wouldn't ask people to bring them anything. I spoke with Immigration. I asked them, 'Isn't it Serco's job to provide all the clothing material to us here?' And he said, 'Yes.' I said, 'So, what's happening? We put a lot of requests to bring them and nobody cares. Why?' Ten minutes after the meeting, they told me, 'Okay, we've got socks for you.' But it wasn't about me, they should give them to everyone. It was like, you're missing the whole point.

Some of the officers were nice, the minority. And the majority were the opposite. Being a good officer doesn't mean doing something illegal. He's still doing his job. But they would not be nice in public. Because if the management knew that someone was being nice to detainees they would sack them straight away.

I was speechless

During my first meeting with my case manager, she was trying to convince me to go back to my home country. She told me, 'You are gonna lose.' She was saying things that made me feel like, *Alright, they're gonna smash me*. She was trying to get me to sign a paper saying I would voluntarily go back. I told her, 'I'll go voluntarily somewhere else, but I can't go back. There is no way I can go back.'

It had never crossed my mind to seek asylum. It's a 45-page application. And that's one of the things that is really difficult for asylum seekers. Because you give this application to someone who doesn't know any English, and ask him to fill it out. And then the whole case is going to be based on what he wrote on that application.

Luckily, that wasn't a problem for me, because I have some English. I filled the whole application and I wrote my own statement. After one hundred days of waiting they sent me the rejection letter. I was devastated, because of how they dealt with my case. I felt it was unbelievably unfair. Everything on my side he just ignored, and everything other than that he doubted. So, I applied to the tribunal.* I said, 'Alright, I'm gonna do it myself.' I started to study how to write a legal submission and to read about tribunals. I read some legal books, from universities.

The tribunal member was very professional, an old man. He didn't ask me much. Whenever I talked about my case he said, 'I don't want to hear anything about your case. You're here for only one question. "What do you fear, in case of your return?"' So I started telling him, 'I was tortured . . .' He said,

---

* Asylum seekers are able to seek review of Immigration department decisions to refuse to grant a refugee protection visa, by applying to an administrative tribunal.

'Don't tell me what happened to you, I want to know what is *going* to happen to you.' I told him, 'I'm going to be tortured again, all kinds of torture. They are going to be laying more sentences on me.' Because at that time that's how it worked. Once they get someone, they start laying more charges.

So, that was it. I went back to Villawood with Serco officers. I was exhausted because I hadn't been sleeping for the last days. I'd been preparing myself and thinking about what was gonna happen. My whole life was depending on this hearing. I slept for a couple of hours, and then Serco officers came to wake me up and hand me a fax. It was the decision. He gave me refugee status. I was speechless, I was going to be released. I was going to get outside.

You don't have anything in mind to work for

So, I was waiting, and waiting, and waiting. Nothing's happening. I keep asking, they told me nothing. Finally they said Immigration wanted to see me. So, I went to them with expectation of good news, but they said, 'You're going to be transferred to Yongah Hill in Western Australia.' I said, 'Why? How long am I gonna be there for?' They said, 'It's just operational matters. You're going there.' That's the only information I got.

At that time I started to develop like a form of PTSD. Basically, I was having a fear that I was going to be deported. And I was thinking, *They are just telling me that I'm going to be transferred to another detention centre so I won't be violent or suicidal maybe.* I prepared my stuff and I found that there was another guy going with me. They didn't tell him where he was going. He was from Tonga, and he thought that he was going to be sent to Tonga. So he was having a nervous breakdown. He was having—I don't know what you would call it, medically—a severe diarrhoea condition, because he was so stressed.

When we got out on the road, it was like you'd landed in a different country. It's very yellow there. It's all sand, everywhere. We went from the airport to the detention centre which is like, one hundred kilometres away, and all the way was just a desert road. The officers were wearing the round hat that they wear when they're playing cricket. So that was weird to me because it's not common to see someone in a detention centre wearing these cricket hats. And when we got to detention centre the first thing I saw was a sign stuck on the wall warning you about different kinds of snakes. So it was, *Oh my god, what is this place?* It was like a high security prison. And you'd see warnings that the fences were electrocuted. It was just, like, big fibreglass containers and then the rooms were inside, so you're open to the desert.

I was there for several months. The impact was overwhelming. Because when you are waiting for a decision, you have a cause you're fighting for. You have a case, and you work on that case, and you have a deadline. But after getting the decision and then getting to know that I'm gonna be staying here in limbo until god knows when, that's like crushing feelings. Where is justice? The tribunal gives you a decision that you are a genuine refugee. At that moment you don't have anything in mind to work for. All you have to do is just stay alive—sleep, eat, just do whatever it takes. Because you don't know if you're gonna get out after a month, six months, a year, two years. You will never know. So that's where you start getting depressed and stressed, and you start getting this feeling that you don't want to talk to people anymore, you just want to stay in your room.

THEY CANNOT TAKE THE SKY

Try to be patient

At least in Villawood I had some friends that would come to visit, but in Yongah Hill it was different. It's very rare over there to find any visitors because it's a hundred kilometres away from the city. In Villawood I used to contact my family with Skype. Just as audio calls, because cameras are not allowed there. But that became harder in Perth, because there, every detainee had one hour of internet a day, and your time changed daily. Of course my family were worried about me. But they thought that for me to be there in a detention centre was better. Otherwise I would be in my country and that wouldn't be safe for me at all.

At Yongah Hill I remember a Palestinian guy, he was playing soccer and he got his leg broken. His leg was swelling and he couldn't walk at all. So they gave him Panadol, and asked him to go lie in his room. They said they couldn't do anything until the morning. The guy was dying from the pain until many other detainees gave him some of their sleeping tablets so he could sleep. Unprescribed medication, of course, but that's what you do for someone that is dying in front of you. Two days after that, an Irish guy, he got a back pain. Not a serious thing. They called the ambulance and they carried him and took him to the hospital. Why are you calling an ambulance for this guy, while the other guy broke his leg two days ago and nobody cared? If we needed anything, we had to write a request and send it to the officer and get it approved, and all this bureaucracy. But for a person from a Caucasian background, they would just give it to him straight away.

It was a tough time because there were some criminals there, waiting to be deported. They had been in gaol for five, ten, fifteen years. When they go to detention centres, they form gangs there. New Zealanders, Islanders, and so on. It's not right to keep us in one place. It's not right. We had to stay alive and try to keep our cool to not have a fight with them.

It's the easiest thing for someone to come up behind you in the bathroom and just smash your head. You need to stand up for yourself. But at the same time, you are going to be blamed, not them. The one who is from criminal background, he's waiting to be sent to his country anyway so he doesn't care. But then this refugee wouldn't be getting a visa, because he failed the character check because he made a fight in the detention centre. It was common to find someone getting a black eye, or bruises over his body, because he was beaten. I remember one guy got his skull smashed. They took him from Yongah Hill almost dead, he was in a coma, and he stayed in a coma for a couple of weeks. I felt just tense all the time. Just like, waiting for some problem to happen.

I'm in contact with some people in there, and they are desperate. The only thing I can say to anyone in detention is, 'Try to be patient, as much as you can. Or at least try not to let what's happening mess with your brain.'

I remember one day my case manager told me, 'I have some bad news for you, I think there is a problem with your security check. You could be in the detention centre for a very long time. So why don't you think about going to a different country?' How am I going to go to a different country, while I'm in detention? Before that, I had hoped to get out someday soon. I didn't know what to do. When people were not cleared by ASIO, they would stay there for five or six or seven years. I was terribly depressed at that time, but I tried to be logical and see what I could do about it. I started to investigate.

I filed a complaint to the inspector-general, who is like a supervisor over ASIO.* They got back to me saying there was

---

* The Inspector-General of Intelligence and Security is an independent statutory role that reviews the activities of Australia's intelligence agencies, including ASIO.

nothing wrong with my security check. I was released from detention three weeks after that.

Deal with life

Actually, the night before I was released I was sitting up late with my friends. I went to sleep at around six o'clock in the morning. I was sleeping, and then I found the client service officer opening my door and telling me, 'Wahid, you have to go to the case manager now.'

At that time I was under the fear that I was gonna be taken to Christmas Island any time. Because they were taking people randomly. They would just come in the middle of the night, and say, 'You have a medical appointment,' or, 'You have to go to Property.' And once they are there, they just handcuff them and take them. So, I panicked. I didn't have good sleep, and then this is coming. I didn't know what to do, if I'm supposed to be, like, getting dressed, or packing my stuff, or what. I went to have a shower, and I came out just wrapped in my towel. And I found this officer sitting on my bed. He said, 'Wahid, you have to get dressed and go now.'

My case manager told me, 'I have some good news for you.' I asked her, 'Are you taking me to Christmas Island?' She said, 'No, you got a visa.' I didn't believe her. I told her, 'You know me very well, and I know you very well. So, if you're going to take me to Christmas Island just tell me that straight away, I'll just go pack my stuff and come back. You know I'm not gonna make any problems.' She said, 'No, you got a visa!'

Actually I didn't believe what was happening. They took me to the airport and that's it. Deal with it. Deal with life.

Well, I was very happy to be released. It was a bit strange, actually, to be on my own again. I think being locked down for more than a year made me afraid of being by myself. It was a bit weird at the beginning, but I just got used to it. I was thinking, *I have no place here, I have nothing, I don't know what to do*. They just told me, 'When you get to Melbourne just contact the Centrelink.' I didn't know what they meant. *What is a Centrelink?* I didn't know anything.

This area is heaven

I'm doing supervising for a construction company. If it was my choice, maybe I would move out of Melbourne. It's a bit too busy. I just realised that maybe I would like to have more quietness in my life. Near Lismore there is a rainforest, and in the middle of it there is a waterfall, called Protesters Falls. First you have to go on the road in a car, until a point. Then you have to go on a forest walk, between the trees and stuff. And then you find a big space with the mountain, rocks and the falls, and there is a big lake, underneath. It's just like, marvellous. I think they call it that because in the seventies they wanted to chop down that rainforest, and then activists went to that place and they protested. And this area is heaven, I love it.

Recently I went to propose to my fiancée's father. I was a bit nervous. But in my culture, when someone needs to propose, he would go to the parents and propose. And seek their approval and acceptance. I know it's different here, but I wanted to do it that way. Because I see it as more respectful to the parents.

Now, I'm having a really good time with my fiancée, we're spending a lot of time together. Not long ago we went to the Mornington Peninsula. Just spent a day there, came back. Yeah, short trips like this. I like it, on the weekend. Sit close to the beach and have a barbecue, and enjoy the time.

They took me to gaol and that was heaven

Munjed

Munjed Al Muderis came to Australia from Iraq in 1999. He arrived by boat from Jakarta, and spent ten months at Curtin detention centre. He is a world-leading osseointegration surgeon, which means he attaches robotic devices directly to the skeletons of amputees to allow them to walk again. Munjed's apartment in Sydney is decorated with alien-like sculptures he has built out of surgical implants.

I hide with my sculptures

At times when I'm in difficulties or need to be thinking I hide with my sculptures. A lot of my family were artists; my uncle was very famous. I enjoy making models and shapes and objects from used materials—in my case, using implants. I have a growing collection of them. It's a hobby I enjoy a lot but unfortunately I don't have much time to do it.

At the moment my life is divided into three different areas. The first area is my day-to-day work, which is the general orthopaedic work, like hip and knee surgeries. That's what pays the bills.

The second area is osseointegration surgery, which is my passion about robotic leg surgery. I'm establishing that field and trying to convert the traditional approach to all these pathologies.

The third area, which is growing significantly, is my commitment towards refugees.

It's a combination of work, academic and humanitarian commitments. And that is what I want to do. In part, you need to earn living, in another part you need to participate in the progress of science, and the other part is to fight for rights.

I'm very lucky to be married to Irina. She's a very understanding person who tolerates my time commitments. I don't know how she puts up with me. Basically, Sunday is for the family. It's one day a week, unfortunately, which is very minimal. Family life! Unfortunately that suffers.

I became an escapee

It was late October 1999. It was a normal week. I was a surgical resident doing a surgical term. I parked my car normally in the university hospital car park and I went to the theatre complex as usual, and all of a sudden everything changed.

Members of Ba'ath Party* and military police came to the theatre complex, escorting three busloads of army deserters, and they ordered the elective surgeries be stopped and that the surgeons commence branding the soldiers by chopping off parts of their ears instead.

The head of the department refused and said it was against the Hippocratic oath. So they escorted him outside to the car

---

* The Ba'ath Party governed Iraq between 1968 and 2003, and was led by Saddam Hussein from 1979.

park and put a bullet into his head and turned to the rest of us and said, 'Ladies and gentlemen, now we have attracted your attention, anyone who shares this gentlemen's views come forward, or otherwise, proceed with our orders.'

From there onwards I became an escapee. I thought, *Should I obey their commands and live with guilt, or should I refuse and face the same destiny that my boss had, with a bullet in my head?* And then I thought about the female toilets and decided that that would be a very good hiding place. So I sought refuge in the female toilet for five hours until everything settled and people left.

I ran away from Iraq with the help of my family; they managed to get me a passport and a large sum of money and smuggled me out of Iraq to Jordan. You have to appreciate that all the countries surrounding the Middle East are not signatories to the 1951 Refugee Convention. So there is no place that you can go to seek refugee status, and knock on the United Nations' door and say, 'Look, I need to seek refuge.'

So I had no choice but to put my life in the hands of people smugglers.

A false impression

Christmas Island was not a detention centre back then, it was a phosphate mine island. We were taken to a basketball stadium and we stayed there for five days. We were given Salvation Army clothes, the same clothes that I had for the rest of my time in detention. It was a fantastic time and unfortunately it was a false impression about what we were going to face, because the detention later was completely different.

The third day on the island the captain came to me and said, 'The majority of people here are Muslims, aren't they?' And I said, 'Yes,' and he said, 'They don't eat ham, do they?'

Do you realise that I've been giving them ham sandwiches for the last three days? Well, I need to tell them.'

He was a very honest guy and he announced it to them and that caused a lot of screaming and yelling that they'd been fed ham. So there was a bit of chaos at that time and he had to fire a few shots in the air to calm them down.

Another thing happened on Christmas Island, which was when I first saw the Australian spirit for real. I was taken to interpret for the federal police as they intercepted another boat. We left in two barges: the captain and his deputy in one barge and I was with another officer on the other barge.

This officer—a person I'd never met before and who'd never met me—asked me a question: 'When was the last time you spoke to your family?' I said, 'Just before leaving Jakarta.' He had a satellite phone, and he said, 'Sit down on the ground. Don't let anyone see you because it's illegal. Dial the number and tell your mum that you're safe.'

I'm forever grateful to this guy. That made me think that there are a lot of good people, because he put his job on the line.

Day five, I was taken to Curtin detention centre. I was kind of upset that I was left till the end and the captain said to me, 'Don't be very upset, because when you go to the mainland it's a completely different story. Enjoy it here while you can.' And he was right. Curtin detention centre was simply hell on earth.

One water tap in the middle of the desert

The first thing I saw when we got into the plane were the ACM officers and they were very harsh, very rough. They treated people like animals, basically. We were like a herd and they were just putting us in places.

Once we got to the detention centre, the plane door opened and there was this wind coming in. It was, like, 45 degrees

Celsius of heat, and very dusty as well. The detention centre was a RAAF base, and it wasn't prepared for detaining people. So there were only tents and army stretchers.

I remember there was one water tap in the middle of the desert, surrounded by barbed wire.

The first thing that happened to us, we were marked with numbers. My number was 982. From there onwards I was called 982. They put tags on us and they put permanent markers on our arms. We were given a towel and toothpaste, thongs and toothbrushes. And that's it.

I was there for ten months. We queued for hours to get food. For ten months we had minced meat with colourless spaghetti. We had it for lunch, we had it for dinner. It's a bit stupid to complain about the food, but when you eat the same meal every day for ten months, it can kind of get to you. That's why I hate spaghetti.

The senior officers were Australians, but the junior officers were from everywhere. They were extremely harsh. My understanding is that this company was running the prisons for America, so they were used to dealing with criminals and prisoners, and they were treating us like that.

There was nothing to do

We got locked into compounds at night. You'd wake up in the morning, they'd open up the compounds and we'd start wandering around until breakfast came. They'd do a headcount at breakfast. They gave you cornflakes and a sachet of jam and butter, and two pieces of bread. You'd finish the breakfast, then you'd wander around again inside the compound.

Then lunch comes and they do another headcount. They give you an apple or an orange for lunch with colourless minced meat and spaghetti. Then you finish lunch, and you wander around again.

Then dinner comes and they do another headcount, they give you an apple or an orange, one or the other, and minced meat and spaghetti. You finish dinner, and you go back to your compound and they lock you up for the rest of the night.

They come around at midnight and do another headcount. They come around to everyone and wake them up, put a torch on their face. You have to sleep with your ID beside you, which has a photo and a number. They match the photo to the number to make sure everybody's there. They finish the headcount around 2 a.m. If you're lucky you get the headcount early, if you're not lucky you get woken up at 2 a.m.

Then the next day comes and the same thing happens. Over and over and over again. People were doing all sorts of things. Walking beside the barbed wire and counting their steps constantly. Other people were just lying down and counting the stars. There was nothing to do.

They did a lot of things that didn't make any sense

They had different levels of secure areas inside the detention centre. Like the suicide watch box, which I spent several days in, which is, technically speaking, a small box with no windows. You get locked up there for hours, most of the day, and you get taken out to see the sun for one or two hours and then put back in.

There's another area called 'the hotel'. That's in isolation, for naughty people who do one thing or other. I stayed there forty days, and the reason I was given was to protect me, for my own safety. Which was obviously ludicrous.

They did a lot of things that didn't make any sense, but were a kind of psychological torture.

On occasions, there was physical torture or physical harassment. I saw people shoved and bashed and held by the neck by guards. Usually that happened to people who resisted, from what I've seen, but it was unnecessary. So there was physical abuse in certain occasions inside the detention centre by the ACM guards. I witnessed that.

I could see the violations of human rights that occur in the detention centre and I vocalised that. I was not violent, I was not aggressive. I used only the legitimate, right approach to ask for my human rights, and they didn't like that.

Gaol was brilliant

I spent a significant amount of time in prisons as well. I was very outspoken and I couldn't keep my mouth shut. They took me to Broome maximum security gaol, and that was fantastic. That was heaven.

The gaol was brilliant: the food was great, the clothes were uniforms like scrubs. People were treating me with dignity, and it was absolutely great compared to the detention centre. I used to love it. Every time they'd take me to prison, it would be like freedom. I had access to the media, I had access to TV, I had access to the radio, I could make phone calls and speak to Amnesty International about human rights.

The guards were very respectful. They called me by my name. That was something very special.

There were a lot of inmates there, obviously a lot of people were charged with heavy charges, because it was maximum security. I met a gentleman who was my companion in my cell. I think he murdered the rapist of his daughter.

Then unfortunately they sent me back to the detention centre. But this time, I was sent to isolation—I was kept in solitary confinement in the detention centre.

It is scary and it is sad

It was a mixed group of people at Curtin detention centre. I would say around 25 per cent—I can't quote the exact figures—were women and children. I felt very bad about the children. There were a lot of children in detention staying there for months and months without any education.

I got a broken whiteboard and I managed to make friends with some of the officers who gave me markers: a black and a blue marker. I started running a school, teaching children how to read and write in English, talking about Western values, how to say 'May I' instead of 'I want'. That got some attention from the adults as well and they started attending the school. But it was interrupted by me being taken to prison every now and then.

A lot of children were unaccompanied minors. They were extremely vulnerable, because they were locked in compounds among adults who were from different backgrounds, and it was extremely dangerous.

I was the interpreter for cases where there was alleged sexual assault on children. I was the interpreter in the initial reporting and I became a witness. It was sad, it was very sad. The cases were dropped for lack of evidence. I mean, how can you get evidence? It's the child's word against the detainee's word, and there were no witnesses. It is scary and it is sad. It shouldn't happen in a society like ours.

I was let go from the door

Miraculously, when the Sydney Olympics were approaching, there was a political move to get rid of this headache that the government had with the detention centre, so they started processing applications. They started processing the numbers;

981 was processed, 983 was processed. I was left alone in isolation. My number was slipped through the system and I wasn't processed. That was the lowest point I have ever had in my life, in my wheel of fortune.

I threw my mum's phone number across the fence to the main compound. Someone picked it up and gave it to their solicitor, who contacted my family in Iraq, and my mum hired a migration agent in Sydney, who put in a refugee application for me, privately. Otherwise I would have been left there to rot.

Even when my visa was issued, the immigration officer didn't release me with the group that I was supposed to be released with. They were flown to Brisbane. I was let go from the door of Curtin detention centre. They took me to the main road and said there will be a bus coming from Derby to Broome, just catch the bus.

It was a mixed feeling. Because now I was free, but I was starting from zero.

They didn't like us to sleep on one bed

Nima

Nima and Ashkan are a gay couple living in Nauru. Nima is 29. His partner Ashkan is 25. Until May 2016, same-sex sexual activity could be punished by up to fourteen years' imprisonment and hard labour in Nauru. It is still legal to discriminate against homosexuals there.

We always live in fear

At the moment my partner and I are in the room not going out. We always live in fear. We are afraid . . . [*Pauses.*] Can you tell me where to start?

I studied engineering at university. Then I became an elevator technician. I worked doing that until I left Iran, so about four or five years. I really liked that job. I like trade jobs wherever I go. I would like to start my own small business—that is my goal.

When I was in Iran I was harassed by people because I am gay. I was harassed at school and in public. I was slapped and sexually assaulted. When my father found out that I was gay he couldn't tolerate me. He was slapping me a lot and also torturing me. I was really tired of living.

Yes, yes it is a crime punishable by death in Islamic law. Neither the government nor society can accept a gay man. I remember former president Ahmadinejad* said that there weren't homosexuals in Iran. [*Pauses.*] After I was tortured and sexually assaulted . . . this forced me to leave Iran and seek asylum in Australia.

When I arrived on Christmas Island, I told the authorities, 'I am a homosexual man. I am gay.' I entered Nauru on 25 January 2014. Everyone knew I am gay. In the Nauru detention centre, asylum seekers have come from many different nationalities. When I went to take a shower they were coming to open the bath door. They wanted to enter the bath by force and wanted to harass me. To sexually assault me. Do you understand what I mean? It happened many times. I didn't feel safe.

The showers were like cells, their roofs were open and they could be easily entered from the top—other asylum seekers did it many times. Though I have reported this issue it wasn't followed up and nothing happened.

[*Pauses.*] One morning I went to the mess to have breakfast. At that time my partner was sick, he did not go with me to have breakfast and preferred to rest in bed. Since I was alone one of the asylum seekers, from another nationality, came and sat beside me and said, 'Hi.' I agreed to have breakfast with him together as a friend. While we were having breakfast, he suddenly pulled down his pants and showed his erect penis to me. He was trying to get closer to me. An Australian officer saw the whole incident. He reported it to my case manager.

---

* Mahmoud Ahmadinejad was the president of Iran from 2005 to 2013. Speaking at Columbia University, New York, in 2007, he said, 'In Iran, we don't have homosexuals like in your country.'

Well, I wasn't in a good psychological condition because I wasn't safe. In detention there were tents. And in every tent, nearly 40 individuals were living without any partition or any room. The tent was shared. When I fell asleep, other asylum seekers were harassing me, touching my buttocks and waking me from sleep. Always I was living in fear. I wasn't good mentally because I was thinking, *Why am I still living in a place where I am being harassed?* I fled Iran for that reason but here again I was psychologically and physically abused.

I love him

Well, my partner, Ashkan, was one of the first single men who arrived on Nauru. He is a Kurd, from Iran. He arrived three or four months earlier than me on Nauru. He had more experience about what was going on in the detention centre, he was familiar with detention affairs and he was showing me around.

Slowly, slowly we started to become normal friends by sitting together and talking. At that time we didn't know about one another. But when I realised that he understood me—that when I needed something he helped me—I started to trust him slowly. I slowly started to confide in him and I shared the truth about myself. He promised to be by my side, to always take care of me and support me. After that we shared our relationship with our psychologist, our case manager and immigration authorities. Everyone was aware of our relationship. From that time on we have kept our relationship going. Ashkan is very good. I love him. He is always kissing and cuddling me. And we have loads of sex. [*Laughs.*]

He is in touch with his family. They don't know about our relationship. This relationship is forbidden in our culture and people can't talk about it openly.

We were living in separate tents. We—my partner and me—had no place to live, to have private time. It was all a shared place, even the showers were public. We told Immigration authorities and Transfield that we needed to live together in the same tent. We needed a place or room where we could have privacy, but we received the answer that it wasn't legal for us to live together. Because other asylum seekers had complained about us, they said that they didn't like us to sleep on one bed. As a result Wilson security guards came and warned us not to sleep together in the same bed because it was illegal here. They said, 'If you persist we will inform the Nauru police to arrest you.' We were told this. We were threatened.

Look, we were scared. All the asylum seekers knew about our relationship, they knew that we were partners. Some people were religious extremists. I was in fear, and I thought they would threaten my life because of their beliefs. They said, 'We will kill you.' Or they were shouting at us saying, 'Don't talk to us. You are dirty people.'

When it was eating time we would go at the last hour, so that we were the last people. At that time it wouldn't be crowded. So my partner and I would go to a corner and eat our meal.

Two or three times a week we could contact our families. For this purpose we used to queue in lines for many hours. Sometimes, I stood in line from 8 p.m. till 4 or 5 a.m. Most of the time it was like this: we had to wait from evening till morning for five or ten minutes talking on the phone. Sometimes, other asylum seekers in the queue wouldn't stand next to us or stood a distance away from me. They didn't like to talk to us, saying we were dirty. They meant that they are human but we are not, because of our relationship. I was under pressure in Iran but still I had to face it in the detention centre.

Ashkan left and I remained

When I entered Nauru detention centre, my partner's case process had already finished. He was waiting to receive an answer, whereas mine was newly started. The first time when I visited Immigration, I was asked why I left Iran. I said that I am a homosexual person. After waiting months for the second interview round, I declared to my case officer that, 'I am living with my partner and have a relationship.' The case officer said to us that if one of us got accepted then the partner can also be accepted. Like, I could go out of detention through Ashkan's acceptance. The law was like this. It meant that families—like, brothers and sisters—could leave detention by this relationship if one of their family members got accepted.

When we were in the camp and Ashkan had yet to receive an answer to his case, the case officer called us to visit them. On this visit we were handed a letter in English which said not to reveal our relationship to anyone, including the government, police and the people of Nauru, once we started to live in that community. The letter was interpreted to us by our interpreter, and our case officer gave us the letter to sign it. We didn't sign the letter and did not accept it. We said that we are homosexual and partners. There is no reason to hide it. We don't hide our relationship.

After many months, Ashkan received his answer: he was accepted as a refugee. As I said, according to the law I should have been able to go out of detention with my partner when he was accepted. But Ashkan left and I remained in the detention centre. We were both devastated. I was crying and I went to his bunk to smell his bed. He had long hair and I searched for his hair. This separation lasted for a month. I was in love with Ashkan.

I asked my case officer why I was left behind. They said, 'It's illegal for you to live with your partner in Nauru.'

The day Ashkan left the detention centre, I shouted a lot for them to take me as well. I shouted so loud my scream echoed around the whole camp and people came and watched from behind the fences. I shouted so much I felt my throat tear apart. I hit my head with a stone and fractured my skull and I became unconscious. Then I was taken to hospital, and my head wound was dressed. After I came back I still wanted to hurt myself. I did not eat and did not go to the bath. My condition was so severe I was put on high watch. It is when an asylum seeker or refugee goes to such a severe condition that two Wilson security guards were with me for every step and every second. They were taking notes of my behaviour and condition submitting it to a psychologist. I was in a severe condition psychologically.

Ashkan was taken out to the Nauru community. He took 30 tablets. He tried to commit suicide. He was taken to Nauru hospital, they put the hose in his body . . . He had not been in a good condition.

Nauruan officers sit guard in front of the gate and check everyone with a metal detector. During the month we were separated, one of those Nauruan officers, in the presence of an Australian officer, pushed that metal detector to my buttock. Though I complained nothing happened.

After one month, I was taken to visit the case officer. I wasn't in a good condition. [*Pauses.*] I was taken to Ashkan.

Immigration replied, it is illegal in Nauru

I was taken to a place with single rooms for refugees. Nearly 50 or 60 refugees were living there. It was for singles, not for families. It was named Fly Camp.* Each room was six square metres, without a kitchen, bath or toilet. It was only a room with one bed. When I was taken to see Ashkan, I was expecting we would be with each other, to have one bed. But when I entered Fly Camp, Ashkan was in room number nineteen and my room was number 27. There was a long distance.

If I wanted to go see Ashkan I had to pass many lines. It meant that we were still separated from each other. After one week, Immigration came to visit Fly Camp. I asked them, 'Why our rooms should be separated? We would like to have one bed and live together.'

Immigration replied, 'It is illegal in Nauru. You cannot have one room together. It is designed for one person.' Months passed. For seven months we lived in separate rooms, but most days Ashkan and I were together. We had a refugee from another nationality next to our room. One night he came and knocked the door and said, 'Why are you together? This is a bedroom for a single person.' I told him that, 'Ashkan is my partner, that is why I come to see him.' When I said this, we argued. He punched me in my chest.

In another incident, in the kitchen, most of the times Ashkan wasn't wearing a T-shirt. The kitchen was warm and had no cooler. One of the refugees sent a text message to another one saying, 'Tell him to put on clothes. Otherwise I know what to do to him.' When the other refugee gave the message to us, we went to him and spoke to him with respect. While we were speaking to him he said, 'You are dirty people and you have to be eliminated. You have to be removed.' We spent such a difficult time in Fly Camp for seven months.

---

* Fly Camp is an accommodation facility for refugees living in the community in Nauru. It houses single men and is in a relatively remote location.

THEY CANNOT TAKE THE SKY

We lock the door

When we were in the detention centre everyone knew us. Nauruan officers knew us. When we entered the Nauruan community, when we went out for shopping the Nauruans knew us—they knew that my partner and me have a relationship. They could not accept that. If we were walking on the beach they were swearing and harassing us, throwing rubbish on us, spitting on us. They threw rubbish on my face. Once, I was punched in my head. When we were in Fly Camp, one night around two or three o'clock one man came to our room, he wanted to break in and assault us. Well, we have reported all these incidents and complained but no one has followed them up, nothing has happened.

Finally last year in March we came to the new place where we are living now. The last time we were beaten was on 14 July 2015. Anna, our lawyer in Melbourne, knows better. I don't have a good memory now.

It was six o'clock in the afternoon. We went shopping. It was about fifteen minutes' walk from our home. We did our shopping and when we returned the path was dark and full of trees. Three Nauruan people, they stood in our way. All our body was under stress. They said, 'Are you partners?' We said, 'Yes. Everyone knows that.' We did not like to hide it. They said, 'You are dirty people and rubbish.' They abused gay people. It may have taken about two minutes or less, or one minute or less. I don't know. It was sudden. They attacked us with sticks.

From that time, 14 July 2015, Ashkan and I do not go out. We are in a room where it is closed from all sides. We lock the door because we are scared. To buy something, shopping, our case manager goes with my partner once a week for half an hour and they return back to the room and have no other activity.

We have neighbours, from Iran and other nationalities, but we don't have any relation with them. We are really getting tired and crazy. We are losing our reason. Now in the room, for this long, we have mental problems. We are hurting ourselves. We are tired mentally and physically. I have been seeing a psychiatrist and I am taking medication for the trauma I suffered in my home country and in Nauru.

When Ashkan and I became refugees we could not go for work. The money given to us is insufficient so we cannot buy most things. In the case of the internet, we cannot afford to use the internet a lot. We use it only for talking and no more than that. To say to you, 'We are really tired.'

I thought I would leave detention, but my heart is there still

Lina

Lina is an artist who came to Australia in 2013. She had always wanted to study architecture. In Syria, hiding with her family, she began drawing. During a period of relative calm, she completed a course in drafting software. But then, as the war intensified, she wasn't able to leave their apartment for a year.

Every colour is a story

I started painting when I was in detention. Everyone was surprised. I'd never done it before. In detention, we had nothing—I mean, we just sat and thought. Some people, they were thinking about bad things, they'd been sad, and some people, they just started writing poetry and painting and drawing. They just found themselves, how talented they were, through the hard pressure.

One painting I made, it showed a strong woman and all the officers were like, 'Wow!'

The manager came and saw it and she said, 'Do you like to draw and paint? We can provide you painting stuff if you like.' They gave me colours and I said, 'I don't know how to paint, I know only with the charcoal and pencil.'

But when the colours came to my painting, I saw many things—I saw hope, I saw . . . Every colour, it affected me, started affecting my painting . . . Like, I needed to choose exactly what colour I needed to paint with. Every colour is a story in itself.

[*Deep breath.*] Like, green is important in my painting. Without green, without the colour that I want, I won't get the results . . . So I have to mix blue and yellow together—green. And blue and red together—purple. Playing with colours keeps me busy and not thinking about any bad things.

In Syria, when there was war I started drawing. When you build a house, it's like, because you don't have anywhere safe, you try to build to feel safe. I feel safe when I draw and paint. I could show the immigration officers how we feel, that we're not dangerous. [*Laughs.*] It's like we are normal people.

I had one drawing that's a woman with her mouth covered. I did this in Darwin. I showed everyone and they said, 'What you mean by that?' And I said, 'You just need to understand what I mean, I don't have to say.' It's really clear that I can't talk. She can talk but they covered her mouth. [*Pauses.*] I hate politics. Yeah, I hate it. Humanity is more important than rules and politics. All my paintings are about people.

That pressure

So, before I came to Australia I was in Syria, and before that in Iran. In all these years we tried to find a place to feel safe.

In Syria, in the cities, you walk around, you go shopping, people are selling stuff, drinks, everything is okay, and suddenly you go back to the same places and they are totally different, all collapsed. My father, he had to leave the house to bring food for us and every time he went out my body was shaking. One day, we were sleeping and we heard some noises, like bombing. Then at 5 a.m. we saw a helicopter. I saw the fire coming from the helicopter and we were just scared. [*Deep breath.*] The worst thing is the noises of the bombing. In war you feel no one can hear you. It's like you're screaming and no one can come and help you . . . During that time, my best friend, she died. That pressure, it makes a bomb in my mind.

Every time we left a place we had to leave our stuff. I had to throw out many things I loved, from my childhood, everything. To leave Syria it was impossible to take them. Photos, birthday gifts, my notebooks. I love to write, I love to read poems in Arabic, so I had many things in my books. We couldn't even leave the photos as they were, so we had to cut them. Cutting the photos from our life, the people we loved, it was emotional. But being safe was more important than photos. At that time, they were nothing for me, I want to be safe. But when we get here, safe, I thought, *Why did I do that? Why did I throw them away?*

And then we left Syria and we went to Indonesia. We went to the boat. On the third day, the boat broke down, stopped moving and there was nothing. Nothing. It was all water. We couldn't see anything. And I felt that a human, a person, should have more value than that. It was like, *They shouldn't treat me like that.* Why do people have to choose the worst way to get in a safe place? Why they didn't provide a better option?

Everyone who has power is responsible. I'm not focusing on anyone, but people who have power, they can do everything to make things better. I don't believe in human rights. They did nothing. They're just words: human rights. What's going on in Syria now, what's going on everywhere, it shouldn't happen. If human rights did anything, then ah okay, I would believe in them. But if there are rules, if there is something like human rights, but they did nothing, then what's the point of calling them human rights? I don't know. I'm not old enough to understand. But what I've seen is not right.

I was praying a lot

In Syria, I researched Australia, about the language. I was scared of learning the language because they said it's different from English and American language. I was watching YouTube clips of the Australian accent. It's really difficult. I told my family, 'I like Melbourne.' And in detention the English teacher was nice. He tried to educate me and tell me more about Melbourne. He was telling me good places, nice places . . . he told me when you wanna do shopping you just go to the cheapest one: Aldi!

On Christmas Island there were so many people with many hard backgrounds. Some people came from war, some people were so upset. I couldn't feel safe, because I didn't know the people and they were all around me. They were, like, next to my room where I sleep. Different people. Later, I used to help people, so I could feel safer because I was helping them.

I tried to be active, rather than sitting and being upset. Some people, they used to sleep in their rooms for hours . . . Some people started smoking. I saw many girls, single girls, they'd just smoke, smoke, all the time. Some people, they were just happy, dancing and singing like it's nothing . . . But inside, they were so sad.

I believed that if I showed I'm weak my parents would be sad, so I decided to show them that nothing had happened and I was fine and not upset because they chose this way to come. It was not their fault. We had to. So, seeing my mum made me stronger, to show her how I wasn't upset anymore.

I was praying a lot. I found that I was so close to my god, at that time. And I was also feeling just, like, I didn't feel . . . I had no feeling. It was like, I didn't care for me, personally. For my family, I did care. But it's okay. I thought, *Let's see what's going on, what will happen*. And it made me feel comfortable, relaxed.

I couldn't leave her

So, we arrived in Darwin. It was late evening. People were trying to tell us, 'Yeah, here is better than Christmas Island. Everything is good.' One lady, she told me they have good makeup, because on Christmas Island they couldn't wear makeup as they wanted. And the food is nicer. People were so excited to be in a better place than Christmas Island. And I could see how happy they are. I was happy, but I don't know . . . because in my mind I had many things . . . I had my plan . . . I wanted to reach the aim I came for, to study and work. I couldn't understand why they were so very happy. And most of them, they were sick. They had problems. One of the first I met was Ranya. Oh my god, so many things happened with me and Ranya.

I was sitting with my family. My mum was cutting fruit and giving it to us. I was drinking tea. And suddenly they brought Ranya from the hospital. She was sitting in front of the medical room. I tried to help her because she was alone and I knew that she was new. I asked her if she needed help . . . but she wouldn't talk to me. Later, I asked her, 'Why didn't you talk?' She said, 'I was afraid of talking. I didn't know who you were or where I was.' I thought that maybe she was waiting for the nurse. So I stayed with her. I couldn't leave her.

The nurse came and gave her her tablet and I was trying to know her and why . . . what happened to her. When she saw me with my family she felt safe. She thought, 'Okay, I found a good family.' Slowly, we became friends. Day by day.

I asked her how she came and she said, 'I've never told anyone my story.' I wish I can be strong like her, she has made me stronger. And I have learned many things from her. She's a real woman. Strong woman.

One day, she needed to use her email and she had forgotten her email address. I let her use my email address and she was surprised how I trusted her to give her my password. Even I thought it would be too hard to find friends in such a strange place, but I did. I think detention is the best place to find real people. In hard times, you can see the real people. There, we're not sharing our happiness, we're sharing our pain and everything, the sadness.

So, we were together all the time and then I found out she was sick. Yeah, she started feeling bad. They tried to take her to hospital. I don't want to tell her private story, but I tried to be with her. Sometimes, ah, when she fainted she hurt me, like my hand, but when I saw her I couldn't feel mad, even if I was hurt. People in detention, when they see sick people, they stay far away because they think it will affect their immigration status. But I didn't care, it's about human with human. I don't care about any immigration thing.

We were the craziest girls

Do we have time? I mean, because when I keep talking I'm not feeling the time. This is a true story. Truth takes time.

Some people thought that I was from Ranya's country because we were always together, we ate together . . . Yeah, we were together and because she was sick, I couldn't leave her long. She trusted me and I trusted her as well. But officers, they told her, 'You are doing this because you want to be famous.' They thought she was acting. And one officer told her, 'You need to get married so your husband will take care of you.' It's crazy things she was hearing from them.

They separated us [*sighs*] in Darwin. They sent her to a different detention centre and, ah . . . I was crying. It was first time I had cried like that. In that detention centre there were many people. She gets tired of being in crowds and . . . maybe there no one can help her like I did, like I was supporting her and being with her always. They separated us. They closed the door. She fainted. And I was crying, crying, crying . . . The officer, he . . . he didn't let me see that she had fainted . . . he didn't want me to see her, to get more upset.

Everyone knew about me and Ranya, like how we loved each other, how we were supporting each other . . . Ranya was thinking, 'No, they mean it, they want to separate me from you.' They saw that she was getting more and more sick, more than before, and that her health was getting worse . . . in that new detention she fell from the second floor and that time, ah, she was feeling very bad. She broke her body.

On that night I just heard that Ranya fell down from the second floor and that she was in hospital, that's all I heard. I was . . . I wanted to know if she was still alive, you know . . . And I didn't know anything about her until the next day an officer, she came and told me, 'She's in hospital and she's fine.' I requested to go to the hospital and visit her. After two or three days I was allowed to go with my family. She couldn't speak, I was just talking to her. I used to visit her always, always, till she got better.

Ah. That makes me tired. She made me tired. I'm so tired of her. [*Laughs.*] I don't know, but she was good girl. I mean, she is still a good girl, but . . . Immigration doesn't care about 'good' people or 'bad' people . . . She used to come and visit me as well . . . and then we did many crazy things. We were the craziest girls. [*Laughs.*] Darwin has two seasons, one dry and one wet. In the wet season it always rains and at night when it rains we were just playing in the rain. She was crazy. I love her.

When anyone gets sick they call 'code blue', and medical, they come . . . So, code blue was the worst thing I heard in detention, always code blue. [*Laughs nervously.*] Ranya, code blue . . . when I heard code blue, I knew that it was Ranya . . .

One day she fell down the stairs. Yeah, a time before the other one. Sometimes I was glum in myself: why wasn't I with her so she couldn't fall? I was so sad because of her. Why do I have my family, and she doesn't? Why do I feel healthy and she doesn't? All the bad things in her, why's it like that? But, that's life. I've never met anyone like her.

All the night talking, talking, talking

Immigration told my family, 'You are going to Melbourne.' We were so happy. My mum, she was crying. We were so happy, I was happy, but . . . I didn't show that I was happy. I was normal so that other people wouldn't be sad.

So, three days before my family transferred to Melbourne they brought Ranya to see me. I was surprised like, *Wow, they brought her here because they know that I'm transferring*. For three days, me and Ranya, we didn't sleep—we were talking, we stayed awake all the night talking, talking, talking . . . [*Laughs.*]

The morning I left, Ranya was sitting on chair because she couldn't walk . . . but I told her, 'I am sure you are coming too.' They wanted to send her to Nauru. Even I thought that maybe they would send her, but I told her, 'I feel you are not going there. I promise, I promise you are not going to Nauru. I feel that I'm going to see you,' and she was smiling. And she said, 'Yep.' She was always . . . she doesn't want me to feel that she's sad.

Yeah, and the last piece of my painting, I couldn't finish it because there was no time. The activity officer, she told me, 'You need to finish it,' and I said, 'No, just leave it.'

'Are you an asylum seeker?'

We went to Melbourne. It was windy and cold, but it was good.

The second day we went to finish our Immigration things. I saw the city, we started taking photos and everything. It was so good. I was walking with my family in the city and I felt free.

I found people are friendly, nice . . . but the worst thing is that I always need to say that I'm an asylum seeker. As if there is a difference between an asylum seeker and not being an asylum seeker. When I go to any organisation, they always ask, 'Are you an asylum seeker? Where did you come from? What was your boat number?' It's like they remind me all the time: detention, detention, detention. It's easy for them because they just say the word, but for people there . . .

About being in detention, at first I was ashamed to say . . . but later, I felt like, no, it's okay. I was even thinking about what to tell my future kids. *How did I come to Australia?* I thought, *Yeah, they will be proud of me because I'm proud of my parents.* It was very complicated, what to feel about our being in detention. Because I now know what I learned, I'm not feeling ashamed.

They gave us bridging visas but without study and work rights. They told us, 'You have study rights, but you need to pay yourself. But it means I can't study, so what for? I used to look for centres, education, everything. I was looking, asking, 'Where can I go to learn and study?' But wherever I went was expensive.

So, first I did more painting because I was still in the mood of detention and then . . . I felt that I needed to do more than paintings. I needed to volunteer in some places. There was a support and housing service, I volunteered for one year there. Some people who came didn't know English, so I used to help them. I used to give food parcels and vouchers to people. And that was a good start for me, to be in a community.

I talk to Ranya. I can't see her because they sent her to a different state, seven or eight months after me. She's in the community. She's suffering . . . I mean, she's not well.

Because she is far away from me I can't see her always. But she doesn't have anyone to trust more than me. Yeah, that's what she says. I hope we can be together again, she needs someone to support her. I've never asked myself this question, why should I feel this way. But . . . I just feel she's close . . . close to me. She feels good when she talks to me. So, when I see her she feels good, and it makes me feel good too. I miss her. Lots. [*Laughs.*]

I used to . . . I knew everything about what was going on in detention. [*Laughs.*] I used to follow the news and know about people there who transferred, who stayed . . . I thought I would leave detention, but I couldn't leave it. My heart is there still.

Voices

On boredom, freedom and blockading the gates

REZA YARAHMADI arrived on Christmas Island in 2009; after being released, he began campaigning for detainee rights

People don't know, even activists, no one knows until you live there one day: everyone is sick mentally. All people do is smoke. No one sleeps at night-time. It's just unbelievable. Just imagine you're walking and one hundred other people are walking and no one is talking to each other because everyone's thinking. Everyone's just walking with a cigarette between their fingers. I remember many times, for half an hour or hour, I did not know where I was, I could not see anyone around me, and then I was like, *Wake up!* It was like a dream. I would wake and then I would see people around again, no one talking to anyone else.

Night-time was like thinking time. You'd just think; just smoking, drinking tea and coffee and walking around. It was very strange. I did not feel it when I was there, but now, when I think about it, it is actually strange. It's crazy.

There was nothing to do, nothing to do. There was a very small gym but the facility was terrible, not enough for even ten people, and there were 1800 people there at the time. So I was doing nothing during the day. I would sleep for a few hours because I couldn't sleep at night-time. None of my friends could. We would just sit there, telling each other our stories and talking about issues and our dreams. I'm gonna do this when I get out, I'm gonna do that when I get out. I was not a smoker when I came to Christmas Island, but on Christmas Island I was smoking 40 cigarettes a day.

―――――

ZARA was smuggled out of her country with her daughter ATHENA, who was then seven years old

Zara: Every day we go and wait for Immigration. *Why don't they take us?* And then again they moved us to another camp in Christmas Island. If Immigration comes, everybody goes and waits there. First they call the names. Whose name is coming, you know? I always go and ask these Immigration people, why? Why? They don't have answers.

Athena: They have no order of doing things. They just do them randomly, I guess.

Zara: We think, *We came first, so we have to go first.* But people arriving after us, after one week or two weeks, they get transferred. So fast.

Athena: There was like a mini place where there was a teacher. And there were, like, a million kids. There were heaps of kids and she taught them all. And all grade levels. I was the only one that knew quite good English. And, yeah, I used to just help the teacher, because I already knew what she was teaching. [*Laughs.*]

Zara: We were a long time in there and Athena could not study properly, you know? Some, they don't know English... So I ask the caseworker to send her to the Christmas Island school.

Athena: A Christmas Island school. But we had our own class, like, a teacher taught us. We were all still in the same grade, I'm pretty sure, but separate from the local kids. I didn't get to go to school for long.

JAWID arrived aged nineteen after years avoiding Taliban violence

Most of the detainees didn't wake up until lunchtime. Because there was nothing to do, you know? There were a lot of people in that situation, especially the older guys. Some of them used to sleep in the afternoon as well. After having lunch they went back to sleep until dinner time.

For myself, I was always interested in sports. I made a decision that I have to stay active because there was nothing else to do there. You don't have any freedom, you can't even cook your food. Whatever you need you have to ask someone else to provide for you.

In the morning I got up around eight o'clock or nine o'clock. I used to go to the football ground and usually I would try to go for about half an hour of running and then have a shower and have breakfast before ten o'clock. And then after lunch, around two o'clock in the afternoon we had an English class. After that we had volleyball until dinner time, which was about six o'clock. Then we had football on the basketball court, five a side, from ten until midnight.

The Iranians had a team, the men of Arabic background

had a team, the Hazara and Afghan guys, we had a couple of teams, and there were other ethnicities as well. Teams played against each other to get to the final. I couldn't imagine what to do without sports.

SOLMAZ came to Australia with her son

I got transferred to Curtin about ten days after my son was transferred. At first there were a lot people and I didn't know if my son was there. So I kept asking around and it took a few days for me to find him.

But we were separated by a fence. So every day I would go to my side and we would see each other through the fence, sort of like prison, and we would talk to each other even though that was not allowed. We were a couple of metres away from each other, by the fence, just in case the officers saw—maybe they wouldn't suspect or at least we have time to walk away. We tried not to sit too close, but we were on the two sides of the fence. We tried so hard to talk to each other.

We would talk, mostly about our daily lives, what we do, he would talk about what food he ate. Then we would talk about all the months in Indonesia, everything we went through, all the difficult times, how that was over. We hoped we could have a normal life here.

MOHSEN is a twenty-year-old refugee from Afghanistan

The detention centre is like your home but you can't get out. You are not free. They have fences around you. You can see a playground but it is only open during certain hours. When you go for lunch you hold your plate and you stand in a queue and you sign your name and you get your lunch, breakfast or dinner and then you go back to your room. It's not a very human experience.

Some of the Serco guards were good but some of them were very bad. They would talk to you like you were a criminal. That made the boys, the refugees, feel more uncomfortable. Some of the guards used to say, 'Why did you guys come here?'

JAWID

The only people we could speak with were the guards. Some of them were telling us that there was no order in the process, so not to worry. Just because someone has got their visa a month earlier than you it doesn't mean there is a problem with yours. This system, this immigration system, has no order. We didn't understand at the time—that there was no order—but after thirteen years being in Australia I understand it!

One thing I realised in the detention centre was that I never saw a guard who did not smoke. I used to ask them, 'Does everyone in Australia smoke?' and they used to say, 'No, we smoke because we have a tough job.'

JOHN GULZARI fled Afghanistan in 1999

I remember one of the soldiers said, 'G'day.' Aussie slang. I said, 'G'day,' and then he said, 'How are you hanging?'

I was so pissed off. *How can he say that?* I said, 'Why did you say that? What have I done to you?' And he tried to explain himself but I was not very happy. Then later on he said that to another guard, 'How you hanging?', and the other guard said, 'A little to the left,' and I go, *Oh, that's normal here, making fun of each other.*

MAYA left her country with her mother and siblings

Sometimes officers, when they talk, try to get information about you to write it in a report. Some are nice, you can talk friendly with them, trust them. Some are doing their job. This is their job: to write reports all the time. I used to go behind the rooms, and sit there. There are a lot of cameras but it's a quiet area, no one's there. You know, sometimes you wanna be alone. Our room's very small, you feel like you can't breathe. You just wanna sit somewhere and not talk to anyone. And everywhere there are cameras.

Sometimes I shouted for no reason. [*Laughs.*] Because when you shout it makes you feel better. We did it once, me and my friend. They said, 'Why are you shouting?' They wanted us to say something like, 'I'm gonna hurt myself,' but we didn't. We don't want to do that. It's just something to make us feel better.

I was annoyed by that . . . that I can't sit alone. I can't be in one place without an officer coming, walking around, wondering why. Sometimes me and my friend would just sit. We have MP3s. We would listen and not talk. There would still be officers around when we weren't talking.

That's why I shouted, just to not lose my personality and become someone else. Because if your brain sleeps, that's it.

SARA was a translator and interpreter in Iran, living with her husband and sons

There is a request form or complaint form. These complaints might be considered. Most of the people wrote it down in their own language. That was one of the jobs I did—writing different complaints or requests in English. Some wanted to go to the medical centre. Some wanted to go to the shop and there was no interpreter in the shop. One of the girls didn't feel good so they called ambulance and there was no interpreter at midnight so they asked me to be with her.

There was one woman who had a handicapped child. One day she came to me. She said she wrote down several requests asking for her child to be taken to the hospital because the child was diagnosed with epilepsy. The child didn't feel good. She took it to the doctor, to the nurse, no use. So I went directly to the CEO of the detention centre. Other people said to me, 'Don't make a complaint to the CEO. They're gonna keep you in the camp forever.' I said, 'It's okay.' I didn't know where this courage came from. I went to her, and said, 'I have a complaint. I want to give it directly to you.' Exactly two or three hours after that, the child and mother were taken to the hospital.

For 45 days I was in a detention centre. I think the best thing I did was helping people. I loved it. I thank god for it. I ask god to give me strength, all through my life—and this is what I like to do.

REZA YARAHMADI

I had kidney stones, and I was in pain every single day. For a week I was crying, going to the medical centre, and all they were telling me was to drink more water. I don't know if the water there is magical, but the water couldn't help me.

Every day I was going there at 9 a.m. until lunchtime and then I had to go back to my compound. They lock the fences at lunchtime. And then after lunch I would have to go back to the medical centre and ask for help. No one actually cared about you. No one gives a shit.

I am a man and in my culture a man would not cry unless your loved one died. In my culture it is very embarrassing for a man to cry. But they made me cry in front of my friends, in front of many people, crying every day for a week 'cause of the pain, so they broke my heart. This is not the way you treat a fellow human being—I would not treat anyone like this, not even my enemies.

Finally they sent me to hospital. I was in hospital for two days. On the way from the hospital back to the detention centre I was thinking about killing myself, because I didn't want to go back to that hell. That was my lowest point, you know why? Because after a while of being behind the fences, I saw the freedom in hospital: people coming and going from the hospital, with their kids, laughing and eating, drinking. I saw the freedom and it made me sick. We're all people created by God, why should some have the freedom and someone like me be in gaol?

In the hospital it was so nice, because there was a nurse who was just lovely. She would sit and talk to me. I mean, I couldn't talk because I had no English. She was just telling me stuff, even though I couldn't understand her. It was so nice to have someone talk to me, a friendly face, a nice person. She would laugh and talk and clap, it was very good. I could understand she cared.

JOHN GULZARI

We were living in the cabins. It was very hot, like, 40 degrees Celsius always, but they gave us a small cooler. When the camp exceeded 1000 people, the women and children were just sitting there in tents, like military tents, without any fans or air-conditioners.

There were a lot of people in distress—children, women struggling—but nobody there to listen. Whenever you go to doctor and say you are sick, they say drink water and Panadol. Sometimes if you just have an upset stomach, or body pain, some sickness like that, you go there, and they just say, 'Drink water and you will be fine.' I say this is not magic water. You need treatment.

―――――

SARA

Some girls had private rooms. I witnessed that the security guards had relationships with young girls. One of the security guys was doing favours for very young and beautiful girls all the time. Not only him, most of them had relationships with young girls. As I came out of the detention centre one of these girls told me the guy she had a relationship with always let her use the computer or internet from midnight until morning. Of course the girls are satisfied with it too. I cannot blame only the security.

―――――

OSAMA DARAGI fled Iraq, arriving in Australia by plane

I had been in Maribyrnong for six months, I think, when Serco woke us up in the morning at eight o'clock and took us to the visitor area. I didn't know what was going on. I saw all the people, maybe 51 people. Then the detention centre manager came to speak to us. He said, 'Guys, we're gonna send you to Sydney.' We rejected that, because we had nothing in Sydney. In Melbourne, we have some friends to visit us. But Sydney, no way.

We were yelling, shouting, 'We don't want to go there.' We were so upset, so angry. They said, 'No, you should go. There's no place here for you.' We were so shocked and then they just pushed us inside the bus to the airport, like animals. I was so upset, I was crying. No one cared about me.

At Villawood detention centre, they put me in the place they called Stage One. For the angry people. It was really messy, really dirty. There are no rooms, just a big hall with beds.

This area is used for people who were in gaol. Before they send them back to their countries, they put them in a detention centre for a little while. Hooligans, these people. It's high security, and high fences with electricity. I was really scared. Everyone was like, 'Hey, what you looking at?' They were serious people, man. And I hadn't done anything, I had just asked, 'Why are you sending us to Sydney?'

Some people burned out the detention centre, all the buildings were on fire. Those people had been a long time in the detention centre with no answers, nothing. They were one hundred per cent fully stressed, but they shouldn't do that, because that crime was no good. It was a huge fire. We were watching a movie inside the room, and then we heard shouting. All the officers ran away. They locked all the outside gates.

We ran to the visitor area. We knocked on the door for the officers, because they knew what was happening—they could see everything on the cameras. We said, 'Open the door! We wanna go!' An oxygen bottle exploded—it was like a bomb.

ZARA and ATHENA

Zara: Finally, we were transferred to Melbourne. That was a new camp, at the time.

Athena: The food wasn't good. There were, like, two hundred people waiting. And you just wait out the back of the line thinking, *Oh my god*.

Zara: All is shipping containers.

Athena: They put a little window on it . . . and then that's it. You can actually visit the camp. Usually you have to stay in the visitors centre, but there's a day you can go into the actual camp. But there are some men, the ones that are by themselves, with no families. They stayed about there for six years. Most of them are out. There may be like one or two left there.

Zara: Ah . . . the men were jumping from the roof.

Athena: Some people, like, they don't want to stay there anymore, so they just jump from the roof.

HAL-HAL writes, sings and dances; she arrived in Australia in 2013

We followed the news on Facebook, plus people's rumours. But mostly it was Facebook because we were allowed to use the internet one hour a day—that's if you could find a space or an empty computer. Also sometimes, case managers they talk and they say that visas will not be allowed until July, or for five months, six months, or until blah blah, and then we had no hope of going out anymore. Waiting, and waiting.

When it's general news like this, we talk about it and all the other people talk about it, 'cause you have nothing to do inside detention other than talking so you talk.

In the beginning, the first six months, getting visits in MITA* was okay. It was very interesting to see people from outside, telling you about the world. But I found at the end, like the last four months you feel a bit, ah, unsatisfied. You feel... how can I put that into words... You feel like you will be stuck here, and then when those people visit you, you feel worse. I remember even at the end, when people tried to ask if they could visit, I was saying, 'It's better not to come.' It's a bit rude but it's better for them as well, 'cause when you're very frustrated and very sad, then you prefer to be alone.

ALI REZA grew up on the border of Pakistan and Afghanistan and travelled to Australia alone

There were excursions to take us out and to show us the community. We would go to places that Immigration had chosen, like beaches, art galleries or parks. But after a while, we had been to all the same places many times. I did try more than other people to go on the excursions but to visit the same place many times—like more than twenty times—it was just

---

* Melbourne Immigration Transit Accommodation, a detention centre, was opened in 2008. It is located in Broadmeadows, 15 kilometres north of the CBD.

craziness. Even the officers who took you to the excursion were tired and sick of their job.

I did build up a little strength but it went wrong again. Slowly other people's actions infected me and I became like them: very dumb and sad. I didn't want to do anything. I would stay up all night and sleep through the whole day. Once I became familiar with the people and the environment in detention, again I saw the same life and the same things happening in detention. I would make friends, then some of them would get out and I would feel hopeless and wonder what was happening with my life. During that time food didn't have any taste. Slowly, gradually, I was losing every sense. I didn't want to do anything or eat anything. I was just feeling very depressed.

I was mentally in pain. I began to think that non-living things were better than me. For example, chairs, tables at least provide people something, but I was not doing anything, not helping anyone.

I saw people from outside visiting people in detention. I saw their faces, they were happy. It made me distressed because I could see from their faces how life was different being outside. Their eyes were different.

JAWID

They came one day at 5.30 in the morning and told us, 'You've got twenty minutes to pack all your stuff. You got your visa and you're going out today.' There was a group of about eight or nine of us, mainly people from our boat. They told us, 'Your bus is going to go to Darwin, and from Darwin to Melbourne.' The bus took three days, and three nights. We got out of the bus to eat and the driver would pay, and then we would get back on the bus. We didn't have the chance to speak to anyone. But I was speaking to the drivers, along the way. The drivers were funny guys, typical outback Aussies, in their short shorts, making jokes. We were just happy to be out. We thought, *We will go anywhere as long as it is out of this place.*

HAL-HAL

I never lost hope. It was like the only thing you can have—no one can touch it, no one can play with it, as they play with all of our news, all our visas, our life. Hope is the only thing you have. So, sometimes when we'd sit, me and my friends, we'd dream that we'd go out and we'd go to our work and study. All the basics of what humans want in this life.

Unfortunately a lot of people are still there—it's been years and years. I don't know how they survive. And even if they go out now, after all these years they would be broken down inside.

When I hear that other people are still in detention, I say, 'That person could be me,' and I do a prayer that one day they will be released. I try to stand and fight all the obstacles around. If we've been through all this from zero, we can do something. I can be what I wanna be. I remember when I was in detention I was saying, 'If they just release me from here, I would never complain.' And until today I haven't complained. To live your life in a way you want, freedom is everything.

When someone came from the Immigration department and they said, 'Now you're all released,' I didn't hear any other word [*laughing*]. I heard 'release' and I was crying for hours, my eyes got so red. And I hope that people who are in Nauru—

and anyone in any detention in the world—will feel the hope that they will be released one day, to the gorgeous world.

OSAMA DARAGI

I called some friends. They had been inside with me in detention, but were released before me. I called them, and then I was waiting from twelve o'clock to four o'clock. Oh my god, I wanted time to run, but it was stuck. Then some officers were looking for me; 'Osama, Osama, let's go, let's go, outside, outside.' Oh my god! I went outside and I saw my friends. Unbelievable, man.

My first job, it was at a wreckers. I saved money and I bought a car. It's a BMW. I had one in Iraq. If the car worked it would be worth more than six thousand dollars. I don't have that money, but I'm a mechanic. I was looking for a broken car to fix up, and I found this car for, like, one thousand dollars.

I drove my car to Adelaide, and to Sydney again. I drove to Queensland. Just to see around. And I flew to Perth as well, just because I wanna see all the states. And then I started to love this country, because this is my second country. It saved my life. When I left my country I was nothing.

JOHN GULZARI

When I was taken out, you had a choice: you go to Sydney or you go to Queensland or you go to Perth. I wanted to go to Queensland, and instead of taking us by plane they took us by bus. It was a long, boring and tiring journey from one side of

Australia to the other side. Then we settled in a government hostel in Brisbane, which was not too far from the city. We always walked the Story Bridge to buy some food and bring it back. We did not know how to use the bus, or ask anyone for help. We felt very scared. I have fond memories of this Story Bridge—I had never seen such a big bridge with so many lights, so strange to me.

MOHSEN

I find Australians are very good and they are very nice but they always have some kind of stress. I don't know why they are always stressed. Most people want to live luxury lives and maybe they have a lot of mortgages and they have to work, work, work. It's kind of a bit silly.

Personally, for me, I've learnt from family, from my elders, that you should not stress or think about things that are temporary, something that one day will finish. If you have love, family and human connections, you will always have everything you need. For example, if your father dies, he lives in your memories, in your mind. Love is forever. This is permanent. What you leave behind in someone's mind and how you touch their heart is all that matters.

REZA YARAHMADI

I've visited detention centres regularly since 2010. Getting visitors never happened for us on Christmas Island. The first thing I did, after being in Melbourne for one month, was I went to Sydney, to Villawood, to visit people. And then I visited people in Maribyrnong and Pontville detention centre in Tasmania, and I'm still doing it.

I take them meals, Persian meals, because they haven't had it for ages. If you are away from home a while, you love to have traditional meals. When I visit we talk about different things, but I always give them hope. I tell them, 'Someday you will be in the community. You will have a job. You will have a future. You will have kids. You will be married. Just wait for the time.' I know these people are being tortured but it is always good to have hope, to hear, 'I came from the detention centre, like you.' And when I tell them, they say, 'You are one of the lucky ones. We are not so.'

ALI REZA

Sometimes I dream that somebody keeps me in a cage and doesn't provide me with food. In my dream I am stressed and thinking about how to escape but if I do that, my life will be in danger. So I just sit in the cage, waiting for someone to help.

It's very hard to adjust as a refugee with permanent residency in Australia. I think about my family. No one wants to live without their family, you know? We were just unlucky in life. Freedom is something different.

REZA YARAHMADI

Once, they were going to deport people to Nauru. We took action, and I was leading the action with someone else. The day after, when I went to college I was very tired because I hadn't slept all night. One of my classmates, an Australian lady, said, 'You look very tired.' I told her the story, and she had no idea, she did not know any of those things about the detention centre system and policies. She told me, 'I really want to be involved.'

We took those actions three times. We were locking the gates by lining up and holding each other's hands, and checking the cars going out to make sure there were no detainees in there. We were ready to go to airport and hand out papers to people so they could read what was happening and please stand off that flight. Because I know everyone, I check the cars to make sure there is no detainee, I am the person who is in touch inside. Now Serco call me 'the troublemaker'.

I am not scared, not at all. First, I believe actions will be louder than words—we have to do something rather than say something, or sit behind a computer writing something on Facebook. And the second thing is, I believe if I am silent, I am a dead person, I am gone. What I believe is: we are all human beings. If they abuse you, one day, they will come and abuse me. So we have to stop them.

PART III

When I was a kid I had heaps of dreams in my mind

Aziz

Abdul Aziz Muhamat is 24. On his first attempt to reach Australia, five of his friends drowned. He was taken to Manus Island in October 2013 against his will. Aziz told his story on a smuggled phone. The signal in the detention centre was too weak to call, so over the course of several months he left thousands of short voice messages. These are some messages from March and April 2016.

4 March

Yeah bro, how you doing? Good to hear from you.

My day? Actually, what can I say? It's really not so bad. I spent half of my day just pretending to be sleeping. I just lay down on my bed, because there is nothing you can do outside. And the weather was really hot today. I spent a couple of hours outside, just chilling around with some of my friends, and, as you know, there is nothing here we can do. Sometimes we don't have the motivation to do anything, so we just sit around and we have a coffee and talk to each other about different things—not about the resettlement process or about the problems that we are facing every day.

I've been through tough times. During the hunger strike, I was suspected of being one of the ringleaders and they sent me to gaol for 25 days. Since I came back I've been under supervision from the Wilson guards.

Why should I be scared? I'm not doing anything wrong, I'm not breaking the law. This is part of my rights, and I have to do that. I want to tell people that there is something wrong happening.

The phones we are using are really illegal and when the expat guards find out we have a phone they can confiscate the phone from us.

We made a relationship with the local guards who are working in the detention centre. We buy cigarettes from the canteen and give them those cigarettes and they sell them outside and bring back the money to us, or sometimes we ask them to buy a phone for us instead of bringing money.

The first time we had the phones actually, we started using them under the blankets. You cannot use your phone in public, or even inside your room, so you have to cover up yourself with the blankets. You cannot make phone calls. The only thing you can do is send a message to your friends or to your family through WhatsApp or Viber or other apps.

Our situation with the phone cards was good before but now it's really getting harder. When you are found to be a refugee they cut off your points so you will have no more access to the canteen and the cigarettes will be hard for you to get and trade.

11 March

Our situation at the moment is getting worse and worse. The pressure is increasing day by day, and people are really flat and tortured by this place. You know being in a cage for a long time is always affecting your brain.

So we have only one option left: every single night, more than three hundred or four hundred people go to IHMS and take sleeping tablets. Actually, you have got two options: either you be a drug addict with sleeping pills or you will start smoking some marijuana just to spend the night.

My situation, personally? Number one, I'm not a smoker. Number two, all my friends are smokers so I'm trying to help them. I'm doing all my best just to help them, so . . .

The only thing we can do right now is just . . . You do a lot of exercise and you feel very, very tired so you can just lie down and sleep. That's the only thing that can help.

12 March

I'm the kind of person who, since I was a child until today, I haven't had a good life. I've been through a lot of miserable things. You know, I don't know actually how to describe it, but well . . . it's really a dark life I've had.

As I'm talking to you now, this is the only thing that I can remember and describe because of the pain I feel inside me. I feel now my chest is beating up into my mouth. I wish I could describe the situation more than that, but the problem is I cannot, because I have forgotten everything. My brain has been formatted by this situation.

This environment takes control of every person in this place. If there was anyone here who said, 'My memory is okay and everything is fine,' I would not believe them, actually. People here can't remember their name. They can't remember their name.

I was standing in front of the gate with one of the fellows, and one of the security guards held the fellow's ID card and the guard was calling his name. And the guard did it three times or four times but the fellow, he didn't even reply to him. So what does that mean? The security guard was thinking that, *Oh, this guy he is just pretending*, but I said to him, 'Look, man, no one is pretending here. Why should he pretend to you? We forgot our names.'

15 March

I'm good, thank you, brother. Thanks for checking up with me. I'm doing alright, actually. I don't know what to say but I can't complain. Different day, same shit—but still alive.

17 March

When I came here in 2013 they made an appointment for me to see the dentist and I got approval to go only yesterday. So it means two and a half years I have been waiting for this appointment.

I had only one tooth out—number five on the bottom—and I feel I will get better soon. I haven't eaten anything so I'm just trying to drink something cold instead. I don't want to bite anything and feel the pain at the moment.

I'm still trying to get back on my feet from the pain, actually. Last night I took four Panadols just to help me sleep.

The only easy appointment you can get is just to get Panadol from the gatehouse—that's the only appointment you can get. You cannot get access to see the GP if you are sick. You cannot get access to see the nurse if you are in an emergency.

23 March

What I can remember at the moment is, it was a very, very long journey that I took when I fled the country.

The incidents took place in Sudan, where as you know, we have been through a very, very horrible conflict. If you google now on the internet you can find some more information about what happened in Darfur.

At that time I was between fifteen and sixteen years old. The smell was just the smell of dead bodies everywhere and the guns . . . You could see just smoke because most of the villages had been burned down and people had been shot down dead. The only other things you could hear around you was people screaming and shouting and crying. They needed someone to be very close to them and to help, but we were running to find shelter for ourselves and we weren't even able to help ourselves.

And, ah, I just turned left and right and the only things that I could see or hear was smoke and gunshots. My parents told us not to stop, to keep running. When you're tired of running so they asked us to keep walking, to not stop, because those militias had horses, so they could chase us as far as we can go. They could kill us or if they needed us, they could take us with them, especially the young people like me. That was the order they had from their bosses: don't kill them because we need to recruit them.

And we ran, we ran, we ran from the village. Even the animals were a bit better than human beings at that place. You could see human bones where some people couldn't bury them, and you could see other animals, like eagles, flying and eating human beings' bodies.

As I am talking to you, I am one of the lucky men, that I survived that genocide and I got a chance and I just ran away from that.

Let me have a break and let me have a coffee because, ah, I get a shock when I tell the stories and I start feeling like I have got flashbacks from that incident . . . But anyway, it doesn't matter. I can continue. When I start feeling that pain, I can relieve it, because I don't want to keep things inside me. I want people to know about me, what happened, how I ended up here, and what kind of person I am.

27 March

Well, the walking group is nice. I really enjoy it. I normally do this kind of walking group once a month. At least you can see the people outside, smell a bit of breeze. This is a navy base, so we walk to the main gate and we come back.

We stop near a tiny market, which is located about half a kilometre from the compound. Sometimes we sit there and talk with the locals. It depends on the Wilson guards who are escorting us. If the person is really nice he will allow the counsellor to buy coconuts or chewing gum for us. Otherwise, if the guard is really awful, he will probably write a report on the counsellor. That's why they stop now—some of the counsellors, they don't do that anymore.

Today's one of my bad days actually. I woke up and, I don't know how to explain, but it looked like, oh, a dark day. So I went for a walk and when I came back I felt a bit better. I'm trying to gain a bit of the energy that I lost a long time ago, so that's it . . . but really, I like the walking.

Human nature? To be honest, the environment that we are in is very harsh so it requires individuals to look after themselves and do whatever they can to just protect themselves from letting their mental health deteriorate. You witness some people harm themselves and some people fight over only small things. Why are people fighting because of just one spoonful of sugar?

People swallow nail clippers. Some people drink shampoo, washing powder. I ask myself, *Why would I do all this? Is that just for me to go to Australia? Or it's just to show people that I'm innocent? That's not a good way! Why should I harm myself?* I have got some people there waiting for me. They love me, they want me to be with them. So I have to be patient. As long as you are patient in any circumstance that you face in your life, one day you will succeed.

I'm talking about my family. They are still living in a refugee camp. That's the place where I left them in 2013. I'm so lucky because the day before yesterday I was in touch with them, for the first time in a long time, after six months. I got in touch with them and I spoke with my mum.

I was trying to explain to her my situation but I thought about it several times and I decided I couldn't put more pressure on my mum. If I started to explain about everything I've been through, probably she wouldn't be able to eat, or sleep, she might get some kind of heart attack. I don't know whether it is good or bad, but I told her a white lie—I covered it up, and I told her different things. I started by greeting her and she recognised my voice and she just started crying and, like, oh, I cried with her! For ten minutes we were just crying on the phone, you know? And finally I just told her that things were fine and she said, 'I've been worried about you and I thought that maybe you have been sick or something bad happened to you.'

My family don't know where I am exactly. The first day I reached Christmas Island, I called them and I said, 'Oh guys, thank god, I reached safely to Christmas Island and now I'm in Australia.' They still believe that I'm in Australia. I'm not able to tell them that I'm in Manus Island. I'm just trying . . . I'm lying to them but it's not like . . . Whenever they want to talk to me about the place or the environment, I'm always trying to avoid that conversation.

And it's not just me. There are hundreds of guys in here who did the same thing. You can't tell lies to your parents, but in some cases you can't tell the truth. Whenever I go to the phone I'm trying to be more flexible and I'm pretending like I'm really happy and laughing so they feel like, 'Oh, my son is really living in a good environment.'

I told my sister everything because she is older than me and she is a bit wiser. She is always trying to calm my parents down, telling them not to get upset with me or not to worry anymore. And she is just telling them, 'Oh, he's doing fine, but he is waiting for his visa to come. Once he guarantees his visa he will be free and he will start to do all he can to help the situation back here.'

A lot of people back home think that because these guys are in gaol, they must have broken the law. A person seeking asylum would not be detained for three years. The maximum is six months. Whenever you explain it to people, no one will believe you.

You can't even tell your close friends the reality, because if you do, they will find a lot of information about this place and they can ruin your reputation or they will reveal everything that you've been hiding from your family. That would be a disaster for us. That's why some of the people here just cut off the phone calls. Some of them haven't called their family for almost two years now. They don't want to call until the final day they get out of this place.

30 March

We had a big meeting yesterday morning. They told us that they're going to separate us: the refugees on one side and the non-refugees on the other side. According to what I heard, if they refuse to move, they can force them.

I'm still trying to find out why they want to separate us and what they want to do, actually. You know, I spoke with many case managers here but they don't tell me actually what they are planning to do.

They are planning something. They were trying to put a bit of pressure on the refugees, including even the negative guys. Once you have received a negative determination, you will probably be forced to go back to your country. But they put extra pressure on the refugees so they will accept Papua New Guinea as a resettlement country. So this is what's going to happen.

6 April

How was your day? How are things going with you? I'm sorry I didn't get back to you. I have been really busy since this morning . . . One of my roommates, he has got a negative assessment. He was resisting and finally they just brought the police and they convinced him.

You know, when the police are involved it's really scary, not just for me but for many people. The police were serious this morning and they have got instructions from Wilson Security that they must move everyone who refuses by force, either by beating him up or, if he was misbehaving, by sending him to gaol.

9 April

I'm just, you know . . . I'm really sorry, I don't know what to say, but there has been a lot of things happening here. I couldn't get a time, actually, to even open my phone or use my phone because of what's going on around here. I don't know where to start but there's heaps of things happening.

Heaps of guys are trying to commit suicide. Some of them were jumping over the fence. Some of them they were doing a lot of shitty stuff, swallowing nail clippers, trying to harass the others. And some of them are fighting with security.

Most of the guys who are hurting themselves are the guys who have got a negative refugee assessment. Some people, when they finished the interview, were told that they were positive. And suddenly, later, they just told them, 'Oh no, you are not a positive. You are a negative.' So that is why people are hurting themselves.

Everybody now is scared that this is not a real process, that this is just wasting time. That they have been keeping us here for three years, and finally we've just figured out that the process, it was just fake.

When we see someone who is trying to commit suicide, sometimes you just drag yourself away to avoid getting the pictures in your head, and sometimes you can get close, to help.

You just hide yourself and you pray. Or you try to keep yourself safe and you hope that this is not going to happen to you, and you are not going to do that. But it's really very tough. I don't know even how to explain it whenever I see things like that happen in front of my eyes.

10 April

This is my destiny. You know every human being on this earth has got his own destiny. Sometimes, life will turn its back on you. So you will be suffering, suffering, suffering, from the first day you are born until the last day you die. And some people, they are lucky, they're fortunate, they are born and they find everything in front of them. Some people, they have to dig and dig and keep digging until they get what they want.

Maybe after this prison I will end up in another prison, or I will have a better life. I don't know what will happen. But from what I can see now, I'm still having a dark future.

11 April

I was really following the process of the court case in Papua New Guinea but guess what? I stopped following it and I stopped reading about it. Even now Australia is manipulating the Papua New Guinean court. Guess how many times the court put a date to finalise the case? Every time they postpone the final decision for an extra three months or four months.

There are not many people here who have a hope with the court case. We just have a hope for one thing: we know we have been brought here because a new policy had been introduced to Australia's immigration law, and we believe that one day this law will be changed. That is all. But we don't believe in the court case and we don't believe in anything else. Everyone is scared about what is happening right now in Europe.

14 April

When I was a kid I had heaps of dreams in my mind. When I went to the hospital with my grandma—I think I was ten or eleven years old—I saw the doctors and everything and I was like, 'Oh look! I want to be a doctor one day when I grow up.'

I said, 'If I fail to be a doctor, I want to be a pilot,' and that was my Plan B. And my Plan C is I want to be a person that can help other people.

But, you know, sometimes life is like that: you can't predict your future. You don't know where life is going to take you.

17 April

Last time I called my mum I heard very, very bad news which hurt me and I was just crying by myself all night, I couldn't sleep. She told me, 'Your grandma, she's just crying, she's crying.' She asked my mum, 'Why did you send your son away? Why don't you do something and bring him back to me?' When I heard that news from my mum I just started crying, I couldn't hold my tears.

And I'm still feeling that, I'm still regretting . . . Why, why did I just leave them behind and why am I not able to do anything to help my grandma? She did all she could to bring me up safely and politely and to be a respectful person. She taught me a lot of things and I'm not able to return that favour to her, not even one per cent.

I understand that the situation is not in my hands, but I need to do something. They are just suffering. They worry about me more than they worry about themselves, and from where I am now, I worry about them. Like, I feel every time I go to the mess I can't even eat properly. I feel like, *Oh my mum and my grandma, they haven't had a dinner so how come I'm going to have a dinner like that?*

Believe me, it's a really tough moment that I'm in now, and I feel like the room, it's just getting narrower and narrower every single day.

Before we had the conflict and many people lost their lives, I never imagined that one day I would leave the Sudan and I would end up in a place where there is no way I can do anything to help myself or to help the people that I love. So this is something really, really terrible. I'm just trembling and it's really touching my heart. Every time I start remembering about those things I feel like, *Oh my god, why, why, why?*

I have got a bunch of questions in my head and sometimes I talk to my room, I talk to my bed, I talk to my pillow, my mattress. Everything I see in front of me, I talk to it, but I feel like there are not any answers.

Well, ah, I can understand it's not really my fault but deep in my heart I feel like, *Oh I did this for myself, I searched for it.*

I still feel like my heart, like every part of my body, is just saying to me, 'This is your fault, this is your fault.'

To be honest, I feel like, what is the importance of my existence, if I am not able to do anything?

26 April

I have just heard the news! I checked the link and I saw that it is true, the Supreme Court ruled that this place is illegal and Australia and Papua New Guinea, they must take these people out.

I don't know how to describe the happiness of everyone and . . . I just walked in and I saw everyone was smiling and I was astonished and I said, 'You guys, what's going on?' They said, 'You just go and check your phone and let us know!' This is really good news for us and I feel really happy.

I can say what I can see right now: everyone here is shouting and clapping and whistling and their voice is really over the sky and they are really happy about this news! The Wilson guards closed all the gates and I think they're trying to evacuate all the staff. They don't want to let any of the case managers walk in for the time being.

I'm really proud. I'm really proud because we have been fighting for this, day and night and day and night and thanks that finally we did it. We never expected to hear something like this.

To me, it doesn't matter whether they come out with anything else. We know the real thing: Papua New Guinea ruled that this place is really illegal. It's really illegal. We don't care about whatever manipulation that they want to do, let them do it. Their plan is not going to succeed anymore.

I'm really excited. I haven't been excited like this since I came to Manus. Today is the first day that I'm really smiling. I'm not pretending, I'm really smiling from my heart. And I've seen every man is just smiling from his heart. It's as if people were thirsty and you gave them water.

This is the first step. From now on when Papua New Guinea or Australian Immigration talk to us, or the guards or whoever, we can say, 'Look, stop there, this place is illegal and you've been holding us here for three years and this is enough. You've been fucking us here for long time, so you have to stop now.'

I'm sorry for my language, but this is the point of view of everyone. Everyone is just astonished by this news and they don't know even what to say. You laugh, but really it's not enough. People are just hugging each other and cheering and walking around and spreading the news. We don't know what's next, but this is really the first good news that we've heard.

I learnt all people are equal

Sajjd

Sajjd is living in transit accommodation in East Lorengau, Manus Island, having moved out of the detention centre months ago. He did not accept resettlement in Papua New Guinea, and has no visa, but he is there.

The sting of the cigarettes

This? This is one of the local cigarettes that we find here. It is cheap, and you know, one of these local cigarettes is equivalent of five other cigarettes [*laughing*]. So that means it is a very strong one.

I smoke one packet a day, or one and a half packets a day. When I was in my country, I didn't smoke. I smoke because of the stress and depression. Sometimes, when you smoke you feel like the cigarettes can help you to reduce the stress and stop you thinking, and make you relax. You live on the sting of the cigarettes. Yes, I just live on the sting of the cigarettes.

Any moments of happiness? [*Laughs.*] How can you feel happy here? Sometimes when I see the guys and they tell a joke or tell something funny I feel like I'm really, really laughing, from the bottom of my heart. And I feel like this is weird from me—I'm just laughing, but I don't know, it's just weird. I don't feel there is anything here that can give me relief. Just sometimes my friends or the people who are surrounding me, they sit and talk to me. That's it.

I haven't done anything today. I just spend all my time resting in my room. Just doing nothing. I spend my time doing nothing, either using internet or reading a book. We don't have any alternative and we don't know what's going to happen to us. So we are just sitting, and waiting to see what will be next.

I'm a refugee from wars and I came to Australia as a refugee. I grew up in a country where there is no freedom. I went to this school where they speak a language that is not my own language. And most of the students were laughing at me because I could not speak the language . . . This is the most . . . One of the memories that I have of my childhood.

I lost my father seven years ago. Only my mum is there now and one brother is there to look after my mum, my younger brother.

I last spoke to my mother, ah, it was twenty days ago. I just said few things like, 'How are you?', 'How you doing?', 'How is life with you?' She just said she can't complain. Ah yes, she did ask me about what I'm doing . . . But I didn't have an answer. She asks me . . . I don't have an answer. She doesn't know where I am. I didn't tell her, no. She is really sick and she is diabetic and if I tell her that I am in this place, she will feel worse and, that's why I just tell her I'm in Australia. Sometimes when I talk to her I pretend—I smile and laugh and express myself as a person who is happy—because I don't want her to get worse or to think about me and to worry. I feel pain inside me, and the same time . . . I'm scared that she can . . . she will get worse . . . worse than she is now, so that's why I tell her nothing. My friend and my cousin know that I'm here and I told them on the condition, 'Please do not tell any one of my family or relatives.'

I don't have an answer

I am 30 years old. I have been on Manus Island 34 months. When we first arrived on Manus Island they told us that the Manus people eat human beings. And the second thing they told us is that they have lots of kinds of contagious diseases. And when the first mosquito bites you, you will get malaria. We come from a place where we didn't even know that things like that exist in the world. We live a life full of fear and worry because of the information we were given when we arrived. The Department of Immigration and Border Protection are the ones who told us this. They bring you to the arrival halls and then they start telling you all this stuff. I don't know what the reason is behind this.

One thing I could say about it is that they just torture you and they do whatever they can and they just leave you like a robot. You can't remember anything. Robots are normally controlled with a remote control, so whatever you say, or whatever anybody touches, the robot will move in the direction you want. We don't have any other choice. In the morning they come and without knocking on your door they just walk into your room and ask you to come out, 'We want to search your room.' They have been taking our freedom away from us and we have just been following their orders. They put a lot of restrictions on our life. Why? I don't have an answer and I don't know.

One of the worst times I had was the first day I came to this island. I became sick and I was coughing. I submitted a request to IHMS and I was waiting for a week and hadn't received any feedback. The coughing was starting to increase and I wrote another request. And I submitted another request—the third one—and I explained on that request that I was coughing blood. And I received a response after ten days. And after ten days I went to the doctor and I met the nurse who gave me only antibiotics. I used the antibiotics but it didn't help and I started coughing again and it was getting worse and worse, so I spoke with one of the counsellors and she actually helped me out. She went back and spoke with the doctor and I got chance to speak with the doctor and that was the moment they gave me the right treatment for my coughing. Who am I going to complain to? Am I going to complain to people who gave me the worst treatment I have received? Or am I going to complain to the people who have broken inside and beaten us? The sick person requires the right treatment to be healthy and if there is no right treatment, how would you feel?

I remember the incidents in 2014 when the locals stormed the compound. We had been beaten up and many people were injured and one of our friends passed away. And after that incident we complained a lot: why are we in this prison? And we didn't receive any answer from this complaint, so we decided to go on hunger strike. After several days of the hunger strike the police came in and with the security guards they took us to the Manus gaol. And we asked them, 'Why we have been sent to gaol?' They said to us, 'Because you are complaining.' We don't have a right to complain. To whom we can complain? Or to whom we can speak or describe our anger or frustration? Our protest wasn't violent. It was just peaceful, we didn't say anything to anybody. We didn't want to go and eat because we had had enough of the food they provide us. And they came and took us to the gaol on Manus Island where we spent our time with the prisoners, like thieves and rapists and murderers. We don't even know what we did. I was in the prison, I can't remember, maybe ten or twelve days.

After we were sent back to the detention centre they also built another tiny gaol inside the detention centre and they sent us to that gaol. And if you ask anybody, particularly the guards, they tell you: 'We don't know why. We just have an order from the Department of Immigration.' That's it. I was with the criminals, while I hadn't committed a crime. I was innocent and I didn't know why I was there. I just want to say two things: I'm a refugee. I'm not a criminal.

A fear, growing and growing

When I close my eyes at night, I think about how my future will be. I think, *Why I have been in prison for three years? Have I committed any crimes in my life that I didn't know?* I don't know even what to say . . . I can't even describe more than that. I don't have any dreams, but sometimes I experience nightmares, two or three times a week. I can't remember them particularly well, but sometimes when I wake up in the morning I remember the feeling. It's just a fear. It's just a fear, growing and growing. And I don't know even fear of what. I don't know, it's just a fear.

Here, the only thing that you think about more often is how the day will finish, from morning to evening. In the three years that we've been here every day there is news. One day you hear on the news that they will send you back to Indonesia. Another day on the news you hear you will be resettled in Papua New Guinea. Another day you hear they will send you to a third country, like Cambodia or the Philippines. And it has reached a point that we don't want to think about tomorrow, we don't want to think about today.

I moved out of the detention centre to the East Lorengau transit camp a year ago. I haven't accepted resettlement in Papua New Guinea. I'm living in this country without any documents, without anything, not even a visa. There is no paper for resettlement—there are only the documents that show you want to move from the detention centre to the transit centre. Australia knows I am here illegally, yes. And even the Papua New Guinean government know that I am here illegally. I'm living here without any visa, without any legal document, without anything, and I have only a refugee ID card with me. I did not mean to violate the law in Papua New Guinea but they forced me to do that.

The detention centre is surrounded by fences. There is a fence everywhere you go. I left that detention centre for another one where the fences are wider apart, so you can go as far as you can. This other detention centre is the island.

I have learnt that all the people are equal. I learnt all people are equal, but the politics are different. I learnt that when one of the Immigration officers—she's a woman—she came to me and I talked to her and she cried. And she said, 'I am here just to do my job. I have nothing to do with the policy.' It's clear to me that the people are different from the policy. And any kind of policy implemented in the world has nothing to do with its people.

Education is light

Omar

Omar Mohammed Jack is the oldest child in his family, but he was only seventeen when he left Sudan.

They call me Immigration

Six of us are living in this room and the space is too small. I have a shelf—it's a tiny one—above my bed. I have some books there, the books I borrow from the library. Every two weeks or three weeks I return those books and then I borrow more. And also, I have some sheets that I printed from the internet which are about international law. I love to read, so sometimes I keep myself busy with reading those sheets I printed from the internet. They help me to know the meaning of international law, the history of it. Just basic information. I'm just warming up. I want to study law, hopefully, if I'm still alive one day.

I have three pillows in my bed. One, I put my head on, the other I put my legs on, and the third one I just hug. When I hug the pillow I sometimes like to pretend as if I'm hugging my girlfriend [*laughing*]. Ah! I mean, I've been here three years, how can I get a girlfriend? Yes, some people have girlfriends on Facebook, but I'm not living in Facebook relationships. Maybe they are using a different face, a different name? Maybe men can use a girl's photos? It's difficult to believe [*laughing*].

You know, I have sent too many emails to universities in Australia. I asked them for an online scholarship and I explained my situation: I'm living in the detention centre, and my financial situation is not perfect. I came here to Manus Island, 28 September 2013. I was seventeen. It was a hard decision, but we had no choice.

My name is Omar Mohammed Jack. Jack? It is my grandfather's name. Maybe they took it from the British in Sudan, a long time ago. I was born in a village called Kiskita. In 2013, war started in that area and we lost half of our family. We fled from that village to a big city, El Geneina, the capital of West Darfur. We came to a refugee camp called Riyad, where my family lives now. You know, Darfur is really big. The wars have lasted from 2001 until now.

Some people here are saying to me, 'You are a leader.' I have a nickname from the guys, they call me Immigration. Why? Because when Immigration staff brought us here, they just released us inside the camp and we found our rooms by ourselves. I was helping new arrivals to find rooms and beds. In camp, if you say Omar, not too many people know me. But if you say Immigration, they know me well. Because I'm trying to help people. Sometimes I like to talk politics, and some people are hoping one day I will become a minister of parliament. Even some people are calling me Minister.

I'd like to study instead of doing nothing. I want to study for my future. If you want to change something you have to learn. Education is light. You have to light your life, and you light other lives also. Do you know why I want to study law, and especially international law? Because I want to work with international organisations, like Amnesty or UNHCR. I want to help, I want to help people. If I can't help, just I want to tell the truth, about what is right and what is wrong. I am interested in law because I have confidence I can help my people. Yes, my English language is too slow, but I have ability to learn more. I believe.

My English teacher, David, advised me about scholarships and helped me to write the letter. And then I copied it onto my email, and sent it to several different universities, asking for scholarships for online study. I sent it to Melbourne Law School and Adelaide, and another university in Perth. Always law schools. I forget the names, but they all replied to me. The answer they told me was, 'You do not have an Australian visa.' The first condition to apply for university or to get a scholarship from an Australian university, is you need to have Australian visa. And finally I gave up. They were telling me, 'Just stay strong and get out of detention, and come here. If you get a visa in Australia, then we have many different organisations helping people to get scholarships.' Yep, I remember, but unfortunately I get nothing.

I think about my future, why not?

My family is still living in Riyad refugee camp. My mother is there and my brothers, but my father is in another country, Chad. Have you heard of Chad, bordering Sudan? My father also ran away, like me, 'cause of lack of safety. We are from the Zaghawa tribe. The people who killed most of our family, they are everywhere, and the camp is open. They can enter the camp at any time. You can't guarantee your safety.

I'm the first child, the oldest. I spoke with them last Sunday, I call them every thirteen or fifteen days. They know my situation already. I just ask, 'Are you okay?' And they ask me, 'Where are you?' The same question, every time. Same answer. I'm still in the camp, same as them and I don't know my future. I tell them that I'm okay. In fact I'm not okay, I'm not feeling good, but I tell them I'm okay. The oldest son should look after his parents and brothers. You help them and if the financial situation is not perfect, you should sacrifice to get a job and help them. They need my help.

Sometimes I think back to my situation in Sudan and I know it's not good to go back. I do other stuff to keep myself busy, sometimes studying English in my room, sometimes playing football. Sometimes I read books like Nelson Mandela's—leaders like him, they were suffering a lot and then finally they got their freedom and they achieved their goals. When I look to those people, it's kind of encouragement, you know, to survive.

When I am thinking a lot, I can't sleep well. Some days when you feel good and happy you sleep early, and the other days will be totally different, especially when you hear some news coming out from the Australian government. The politicians, they know we will suffer. Every single word they use to describe us. It's rumours, you know?

Nightmares start. I have nightmares, like action nightmares, people attacking people. Now we have memory problems, we can't remember what happened yesterday, or last night. Our memories are not normal, they cannot record anything. I'm talking to you now, but maybe after couple of hours I won't remember what I said to you. I forget too easily, not like before. I worry about that, yes, of course—that maybe it's getting worse, worse. Maybe one day we will lose our minds. I have seen a lot of people here lose their mind. They arrive normal, like you, but the situation makes them like that.

Yes, I think about my future, why not? Even the animals they need a future. Like anybody else, like any normal person,

Omar

I need a future. I want to study and I want to help myself, my family, my people, people generally. Why not? Seeking asylum, that's a crime? Under what kind of law? If you come by boat and sought asylum in Australia, you are guilty, yes? Why they don't take us to the court if we are really guilty and we really are terrorists? I want Australian people to discover the truth by themselves. I believe in justice.

One day the torturer will get tired and you will win

Ariobarzan

Ariobarzan arrived on Christmas Island only to find out that anyone who arrived after 19 July 2013 would never be allowed to settle in Australia. He is a lifelong democracy activist.

I have two daughters

Ariobarzan is not my real name. My family is in Iran. Due to political problems, I had to leave. I have two daughters. When I left Iran, my daughters were very young.

For a dad, the only happiness is witnessing his kids growing up. Nothing is more difficult than losing these moments. My younger daughter can't remember me at all. The older one has very limited things in her mind, like a shadow of past memories—me being with her and with my family—and she tells her little sister about the joy of those memories. Their mum is playing a very important role in keeping me alive in the minds and hearts of our kids and I am very thankful for her.

Whenever I called my family, people from the intelligence ministry of Iran came the next day and took my family. I had to stop calling them. In twenty months, I have called my family three times. I rang my neighbours' home and they secretly brought my family to their place, and I talked to them. It is difficult, very difficult. If you were in my shoes, what would you do? Would you continue your life? There is no way to be with my kids. It is an absurd, aimless and senseless life I am traversing.

My kids are looking at the door, hoping that it will open and I will step inside the home. But my wife and I, what can we say to these two kids? Is there any convincing reason that we can tell them? They are not at an age where they can understand the path that I took. I live for the day when I can see them and tell them the reason for my beliefs.

Before I left Iran, I had been a fugitive and the government had been looking for me. I was forced to stay hidden and then I departed on a plane. I was in Indonesia and then I left for Australia by sea. Every single moment we expected that the boat would break and we would sink to the bottom of the ocean. Everybody was scared of death, but we left ourselves to our fate and destiny. I just thought about my dearest, that's all—only my family, my two children and my wife.

After approximately one month on Christmas Island, I was taken away like a criminal. Whatever I found out about why I would be exiled to Papua New Guinea, I could not understand it. Two officers were next to me. They held my hands firmly to prevent me from escaping. In that way, they took us to the plane. I didn't know why.

I won't give in to slavery

The concept of prison... In Iran, I had been in political prisons. I fought for the sake of democracy. Maybe many people think that torture is just something with cables, beatings or these things. Look, the intelligence prisons in Iran have two types of tortures combined: physical torture and mental torture. With physical torture the injuries and wounds heal after a while, but mental torture is 80 per cent of what they inflict. The worst type of torture is mental torture.

When I entered Manus, I could compare my thoughts in Iran with the reality in Australia, a democratic country. I lost my family, I lost my country, I lost my friends, my money, my material life. I devoted all I had to my spiritual life. I wanted to know if the pathway that I battled for was right. Was that real, my goal?

I faced worse mental torture compared to the intelligence prisons in Iran. We have been under severe mental torture for three years. We see it clearly and exactly: there is no way behind—to return is a torture—and there is nothing in front of us but hell. There is no hope, there is no future.

What sort of democracy is it? I am confused. After three years, I still can't believe it. I can never believe that this country is the country that we used to watch on TV, that we looked at as one of the countries that built the foundation of human rights in the world. I am still shocked, a nerve-wracking shock.

This is the greatest crime that Australia committed against me. They have made me regret why I fought against my government. Why did I leave my family because of my beliefs? Most of my nightmares are because I was defeated in this pathway. I had hope for victory, but this torture has left nothing for me but an absurd world. I lost my former life because of the absurd propaganda that democratic countries state at their podiums—empty words. I came, and now understand that there is nothing more, nothing except cruelty.

I hope this situation is only in this country, and my belief in democracy . . . That democracy still exists . . . Maybe this democracy exists, yes, in European countries, or maybe in America.

No, it wasn't in Australia. They caught me, tied my hands, brought me to an island, exiled me. They provide us with a choice: torment and torture in the camp, or to return to your country and face death. If you were in my shoes, what would you choose?

By staying in the camp, I will fight, I will tolerate the mental pressure, I will tolerate the lack of freedom, but I won't give in to slavery. It is modern slavery. They brought me to an island and said, 'You should let us sell you like a slave.' They deliver me to another country and try to sell me to put their policy in practice. I won't accept being sold.* And I will fight to death, till I am killed. The only way of defeating torture is resistance. One day the torturer will get tired and you will win, that's all.

One day you will come to our countries

On 17 February 2014, at night, we were shouting that we didn't deserve this situation. It was not a riot, it was a huge protest. When the locals attacked Mike compound, I was in Foxtrot and I heard from a distance my friends' wails, exactly the same as the voices in torture cells of Iran. It reminded me of that situation.

When the clashes were about to finish, I saw a scene that I had seen a few times in Iran: a young man, around twenty, wailing, a bullet in his body. He collapsed in front of me. A young man who was shot only because he was trying to achieve his freedom.

---

* Ariobarzan is referring to the additional aid payments made by the Australian government to the Papua New Guinean government to accept resettlement of refugees who had sought asylum in Australia. This concept—the feeling of having been sold—has been raised by several narrators detained on both Manus Island and Nauru.

I think locals shot him. I don't know who carried the weapon, but he was shot.

The day after, we found out about the death of Reza Barati.

I think this was the starting point of dictatorship in your country. This was like a sperm in the womb of the Liberal Party and this child was born and will grow, and one day, you—because of human rights violations—will come to our countries and seek asylum. I am really sorry for the Australian people.

My words aren't related to the Australian people. Australians are very kind and wonderful people and I really like them. I would like to talk about many things, but the most important thing is this matter: the wound that we experienced in our country was caused by dictatorship. Once we had a good country, full of freedom, full of democracy, but the freedom and joy was taken from us. Don't let the misery we experienced happen to you as well.

Now I don't have the heart for girls

Sami

Sami works out in the gym each morning in the Manus Regional Processing Centre, and exercises again most afternoons. He has been there since September 2013. He is currently living in Mike compound.

She was my lover

I am from Pakistan. I needed to be safe. I didn't need trouble for my family, for myself . . . I was scared. I left the country.

So I came to Malaysia, Indonesia. I gave money to the agent. I said, 'I need the safe countries.' But agent told me lies. For three months I was in Indonesia. I saw hard days. Four times I tried to come to Australia, four times, and each time the police caught me and I gave them money and they released me.

I came to Christmas Island on 6 September 2013. I was on Christmas Island for fourteen days.

After that, Immigration told us, 'You have to go to Manus Island.' I said, 'Where is Manus Island?' So now they herd us like animals. This is a jungle, Manus Island. This is a jungle. Where is the freedom? Immigration always told us, 'Your process will finish.' Two years ago, I got the positive refugee status. I am still here. I just ask, 'Why?' No one cares.

I didn't see a situation like this before, when I was in Pakistan. When I came, and I saw many people in the prison, when I heard about everyone's story in here, I became like a humanist. You know, humanist? Everyone has a lot of problems. So I care about everyone. When someone's telling me their stories, I am crying. So, in here, I love everyone in the compound. I love friends, I am a positive man. I am always trying to be positive to people, to be patient, to help, but my heart is broken.

My love story? My cousin, she was my lover. After I came to Manus Island, when I talked to my lover, she told me: 'When you are free, we will make an engagement and our families will be happy.' I always worried about it. When I call her, sometimes I'm angry with her. I say, 'Why you don't attend my call?' And she says, 'Don't call, please. Just when you are free.' After that I call my mum, every time, and say, 'Why you don't make me my engagement?' My mum says, 'Please, wait, be patient.'

I was living in Foxtrot compound, then I changed to Mike compound. I was there. Then all our families agreed to our marriage, all our families were happy. All my family was just waiting for my freedom so we could marry. I was talking always with my lover. If I didn't call my lover for one week I felt very sad. Because everyone needs love. When I talked to my lover, I felt happy all week. I was doing exercise and I was very happy.

But I'm unlucky. One year ago, she went . . . She was . . . She passed away in an accident. The last night before the accident I talked to my lover. Her last night. I said, 'What's wrong?' She told me, 'We have to go. My mum has to go to hospital in Karachi,' in a different province. They got in an accident in the mountains. After three days, when I checked Facebook, I saw the news, the picture of the car, the accident. I was in Mike compound and many people saw me. I was crying.

Security caught me and they put me in the Green Zone. I was there ten days in the Green Zone, feeling sad. When people are mentally disturbed—when they are angry, or have problems—they catch them and put them in the Green Zone so you can't do anything. There is always security. It's like isolation. When you do something, when you are angry, there is a bodyguard—there is the big, big man. So if you do something wrong they can beat you so you are like a small baby, you can't do anything. I was there for ten days. I was sad. I was very worried every time and any time. Still now, I worry about my family. Now I don't have the heart for girls and I don't feel love. If I was free, maybe I'd forget, but now I am in the prison. They put me in prison. I am tortured because I'm in the prison, I'm always thinking about my lover. I am just thinking, always. I am continuing to do exercise, but my heart is feeling sad.

How can I forget?

Everyone lost hope now—everyone is mentally disturbed. Today my friend is mental, very mental. He was my friend from my city. Today he caught a special flight to Australia. He lost his memory one year ago. He didn't call his family, he doesn't know who his family is. He's . . . We care about him. We always told the IHMS: 'Please, take him. This is crazy, he doesn't know anything.' The security and doctors don't care. Today they put him on the flight into Australia. Why? If he went before, he would be treated, but now I don't think he will recover. He lost his memory.

THEY CANNOT TAKE THE SKY

I don't know how long we will be here in the prison. These three years, and this situation, we will never forget. They are always coming in our minds. They will beat me. And why were we in the compound, why? Why did the Australian government beat us? Do you remember? They beat us, they did wrong things to us, like we were animals. Same now. They abuse us. They can do anything. We are scared, this is true. If I do something, if I'm talking too much, security will come.

So in my life, I will never forget this situation. When we are free, when I can go anywhere, I will never forget this memory. This moment, every time, will eat me. Will eat my mind. They made us mental. So how I can forget? I can't forget for one night, just one day. Now I have been, I think, 1015 days in the compound. In this jungle, Manus Island.

I see the situation, in the compounds. I hear the stories of many people. So I get experiences from everyone, in the stories, in the situation, in our problems, in the security. If I am thinking negatively, I can't do anything. So it's better that I think about positives. If I think about positives, so my mind will be fresh. I am trying, but I have a lot of problems, they eat my mind. So in my mouth I have positives, but in my head they are broken. I don't have any option. Sometimes, when I feel sad, I think, *Why? Why am I here?* So, I just ask you, how you can forget this moment? Never. You can never forget this moment. When I am old I will be thinking about this moment. *Why did I spend four years in the prison? Why Australia, for four years they spent us in the prison, in the jungle?* How can we forget?

I have been tortured and I have been loved

Imran

Imran Mohammad is a stateless Rohingyan man who fled Myanmar as a teenager. He taught himself English in detention on Manus Island.

She moved her fingers over each verse

In our garden, there are many trees: fruit trees, flowering trees, trees with colourful leaves. My mother didn't let me go out because it wasn't safe for the Rohingyan boys, especially the ones who are young. So I would spend my evenings with my mother in our garden and we always talked about her family: her father, mother, her grandfather, grandmother, all those sorts of things. And we also discussed about our future.

In Myanmar they don't accept us as their own citizens. We are not from Myanmar, they say. But we were born in Myanmar, and our parents and our grandparents were born in Myanmar. When I was sixteen I had to flee my country. I had no choice. I was nineteen when I arrived on Manus Island; now I am 22.

When I was back home, my mother was the first person I saw every morning. When I first opened my eyes, I saw her praying. My mother is a very religious person, she taught me many things about our religion. She used to pray five times a day, on time. She didn't go to school so she can't read and write—it was so painful for her because she wanted to read the Holy Quran. When she woke up, she prayed first and she took the Holy Quran and just moved her fingers over each verse and that made her happy.

I used to talk to my mother while she was getting breakfast for all of us. We always ate together: breakfast, lunch and dinner. She used to make flatbreads and different types of vegetables . . . And when she finished making breakfast she woke everyone up and we came to the kitchen and sat together. I always sat next to her because I wanted to eat the best flatbread . . . All I can say about my mum is she was the most precious person in my life. I was scared, I was traumatised and I was persecuted when I was back home. I wasn't safe in my country, but whenever I was with my mum, I found peace in her eyes. I felt the safest person in this world.

Many things happened when I was on that boat

So, I was in Myanmar; I am from Rakhine state. I left my village during the night. I caught a boat, with my friend. We were in Bangladesh for maybe twenty days, then my family arranged another boat for me.

I was on that boat for fifteen days. It was one of the terrible experiences in my life. The boat wasn't very big but there were almost five hundred people on that boat. There were women, older people, babies, teenagers like me. After four days things started to get harder and harder because we were running out of water, food. After nine days people started to die. [*Sighs.*]

You know I saw some babies who died in their mother's lap. The mothers didn't accept that their babies had died. And some old people, they got really sick and died. We just threw them in the ocean.

Our goal was to reach Malaysia, but we reached the Thailand border three times before we reached Malaysia. Thai authorities turned our boat around twice and the third time they started shooting at us and some people died. I felt like I was an animal. Nobody on the boat had a heart that a normal person has. We were put in a position where we had no sympathy for each other. We were dehumanised by the smugglers because they just cared about money. Believe me, if I knew I would go through this hardship after I left my country I would never, ever have left my country. I would rather die in my country than . . . [*speaking quietly*] than die in another place where I don't feel safe. There are many things that happened when I was on that boat. I think people would find it extremely hard to read those stories.

After fifteen days we reached Malaysia. I was underage. I was not allowed to work, but I had no choice because I had to afford my meals . . . so I did construction work. It was very hard work and it was very risky as well. I saw many young boys lose their lives when they were working. I was a stateless person so I had no legal documents. They didn't pay me as much as they should.

I really didn't want to work, I really wanted to study. I cried every morning when I saw the kids going to school . . . I really wanted to be one of them. There are many heartbreaking stories in those workplaces in Malaysia. Really. There are many people there from Bangladesh, from Myanmar, from the Philippines and many of them had no documents. I saw with my eyes the places in which young people are trafficked, woman are raped, and so many other things that I cannot describe.

I wasn't there for long, just five months. I decided to leave Malaysia and I wanted to come to Australia because I heard about Australia—that it was a country in which I would receive my fundamental human rights.

Everywhere I looked was pitch dark

In 2012 I wanted to come to Australia. [*Long pause.*] For ten days I was in a home that was provided by the smuggler and then we got arrested by the Indonesian police. They put me inside a detention centre for seventeen months. It was complete prison. We were locked up.

The camp was very small and it was totally crammed with people. There were families, adults and underage people, and there were prisoners as well, most of them were from the Philippines. We didn't have space to move around. There was no playground, nothing. We were interviewed by UNHCR.* They came every five months to interview some of us. They stayed for four or five days and they went back. During the whole process we were not able to go outside of the compound.

I received my refugee status after fifteen months and my life became much easier. I was released and I was accommodated by the United Nations. I was a refugee and I was free in Indonesia. But I'm a human being. I wanted to study and I couldn't study. I was given one hundred and twenty dollars a month. I wanted to work, because it wasn't enough to survive. But I was not allowed to do anything. I was thinking, *How can I pass my days?*

---

* United Nations High Commissioner for Refugees is the agency responsible for leading and coordinating international action to protect refugees. Its primary purpose is 'to safeguard the rights and wellbeing of refugees' and it also has a mandate to help stateless people. In the absence of protection claim assessment systems in many countries in Asia, for example, UNHCR is responsible for determining asylum claims.

The United Nations visited our accommodation once a month. They never let us know they were coming. When we saw them we asked, 'Can we make an appointment to talk to you guys? To explain our situation?'

'We don't have time,' they said.

'When will we be processed? How long are we going to stay here?'

'We don't know,' they said.

So all these obstacles made me leave Indonesia. Somehow we managed to get a boat to Australia. We were on the ocean for four days. The journey was . . . so, so terrifying . . . Because the boat was so small, so small, compared to the amount of people that were on it. [*Disbelieving laugh.*] There were 295 people . . . the boat was small. And we didn't have food, we didn't have water. After two days, something broke and during the day, we emptied the water from our boat. During the night we couldn't do anything because it was too dark and there were so many waves. I was very, very frightened because everywhere I looked was pitch dark. And, you know, there were many people around me, they were peeing and vomiting. The children were crying. The person who was driving the boat kept trying to escape. Believe me, I thought . . . This is my last time.

We were rescued at six o'clock in the afternoon. If they didn't rescue us . . . we would all have died. That's for sure. It was a miracle.

I had good control over my mind

I arrived on Manus Island on 29 October 2013. It was a horrible experience. They put me in Delta compound, so it was a very small room—there was no space, there was no privacy, so I couldn't study, I couldn't do anything in my room.

I didn't have any book, or any pen, or . . . any materials to keep myself occupied. However, I made up my mind that I need to get something out of this place which will help me in the future. So I started thinking, *How can I improve my knowledge?*

Yep. There were many people in my compound, it was really crowded, people were very depressed and they didn't know what they were doing or what they were saying, but I didn't lose my mind. I was suffering from many things, but I had good control over my mind.

So every morning I woke up at four o'clock, because it was quiet, everyone was sleeping. I used to sit in front of my room and I started teaching myself English. I had no dictionary, no nothing. So, I just got some English papers and I taught myself. What does that mean? When I couldn't figure it out, I went to a teacher and I started talking to them. My English was very poor, but I didn't give up.

After two weeks, I went to a class, there was a teacher, her name was Judith. I was sitting at the back. At the end, she sat with me and asked me about my life. And she said to me, 'How do you have hope, in this environment?' I just told her, 'I don't know. There is nothing.'

She told me to write, 'If you write something every day it will help you. It will improve your English and also it will help you to cope in this environment, because you are not keeping your anger in your heart, you are letting it out.'

The first piece I wrote . . . ah . . . I wrote about my mother. And I wrote about my girlfriend. I did not know I was writing my story and it could be a book one day. I had no notebooks and I grabbed a request form from the guardhouse. I wrote eight lines on the back of this form. There were 24 mistakes.

I didn't suffer from anything

I started writing, but I had no idea what to write. What should I write? I was very unfamiliar with these things. So I started writing about my family. I mostly wrote about what I learned from my parents and how life is back home for a Rohingyan family. It wasn't very clear, in that time.

There were no novels that I could read to help myself. I just did it by myself and I was very proactive. I didn't waste my time, I didn't chat with my friends. I didn't suffer from anything, because I woke up every morning thinking, *What can I write today?*

I used to write fourteen hours a day. It's crazy, really—fourteen hours a day. I didn't have any space, I didn't have any privacy, you know? When I was in Delta there was a table in front of my room, so I was writing on one side and there were other people who were playing cards at the same time. Whenever they needed me they started talking to me. They always interrupted my writing or reading. But you know what? The noise was really annoying, however it helped me to write more, because I was getting angry, then I was putting all my anger on the paper.

They were my friends so I couldn't tell them to go away. They could see I was writing and reading. They are human beings and they have their own brain. You can't make people learn. People need to learn by themselves. They didn't give me my space, but I didn't tell them anything. I was busy with myself.

I have written a lot of things, I have written 23 chapters. It's a complete book. This place is so strange. You can explain things about this place for years and years and it will never end.

THEY CANNOT TAKE THE SKY

I know how to count my blessings

I spent this afternoon studying English grammar and then I prayed. After that I went to gym. I've just come back to my room, after having a shower. Now, I'm ready to speak to you. The other day you asked me, 'Do I fear death or not?' I don't fear death because I have experienced death many times in my young life. I have been tortured and I have been loved. [*Sighs.*] By experiencing both things I have learned something else: I know how to count my blessings.

I experienced death when I was on the ocean. I've experienced death on the land as well. That's why I left my country. And in 2014 when I was in Mike compound during the riot, I was about to die. I was beaten and I was unconscious for 24 hours. I'm a religious person and . . . I know that according to my religion, if we do good things while we are alive we will go to paradise when we die. If we do bad things we will go to hell. However, I don't want to die. I want to do something with my life. When I was back home, I didn't know what I was capable of doing in my life. But now I know—I know that I'm gifted with many abilities and I know that I can do something to help other human beings. And that's my goal, my ambition. [*Sighs.*] I hope it will come true one day.

Since I left my country I have met many people . . . I call some of them my angels, and Rebecca was one of my angels. She was my caseworker for a long time. The first time I met her, she came to Delta compound in the afternoon with an interpreter to talk to me . . . I was very shy, because in our culture we are not familiar with communicating with women. Because we don't see them outside their houses. They are always inside.

I don't know why, but I felt very comfortable whenever I talked to Rebecca. She started helping me. Every single morning at ten o'clock she came to my compound and sat with me, helped me with my writing, speaking and reading. I used to write down the words that I could not understand so that I could discuss these strange words with her in the morning.

She was not allowed to give me anything. However, she got me blank paper every day, and gave me pens and pencils. One day she gave me a dictionary. Oh, it was so amazing [*laughing*]! I felt like I had been given the whole world, because I needed a dictionary so much. I cried for a dictionary.

Whenever Rebecca came to visit me in Delta compound, she sat with me on the floor because there were no tables, no chairs. In my country, and the countries I've been to, the officers treated me like an animal. She treated me like I was a member of her family. I'd never experienced that. I was learning a lot of things. There were many times when I was so scared. I was depressed, stressed and frightened . . . However, I had someone who . . . who helped me during those terrible times. She held my hands and told me that everything will be okay. She is not working here anymore, she left almost one year ago, but she still helps me with my English, with my writing. This is a place that was set up intentionally to torture vulnerable people, but I was blessed with . . . an angel.

I remember one thing that my mother told me when I left my country. 'Son, you will be looked after in your life wherever you go.' And . . . [*crying*] her words were so true. I have struggled a thousand times since I left my country. But I was given help, I was protected, and I'm still being loved. I think that's why I've been keeping myself so strong.

Speaking of my mother's words, I want to say something about Sandra Fulham. She lives in Mount Isa, in Queensland. She has never been to Manus Island. She managed to get my information somehow and contacted me. She is my mother angel. Everything about us is different: language, culture, place, religion—everything. However, she calls me son and I call her mother. In the old days I struggled with lots of things: I didn't have shoes for months, I didn't have T-shirts, shorts. I cried many times, many times. Sandra has been sending me parcels. Every morning when I wake up, I get a text from her. Every night, I fill her in about my day. She has been loving me unconditionally. It is the kind of love that only a mother can provide. There are no words to express it. It can only be felt.

I have been tortured so much by Australia, but I don't prioritise the hardship I have endured. I focus on the love that I receive from these amazing people. And I would like to say thank you to all of them.

I speak to my mother in Myanmar every fortnight. It's difficult to get through to her but I manage to talk to her somehow. I share all these things with my mother just to make her feel relieved. Now she knows that I have been looked after, that I am well, I am healthy.

All we can do is talk to each other

Our situation is getting worse. They are separating the guys who have a negative refugee assessment from the guys who have positive assessment. I don't know why they are doing it, because the gates are open and we can move between compounds. It doesn't make sense at all. I have no idea. All I can say is they are trying to make our lives even more miserable, that's all.

I have got some friends who have received a negative. They are so depressed so I am spending some time with them and trying to give them hope. Sometimes we are really concerned about them because we think they will do self-harm. We don't leave them alone, we stick with them and talk to them and if they need any help writing a request or a complaint or something, then we help them in these ways. We can't do much to change our situation—all we can do is talk to each other. Those who are strong, they need to help the ones who are not strong. I am privileged and feel honoured to be able to help them in some way. I've tried my best. I've done what I could. We are very vulnerable and we get scared about little things in this environment, however, when we stick together and look after each other it helps us to survive.

Our refugee case doesn't mean anything, because we don't have the power. They have the power. When I say 'they', I mean the Australian government because everything we have is provided by the Australian government. They are the ones who are controlling our lives.

We are allowed to take three packets of cigarettes

There are thousands of things I can tell you to explain how we have been treated like animals. We have been imprisoned for the last three years—for what?

Let me give you an example. One day they say you can have an apple. The next day you can have two apples. The third day they say you can have three apples. Then on the fourth day, they say you can't have an apple. You can't have an apple. And they stop giving us apples for a week. After a week, they start giving apples again. And everyone goes crazy about it. It's nothing—but, you know, it's the system that makes people crazy.

They bring one hundred packets of biscuits for three hundred people. So we start buying biscuits from the canteen. There are two hundred people who can't buy a packet of biscuits from the canteen. Then they become depressed because they can see that their friends are eating biscuits, but they can't eat biscuits.

THEY CANNOT TAKE THE SKY

Before I move on to another question, I just want to tell you something more about how we have been treated. We have been traumatised for the last three years, we have forgotten so many things, we don't know how to live normally. Then suddenly, the camp was open and we were able to go into town. So many things have changed over the last few months.*

We were not allowed to have a phone for two and a half years. Millions of dollars have been spent in this environment in our name, however we were not given phones. We have to trade cigarettes in the market and we have to manage to buy a phone by ourselves. Nowadays we are allowed phones but we don't have credit. I spoke to Immigration and told them that we don't want to trade cigarettes. We asked them to give us money, not cigarettes. But they have never listened to us. They want to show the world that we are bad people. [*Sighs.*] When we go into town, we are allowed to take three packets of cigarettes with us. But we cannot take more than two bottles of water.

They change the rules without informing us. Before, everyone from the prison camp was allowed to stay at the transit centre in town. Then they changed the rule and they said we can't stay at the transit centre. After one week they changed it—they said those who have a positive assessment can stay and those who have a negative assessment can't. It lasted for one week. Then they changed it again. They said, 'Okay, no one can stay at the transit centre anymore.'

One night I stayed at the transit centre, then I went to the market in the morning. And when I came back they did not let

---

* On 26 April 2016, the Supreme Court of Papua New Guinea ruled that the immigration detention centre on Manus Island was illegal. The court found that detention breached the right to personal liberty in the constitution. In the following weeks, some rules were changed. The men were allowed to travel by bus into the town of Lorengau, about 40 minutes from the detention centre. They were also allowed mobile phones, and restrictions on movement between compounds were relaxed.

me in. My bag was there. One day they didn't even let me use the toilets . . . This is so ridiculous. Now we can go into town but we have to come back to our prison camp. If we miss the six o'clock bus, we don't have any place to stay.

I talk to myself all the time

I want to live my life. It's really important for a human being to live their life. But what does it mean, life? I always ask this question to myself. I don't talk to other people very much—I talk to myself all the time. And I question myself, *What do I want from my life? What is this?*

I left my country, I've been to many countries, I've been to many detention centres. Now I am here. I'm still not satisfied with my life. Why? Why not? I have clothes, I have shoes, I have food. I have everything that I need to survive, so that's enough . . . No, it's not enough. I should be respected, I should be honoured, and I should have my fundamental rights.

The worst moment of my life was fleeing from my country in the middle of the night, not being able to hug my mother, father, brother and sisters. Not being able to say goodbye for the last time broke my heart into a thousand pieces. If I knew I would never see them again I would never—I would have chosen to die in my mother's lap, rather than die slowly in this strange and lonely place.

If anyone asks me, 'What do you want from your life?' I will tell them I need to feel safe. If someone tells me, 'Oh, this is safe place'—no it's not. Because I'm not feeling safe in my heart.

I sit on the ground so that I can feel the earth

My world was small when I was back home, because I was isolated; now my world is quite big. It is still small, but it is bigger than when I was back home. My father had a dream for me to become a doctor. Now I can see my future, and I believe I can be whatever I want to be. I just need to have the opportunities. I do not know if I will be able to become a doctor or not, but it's my ambition.

When I was back home I had a girlfriend, but I didn't know it was love. Because I was very young, I was sixteen and she was only thirteen. My girlfriend's house was next to my house and she used to come over with her mother, because her mother and my mother were friends. It was like . . . family. We were young and nobody cared because we were young. So . . . I spent a lot of time with her, but we didn't know we loved each other. Because we were too young, we were just friends. As soon as I left my country I realised: Oh . . . It is love. Because I was missing her all the time. She was my first love.

Since I left my country I talked to her a couple of times, and we knew that we loved each other. The last time I spoke to her I was in Christmas Island. I didn't talk to her after I came to the Manus prison, because it was becoming harder and harder for her, and for me too. In our culture, women can't wait for a man for long, so I didn't want to ruin her life. I loved her—love means let someone live their life, not keep them for yourself.

So, I told her: 'Forgive me and just live your life, because my life is stuck in a political limbo and I don't know what will happen in the future. And I'm a person who is stateless and I can't go back to our country, so you'll never see me again. There is no point waiting for me.'

I forced myself to lose her. But she will live in my heart forever, because it was my first love. We are not together physically, but we are together emotionally and it will live forever. I always think about her and I always think about our time we spent together. I am not trying to forget it because, you know, love is something that keeps us alive, so these memories help me to be strong. I can make myself happy just by remembering.

I don't talk to her on the phone because I don't want to ruin her life, but I can talk to myself. And people ask me, 'Hey, are you crazy? Why are you laughing by yourself?'

'I'm not crazy. I'm talking to myself, and I have someone in front of me who you can't see, because she is not here.'

I try to find a peaceful place where I can be myself. I sit on the ground so that I can feel the earth. I place my hands on my chest and bend my legs and keep them close to my chest. I look up at the sky and then recall the memories. I always tell her, *Being in love doesn't mean we have to be together physically. I love you and my love is unconditional for you. All I want for you is a happy life. Always remember that you were the one who taught me how to love. You will live forever in my heart.*

She always tells me, *Imran, although we are apart I can feel you in the earth and see you around me, because you were the one for whom my heart beat for the first time. My love for you will be alive forever. All I want to do is eradicate the suffering from your life.*

We are all convicted to live on this planet

Amir

Amir Taghinia lives in Oscar compound. He has been in Immigration detention since August 2013. He left Iran as a teenager and spent five years in Malaysia, where he once acted as Elvis in a TV commercial. With no visa to stay there, and unable to return home, he fled to Australia.

There might not be a reset button

Okay, yeah, the story of being a scared person. A coward. When I was a very little child, I used to be scared of darkness, and whenever I wanted to go to the upper levels of our house, I used to turn on all the lights until I reached up there. And my father used to tell me, 'You're wasting so much electricity. What are you scared of? Why do you turn on all the lights?' And I used to tell him, 'Oh, I'm very scared of darkness.' And he told me, 'What is the worst thing that can ever happen to you? It is death, and there is nothing to be worried about death. We all have to die one day.' So that was the time I learned not to be scared anymore.

Ah, I wish I had died on the ocean rather than being in here. When I was coming to Christmas Island, we were on a boat for three days. The last day we were out of fuel, we had no navigation, no radio, nothing. So, we thought, *Yeah, that's end of it, we are lost.* The only thing that I could think of was my family. I wasn't scared of dying. I wasn't scared of being drowned. I was scared of when my family would hear that their son had drowned. What were they going to feel? How were they going to survive? Like, what is going to happen to them? But now I am so tired of this life. I have gone through lots of horrible times during this three years, so that thousands of times, or maybe millions of times, I have wished that I had drowned on the sea rather than being in this life.

I haven't told my family that, of course not. [*Laughs bitterly.*] I have not really shared anything from this life with them, because I just feel it wouldn't help, it would make it even worse for them. They already have their own hardships. It's almost nine years since they have seen their son. And now he's in a situation, at least 6000 to 7000 kilometres far from them. They cannot reach their son, they cannot help. So telling these stories: it wouldn't help me, it wouldn't help them, it would just make the situation worse.

They have access to the internet and . . . well, I have told them I am on Manus, and they know what's going on on Manus. But I still have to sometimes lie to them, and say, 'Well, I'm good,' you know? 'There is food, I'm eating,' you know? 'There is a place where I sleep, there is shelter.' But I cannot tell them about the rest of the things. About the filthiness, about the disease, about the mental illness, about the people who are trying to hang themselves, about myself who wished and *prayed* for my own death. For more than six months I used to pray for my own death every night when I went to bed.

Well . . . Many people would ask, 'Why don't you finish it up? Why don't you kill yourself if you really want to die?' I have this feeling that we are all convicted to live on this planet. Some people live a good life, some people live a medium life, some people live a desperate life. If we finish it—if we kill ourselves—we might go to a place that is not a good place. And there might not be a reset button. So, we have to finish this journey, we have to continue. It doesn't matter how hard it is, regardless of whatever we are going through . . . I just wanted it to happen naturally. And so I was praying for it. And I have heard from my other friends that if you truly pray, from the bottom of your heart, for your own death, God may help you and end the miserable life that you are going through.

Before this, I had never wished for my death, even though I was a refugee and I had gone through lots of hard times since I had had to seek asylum. So imagine what I have gone through here, that I now pray for my own death.

In the morning when I wake up, I think, *Ah, oh shit, another day.*

For six months I felt that way, yes, maybe more. Every day, when people asked me, 'How are you?' I used to tell them, 'Desperately tired of life.' That was the only answer I could give them.

It didn't feel good. It's . . . You do not wish to do anything. You do not feel good about anything. Everything is hateful for you, even yourself. I used to hate looking at myself. I used to hate being myself. When I went to bed I would just say, 'Please, I beg you, God—or whoever is out there, I don't know whatever is out there—I'm just asking you to finish it. I'm just tired of it. I can't continue anymore. I am tired of humiliation, I'm tired of everything.'

That was a few months ago. Yeah, it was very recently.

It's . . . It's not better right now, but I have given up on asking for death, you know? Because nothing is happening.

You have to run for your life

I am 23. I was almost fifteen years old when I left my country and flew to Malaysia. I was living in Malaysia for five years on my own, and then I left Malaysia and I sought asylum in Australia.

Malaysia is not a signatory to the United Nations refugee convention, so you can't really stay there. I was a student there. I was not planning to go to Australia. I had to go back to my country if I wanted to apply for another visa, which I couldn't. So I registered with United Nations to apply for asylum, for refugee status. It was the beginning of the war in Syria; there were many people when I went to the United Nations office. They literally told me, 'It's gonna take a long time.' I would have to wait almost three years just to be registered and then your interview would be, like, six months later.

In Malaysia, if you get arrested by the police, and you are stateless, they are going to put you in prison. You do not really want to end up in those prisons. I had to ask friends and within a night or two I decided, *Okay, I will go to Indonesia, get on a boat, and go to Australia.* That is the nearest and safest place.

I couldn't live in that country anymore. Yes, I'm not scared of death, but I'm not gonna stand and be killed. If I can run for my life I will do it. When I was a little child I asked my mum, 'If there is a god, why don't we just pray and things happen?' My mother said, 'It cannot be like that. It's not like you hold a lighted candle in your hand, and go in the middle of the street on a very windy day and you say, "I pray this candle stays lit."' Nah, it's not like that. You will drown if you drown yourself, you will die if you hang yourself, you will die if you jump in the middle of the highway. The cars will just hit you. You have to run for your life. It doesn't matter if you are in the most peaceful place on earth or if you are in a war zone. Yes, you may not be scared of death, but still you run for your life. As I said, that's what I believe—we are convicted to live on this planet. We read this story of Adam and Eve. They did something and so we are here—we are convicted to live on this planet. So we have to go until the end of our conviction and see what will happen.

For eight points you get a packet of cigarettes

It's very hard to explain, but imagine 24/7 someone is around you telling you what to do and what not to do, where to go, where not to go. I learnt these words, *Groundhog Day*, from a guard. And I can never forget this. I haven't watched this movie, but it's just repeating days. And the other saying, 'Same shit, different day, mate.' So, they know very well how to describe this situation.

I used to live in Foxtrot compound. I was taken to the prison during the hunger strike and after that I was forcibly brought to Oscar compound. When I was taken to Oscar compound I saw people are covering their beds with bed sheets and blankets to make a little space for themselves. At first I thought it's just to make privacy, but later on I realised it's because they want to keep themselves isolated. They are not in the mood to talk to anyone anymore. They are not in the mood for listening, speaking or playing—they just want to stay in that little removed place in their bunk.

I have made the same thing. I have covered my bed with blankets and bed sheets. It's just a very small space. I might lie down the whole day looking at the roof of my bed, just listening to music . . . That's all that's happening.

You wake up in the morning in that small space. You come out of the dorm. You go outside . . . It's extremely hot and humid. The ground is so bright because they have poured this white sand from the beach and covered the ground. It's so bright and white that even though you put sunglasses on you have to squint your eyes. And the heat is just slamming into your face. You go have your breakfast. You can feel depression everywhere. People try to find the corner side of the mess, a table where there is nobody sitting. They just want to be alone. They just don't wanna talk to people.

People try to sleep after breakfast. They sleep until lunch; they wake up hot again. You go for your lunch. The sun is so hot, the ground is so white. Then you go to the mess. The food is boring, every day the same thing. Nowadays we have something we call zebra chicken. This zebra chicken is making everyone crazy. It's just chicken with black lines on it, barbecue style. For more than four months—breakfast, lunch and dinner—it's been the same thing.

What can I do to get my mind out of this place? So some people, they say, 'Okay, I'll start doing gym,' or, 'I start going to the classes.' These are the activities put in place by the system: English classes, music classes. For these classes you receive points. People who smoke really need these points, okay? For eight points you get a packet of cigarettes.

The thing is, these activities are systematically planned in a way that will disturb your mind. It is planned in a psychological way that you will feel like you are in prison. You go to the gym—imagine a small, maybe ten-metre wide gym for 500 people. There are twenty people that want to do bench-press and then most of the stuff in there is broken. The gym is not always open; the session happens in the morning and the afternoon. You have to be there the whole session, 45 minutes at least, to get points. So you see, it makes it more crowded. If you're playing basketball outside of the gym you're not gonna get points. You have to be inside that ten-metre area, and you have to be sweaty. Then he will give you one point.

When you go to a classroom, you always have this feeling of being in prison. There is a guard sitting at the back, watching you; his radio is disturbing you. You don't really have that 'escape' feeling in any of these activities. Like, myself, I have decided not to get involved in any of these activities, because it's making me insane.

Sleeping. Sleeping is the best thing. I don't really sleep much. You're not able to sleep much. But I have seen people sleep fifteen hours. And you're telling them, 'Come on, man. You've lost weight. You look very terrible.' But they say, 'We don't care. This is the only way we can kill time.'

I have started to do gym recently. But if I really want to find something that can help me escape from this place, I'll say it's writing. I've written a book, and it needs to be completed. But recently, even though I want to write something, the feeling is so bad I do not have the mood to do anything. So I just prefer to lie on my bed and think of the misery that I am going through. That is the best thing that I can think of, to pass time.

I had my hands beside me

I was going to the internet room to help out one of my friends. It was in June 2016. I was approached by a guard who wasn't letting me into the internet room. When I asked him the reason, without checking the list, he said, 'Because your name is not on the list.' So, what I said is, 'I'm not going to use the internet, I'm just going to help my friend. I don't see any reason for you to stop me.' And then he just let me go in. So when I went in, there was another Australian guard.

He stopped me, came in front of me, and when I asked him why he was blocking me, he said, 'Because you are coming in my way.' And when I wanted to change in the other direction he just pushed me in my chest, and I told him he was not supposed to do this.

So I had my hands beside me, with my palms open. I went the other way. I sat on a chair, helping my friend to use the computer. And then the guard just followed me and started harassing me, started bullying me, telling me that he's gonna cause me trouble and all these things. I couldn't tolerate it anymore so I said, 'The police has to come in here.' A few minutes later the police came and they asked me to follow them. I thought we were going there to write a statement or something. They took me to their solitary confinement and they said that whatever I say or whatever I do is going to be used against me in the court. They threw me in solitary confinement, without any food, for almost 24 hours. The next day, they took me to their own lock-up without water and without any food for another 24 hours. And then, the day after that, they took me to the court, and in the court I was told I had assaulted this guy, this Australian guard, by pushing his chest, by hitting him. And I was very surprised when I heard the magistrate. I pleaded not guilty. So they adjourned my case to another date which was in around one or two weeks.

In those two weeks I was very depressed, and had nobody in there, no legal support. Oh, it was terrible, you know? I'd not been to any court before, I'd not gone to any police station. I asked for protection from these people. I lost almost 6 kilograms within two weeks.

When I appeared in court again, the guard did not come so the judge just dismissed the case. Maybe they did not have witnesses. Maybe they were scared that we had witnesses, or a video recording, or a legal representative, I don't know.

But all I know is they were lying, they were trying to get me into trouble.

The magistrate, he was like, 'If we find out you're guilty, we're going to deport you to your country.' But you know, when I was telling him, 'Look, they have set us up. They try to put us in trouble when they beat us up. Why are these things happening?' The magistrate, he was just like, 'Okay, I do not want to see you in here anymore. Just go and do not be a big-head anymore.' So that's what he was saying. It was very, very weird. Very distressing, you know?

That guard, ah yes, he is still in here. Yeah, he has provoked another detainee to fight. It's very obvious. Like, everyone is telling me the same story. He's not the only one. They plan to get people charged, to get a criminal record for us so we cannot go anywhere, so we are stuck in here.

It's harder but I feel happier

Persian is my mother tongue. Then the second language I learned was English. Then, because I was living in Malaysia, I learned their language, Malay. And I studied a little bit of Chinese, just introducing myself, not very much. And then when I came here I learned Pidgin as well, so I speak these four languages.

I was always interested in studying law. But what I am planning now is, yes, I will study law, but I will get more involved into humanitarian stuff. It is easy to find a very good job, get good pay, go on holidays. But there are people that I can help. It's harder, but I would feel much happier.

Well, I am not sure how to explain this, but I can tell you that I am a very different person than three years ago. I might have been a person who didn't care about others, who just didn't look around. I just cared about my own life.

Yeah. I just wanted to go to school, go to university maybe, study something, find a job. Now I have learned this in here: that I can help others. I might not have money, but I have myself. I can offer help.

You asked me, 'Why do you care now? Why do you want to do these things?' I say because of circumstances. Now that I am in these circumstances. The circumstances in here have made me think of these things deeply.

What I have learned in these three years in here I would never have learned in a thousand years of living in Iran. I have seen people—Rohingyas, Myanmarese, Afghanis, Pakistanis, Sudanese, Sri Lankans and many others—they have lived in harsher circumstances than me. They may not have had food for weeks and months. By coming into this place, I heard from them. I learned these things.

I see these dreams

In these three years on Manus, I have been through times that I had never had in my life. I had never been in prison in my life, but for nothing I have been detained for three years. For nothing I have been humiliated for three years.

When we arrived here, we were 40 people on a plane, and from the airport we were taken to the detention centre on two or three different buses. We were escorted by Papua New Guinean police and military and guards, with these Toyotas at the back and the front. We saw the local people with red teeth, and we were like, 'Why are their mouths bleeding?' We didn't know what it was. They were chewing betel nut. 'Why they are not wearing clothes? Why they are not wearing shoes? Where is this place they are taking us?'

The people were waving to us. But it was scary. Like, there were rumours they were cannibals. The guards were telling us—when we were in Christmas Island, even when we came here—that these people were cannibals. Why? To tell us this place is not good, so we go back home. They used to tell us, 'They will kidnap you. They will rape you. They will cut you into pieces, and they will cook you and they will eat you.' And then we saw these red-mouthed people and we thought they were actually eating humans.

I still remember the first things that we were handed were phone cards and internet cards. Of course, they did not care about us talking to our family or getting in touch with our friends. They cared about the news that we were gonna tell our family and friends about the place that we were in. 'Don't come. This is what is gonna happen to you. Yes, people are cannibals. Yes, they do not have houses, they do not have clothing, they have nothing.' There was a hospital in the town, but they did not tell us that. The guards would just brainwash us, saying propaganda like, 'There is no hospital here. If you get sick you will die,' so that people would get worried and they go back home.

But they never thought about those who *cannot* go back home. There are people who are stateless. There are people that they will get killed if they go back home. They are going to go to prison, they are going to be hanged. But the guards didn't care, they just wanted us to go back. But I believe, on the other hand, they wanted some of us to stay so that they can continue this game. They made lots of bad publicity about refugees. They made lots of bad publicity about seeking asylum.

And for three years, this is what we have tried to live with; a long nightmare that is not ending. Sometimes you feel you are sleeping, you are dreaming; it's a sick nightmare, but you cannot wake up. When I was in Malaysia I had crazy nightmares about home. About being persecuted, being hanged, being beaten by the police and the government. But for three years I have been having nightmares about this place, about Australians. I see Wilson guards beating me up, I see the ERT* guards dragging me on the ground, I see ERT guards turning the rope around my neck and wanting to hang me.

Yes, when I sleep I see these dreams. And I see Australian politicians persecuting us, hanging us, ordering our death, throwing us in the ocean, putting us in gas chambers, burning us with petrol. These are the nightmares, yes, being resettled in Papua New Guinea, being killed by locals.

I'm alright. I'm fine, we can continue.

As I was telling you earlier, we were told the locals were cannibals, that they were wild people. This was propaganda from the system. When I actually met these people outside it was totally different . . . Yes, this is not a place where we are supposed to be living, but it's not a place that the system should ruin in its favour.

Yes, you see I always asked local guards, local people, a very hard question: 'If we are bad people, why are we sent to this country? What does it mean? Does it mean you deserve bad people? You deserve the rubbish? If we are good people, why aren't we taken to Australia?' We have had these discussions many times.

Ah, my local friends sometimes they are saying: 'Look, as much as you scared of Papua New Guineans, a hundred times more they are scared of you. Because they believe you are the one that brings disease here.'

So, if you want to deter people from coming to Australia, are you aware that you are ruining a country? If you deeply think about the plan, you will eventually find out that the

---

* The Emergency Response Team is a group of Wilson Security guards who are called in to handle difficult situations, such as suicide attempts, self-harm, searches, allegations of violence between detainees or forcibly moving detainees between compounds.

government, the system, they are sacrificing Papua New Guinea to save Australia.

I think I have told you enough about things going on in here. And I hope there is someone who hears these things, you know?

EPILOGUE

I can also tell a story

Peter

Peter was granted refugee status soon after he arrived on Christmas Island by boat. Later, he found out that the Australian Security Intelligence Organisation (ASIO) had prevented his release. He is one of over fifty refugees rejected by ASIO between 2010 and 2011, most of whom were Tamils from Sri Lanka. Peter is living in Melbourne, on a bridging visa.

My body had consciousness

When I was released into the community I felt there was a huge change in my body. All that time I had been unable to do anything and all of a sudden I had so much freedom. I was able to feel that my body had consciousness. For six years I had been kept in this cage, where, for the rest of the world, we were non-existent. In that six years we were mentally tortured. I will be able to tell you more about it later.

When I got released into the community, the first question was about my future. *What sort of future am I going to have?*

When I first got onto a train, I felt like I wanted to wear

a seat belt. I have prior knowledge of trains, I have travelled in Malaysia and in Sri Lanka on trains. Why did I have that feeling? Even though I knew it was for my own safety, the way the guards asked me to wear seat belts, the way I was treated when I got onto vans, it left a scar in my mind. All the small experiences in the detention centre remain with us, even in our everyday life once we have been freed.

I am a relatively young man. I was first detained at the age of 34. As far as I'm concerned, I'm a slave—I'm a slave to this world. How do I seek justice for what I have gone through? I am very enthusiastic about writing; I can express my feelings through writing and through that I'm able to overcome the sorrow. Whenever I was hopeful of getting justice, I have been let down. How do I express those feelings? What I see, how do I express it?

I wrote a story about an old lady's eagerness. I tried to write this story as if a mockingbird is telling the story, because a mockingbird makes a great effort to make its nest. The old lady's partner was a busker, but he couldn't make a proper living. He couldn't provide happiness for this woman. They both faced a lot of problems because of that. That was when she was young. He died and when she became old, she needed his love. The only thing with her was the violin he had left behind, so she started playing that violin. By playing that violin she received the love that she would have had if her husband had still been alive. Only when you lose something, and you look for it, do you miss it. Only when I lost my freedom did I see the value of it.

Whatever I see through the camera

I was born in Jaffna in 1974. From the day I was born I saw the Sri Lankan government's injustice towards the Tamils. The first massacre that I witnessed was the *Kumudini* massacre. A three-year-old child was stabbed in three different places by Sri Lankan army men and I saw the photo of it. More than 23 people were killed. It was in the mid-eighties. *Kumudini* was the name of the ship and people who were travelling on that ship were murdered by the Sri Lankan army. I witnessed similar incidents throughout my life.

At the age of thirteen, when the Indian army was present, I had an incident that I can never forget. One day I was reading a notice and the Indian army people asked me who had put that notice on the wall. I didn't know who had stuck it on, but IPK—the Indian Peace Keeping Force—suspected I was the one who did it. When they arrested me and beat me, I fainted. On that day, they burnt the rubber in the tongue of some shoes, and then put them on my feet. I still have the marks on my toenails. The camp where I was being kept was a torture camp where they brought many people to get information out of them. This had a lasting impact on my mind. Even today I'm suffering because of what they did then. I have a lot of stories to share about Sri Lanka, but I don't want to share too much because not a lot is going to happen by sharing.

I worked as a journalist. My job was to take photographs and videos in Jaffna and give them to whoever was interested, to Tamil media organisations. My principle is that whatever I see through the camera should be spread around the world. During that time, the Jaffna university students were quite vocal and started speaking out against the Sri Lankan government. The army felt threatened by the enthusiasm among the university students. They looked for ways to suppress that threat. So what the Sri Lankan military did was, they would arbitrarily arrest and kill certain people and display them on the roads to scare fellow university students.

When we questioned the military about the killings, they would put the blame on certain paramilitary gangs. In a military controlled area like that, for a gang to form, it would be formed only with the support of the Sri Lankan military. When we asked questions, the Sri Lankan military would pass the information to these gangs and then the gangs would threaten us.

The period I'm talking about is 2004. During this time, I also received direct threats from the Sri Lankan intelligence about unnecessarily focusing on some of the issues that were happening in Jaffna. I also had management to answer to; I had a boss, and I couldn't follow what they were asking me to do either. After continuous threats from the Sri Lankan intelligence, I had to flee Sri Lanka and went to Malaysia as a refugee.

The first few weeks were happy times

This was in 2006. I spent three years in Malaysia and Indonesia. I still had that fear; I was living with fear. It's a struggle living in Malaysia: you can't live safely, even if you have a UNHCR card. The police would come and arrest you and then the UNHCR had to come and take us out on bail. I befriended people; I didn't have any relatives or friends with me. We faced a lot of issues, so I looked to try to go to Australia. First I went to Indonesia where I stayed for nine months and then from Indonesia I ended up in Australia as a refugee.

I arrived in Australia on 13 August 2009. I remember that day well. There were 78 people on the boat. It left from Malaysia and came to Indonesia and picked up more refugees. It took 48 days from Malaysia, because the boat broke down on many occasions, but when I got on the boat, we came to Australia within fifteen days. All of the refugees on the boat were Tamils from Sri Lanka. The Australian navy captured us and took us to Christmas Island. Within ten days of being in Christmas Island the interview process happened.

After we arrived in Australia the first few weeks were happy times. We were all full of hope. We never expected that Christmas Island would turn out to be a torture island for us. We felt more secure there. We expected that we would be able to go into the community and live a normal life. We thought that we had found a solution for all of our sufferings. That hope is what made us suffer even more in later days.

When I was in Christmas Island, at end of 2009 or early 2010, the lawyer called me and said I had been given refugee status, so I was very happy. I was quite hopeful that I was going to be released very soon, and I wanted to learn a lot when I came into the community. However, my release was dragged on for so long. First, in Christmas Island. I was there for eighteen months. Then, in a detention centre in Far North Queensland called Scherger. I was there for two and a half years. And then I lived in the Melbourne camp, Broadmeadows, for another two years.

In the early days I used to go to English class. Then I stopped going to anything. When I came to Melbourne, with the help of visitors I started writing stories, and that is how I spent my time.

I wrongly had hope

About early 2010 when I was on Christmas Island, three ASIO officers came and interviewed me.

In 2011, I was told that I had a negative assessment by ASIO and then my detention just continued. There were five people on my boat who were found to be a security threat by ASIO, including me. Talking about ASIO will only make me upset and say unnecessary things and also disturb my mind, so I'd prefer not to talk about it a lot. I have a feeling that by being truthful, I am losing in life. My character, my way of life, is responsible for the losses that I'm facing. I wrongly had hope. Even to this date ASIO and Australian Immigration can't come and tell me I lied, because this is my life and I am telling the truth.

Today I'm asking this question, and it's a really sad question. Why am I living an honest life? Because I was being honest, I was punished for six years. Why did they keep me in the detention centre for this long? What was the reason for them to keep me for six years? Why did they release me after six years? They had no reasons.

Being honest, being truthful, you can't live a normal life in this world. I don't want to go to the other side, because I can't change. Even if I face many more losses, I will continue to be who I am.

A factory to make mental patients

The detention centre life is a tortuous life. Every day they would do a headcount three times: at 5 a.m., at 12.30 p.m. and another time that they don't reveal. It's around midnight, sometimes it's 1 a.m. or 1.30 a.m. This is to disturb people who are sleeping. Even if it's a child, that child's sleep is disturbed.

When you go to the dining area, there are always problems with the food that they provide. For 24 hours a day, you are always under control. In that 24 hours, all those mistakes made by the officers in charge of us, and by the Immigration department, are hurting us. The mistakes made by fellow detainees impact everyone in the detention centre. For example, if someone breaks a TV then it impacts everyone. They punish us collectively. We had to live in fear every single day.

What we faced in the detention centre everyday was structured in a way to make us sick people. During those six years in detention I was one of the few people who did not attempt self-harm or suicide. I tried to be as strong as I could. I guess my experiences as a journalist may have something to do with it—what I saw, my character, and also my will to fight. When I saw certain things, I went in and questioned Immigration rather than keeping it to myself. But every day we relied on anti-depressant tablets. The detention centre is a factory to make mental patients.

Today I have been freed from this factory where sick people are being made. But I haven't been freed from the Immigration department and their laws, and they're chasing me even to this day, while I'm in the community. The name that they have for it is bridging visa. You can search online and see how the bridging visa is affecting refugees' lives.

I'm not trying to talk bad about your government. I'm just telling you all these things because it is my experience. I was treated very badly and then turned into a sick person, and now I have to live as a sick person for the rest of my life. My backbone has been badly hurt. I can't eat properly because all the internal organs have been affected by my experiences. I'm diabetic. I have lost physical strength, I have lost memory power. So there are so many challenges I'm facing to live like a normal person. I feel like I don't have the skills to even work in the community. Very often I'm getting the thought to commit suicide. I'm always thinking about how I'm a loser in life.

They believed in the spirit

During the time I was on Christmas Island there were protests held by Iraqi refugees who sewed their lips. Government representatives came and met with them and gave false promises and after they left nothing really happened. A few months later, they once again decided to protest. Initially, every afternoon they would bang on the gates and shout 'Freedom!

Freedom!' They would just do it every afternoon until about 9 p.m. and they would just go and sleep. But as tensions grew people started breaking things and it became a very violent riot. On the third day, the detention centre came under the control of the police. Police safely got the Serco officers and the Immigration officers out of the camp. There was no food; people were just relying on the noodles and other foods that were in the kitchen.

About the fourth day, I think, the police came and started using tear gas. That's when they started evacuating the Tamils and others who were not involved in the riot. Wherever you queued up decided where you went: some were taken to Darwin, some were taken to Scherger, some were taken to other detention centres. So through that, we were brought to the mainland. The people who were involved in the fight are now Australian citizens, but I'm still waiting for my visa. I'm always hurt when I hear that all the people who caused trouble are living freely but the people who remained silent and non-violent are still suffering. Today, of those who are affected by the ASIO rejection, over 90 per cent are Tamils. They did not get involved in any of the protests. They were begging for help.

We came to Scherger at night-time so we couldn't see anything. They did not tell us anything. It is in an air force base in Weipa in northern Queensland. If you look at most of the refugee camps, detention centres, they are mainly based inside military camps. Refugees who flee their countries are fleeing from militaries, or fleeing at gunpoint, and they face the military here as well.

It's very hard for people to come to Weipa—it's a high security zone. Some of the things that happened in Scherger have not come to light to the outside world. The day we went there, one of the Hazara refugees hanged himself and died in that camp. There were Aboriginal Australians working as guards. They believed in ghosts, the spirit, and they came and tried to clear the spirit in that area, which was similar to what the Tamils do in Sri Lanka.

Scherger is like Sri Lanka, it has the same type of weather and similar types of trees. There were no buildings, they had mainly containers there. Inside the container was a small room and beds where two people could sleep. Other than that there were not many services provided to refugees. It was very hot, with high humidity, and as a result the room was always very hot.

Serco was always blaming the distance from the major city as an excuse to not provide us certain things. Sometimes the food ran out. Whenever we needed things to be replaced, they would just delay it. For example, if the air-conditioner was damaged, it would not get replaced.

There was very limited medical help. I had a bad tooth—it just came randomly but slowly the pain grew and grew. The toothache became really bad and my face became really big but they refused to treat me. It was not removed for more than a year and a half. Imagine how tortuous it was! I couldn't eat, couldn't drink. I'm sure they would have had a dentist outside, but there was no dentist I was able to go and visit in the camp. I was only able to get treatment when I came to Melbourne.

When you blow a balloon, it breaks

There were good counsellors and bad counsellors. There was one, I have forgotten his name. I still remember his face. When you went to see him he would give you a balloon. It's the way he tortured people in those camps. He would make people blow up the balloon to the point where the balloon breaks and he would tell us, 'This is life.' I asked him, 'What do you mean by this?' He would just say, 'This is life,' and then say, 'Sorry, time is up. You have to go.'

There were forms to lodge complaints, but nothing ever happened afterwards. No action was taken. The camps were run through the mindset of people who have business interests. Whatever things we broke when we became frustrated, the management knew how to make more money out of it. The Australian government gained because it was able to portray refugees as very bad people. Refugees are not bad people, but the torture, the mistreatment, is the reason why refugees behave badly in those camps. When you blow a balloon it breaks after a certain point.

In Melbourne you have activities, like watering the garden, but there are no activities in Scherger. I would wake up at 6.30 in the morning. We didn't like to go and get breakfast, but most of the time we would eat lunch, but not always. Then we had dinner. Every day we could use an hour of internet and then I probably go to sleep at about twelve or one o'clock. That's how the day evolved. We stayed, just thinking, and nothing else. We were not dreaming. We just came to the realisation that we had lost our future.

In Christmas Island and Scherger they would call us by our boat ID. It was very bad, I felt that I couldn't use my name. I was a prisoner. They called us that because it was easier for them. Just to make things simple and make it easier for them, they destroyed our lives. I still remember that number.

There were four or five people who worked in the camps who resigned over disagreements about the way Serco treated us, and one of these was Anna. She worked in the kitchen. She actually used to work as kitchen staff for the air force. While I was in the camp I was volunteering to clean the kitchen and through that I met Mother Anna. She would ask me questions about why Serco was treating us like that, and about why we had come to Australia, and through that we developed a relationship. Because they were under the military—she and some of the others—they couldn't speak in support of us too openly. She was in contact with us even after she resigned the job. I still speak to her. When we individually talked to them they cried. They would say sorry to us.

I have a lot of wounds in my legs as a result of the war—whenever I'm in the heat my legs swell. A counsellor sent a letter to the Immigration minister asking him to move me to a colder area and as a result I was brought to Melbourne. For me it was just another move.

Good memories and bad memories

I came to Melbourne detention centre at about 1.30 a.m. I knew some of the refugees in MITA*; they had stayed with me previously in Scherger and some of the other detention centres, so I was looking for them and I went to see them. I saw a child of a Sikh family. This was a new experience. We hadn't seen children in detention centres, but here I was, seeing a child for the first time, after a long time, just right next to me.

Before I was in detention I always saw little children, I was able to mingle with them and talk to them. In those days I didn't understand the value of it. When I saw that baby I felt happy and excited, like there was this feeling I had in my body which had been fulfilled. Only when I was looking at the child, did I come to realise how much I missed seeing children, how important it was.

Then there was another happy observation. The officers in Melbourne were treating me much better than the officers in Scherger. They asked me kindly what my name was and

---

* Melbourne Immigration Transit Accommodation.

where I was from. I first gave them my number, but they told me just forget the number and tell them my name.

Now the MITA camp is like a high security prison, but then the height of the fence was just like a normal house. If we wanted to run away, we could have jumped the fence and run away to the outside world.

I was able to see the Serco guards as part of my family. And then an Immigration officer came and introduced herself. She told me I could call her any time. This Immigration was completely different to the Immigration we were used to. They were more kind. Now it has changed a lot, but I'm talking about how it was. In other camps we never saw the general manager, but in this camp the general manager came to our room! His name was Carlos. We can never forget what he did for us. He would treat us like a brother and ask us whether we had eaten, whether we had slept well. He took good care of us. That's the sort of attitude that changes even bad people into good people. That's the reason why, even to this date, I visit the detention centre. It's a detention centre I can never forget. There are a lot of good memories and bad memories. I go there every Wednesday. I always help as much as I can, but I can't provide them emotional support. I can never give them hope. I know how it hurts when you give them hope.

The first people who came to visit me—Kristalo, Jenell—came as a team to see everyone. That was a new experience. In those days they didn't have a separate visiting area in MITA—visitors came into the area where refugees were staying, the same area where we would hang around. At first it was very difficult for me to communicate with them because of the language barrier. We asked them to come back two weeks later to meet us specifically. Then we had a Tamil interpreter and during that meeting we told them about how we had been detained by ASIO. They were shocked to hear what we had to say. The way we spoke to them, the way we looked after them, they were impressed by it, and they kind of admired us. The government had portrayed us really badly—all the ASIO rejected refugees were seen as terrorists in the community.

A year and a half after being in MITA, an old lady and other people from the church came to visit, with fruit. The first thing the Christian group said is, 'We have heard that there are ASIO rejected people being kept here. Are they bad people? Will they attack us if we come into this area?'

I didn't take it badly when they asked that question. We were all laughing. That's when we said, 'We are the ones.' We told them not to apologise, because it's not their fault they thought of us as bad people. They were in tears. We asked them to drink the tea that we gave. They just kept it on the table, because they were feeling guilty over what they said. Later they came and did prayers for us.

In the early days children were not allowed to be brought to MITA. One of the reasons given to people was that there were high security detainees here and they couldn't let children be alongside them. And the visitors fought against that. They brought their children. They went on hunger strike in support of us. They did a lot for us and they continue to do a lot for us.

We were used for a period by certain people

Every time government policies changed, the way we were treated also changed. For example, under the protection of the guards, we were taken outside, we were taken to temples. Later they would accompany us carrying handcuffs. In 24 hours in MITA, every single minute was influenced by other people's decisions—whether it was the Serco guard or the Immigration department. Sometimes officers would be in a bad mood and they'd show it on us. Sometimes our fellow detainees would attempt suicide and there would be heavy monitoring and a change of rules. They would treat us according to their business needs. Sometimes, when officers wanted to get overtime, the officers themselves would cause problems so they would get the overtime. I have already said that detention centres are factories. They use human lives to make money.

In the previous two detention centres, I was not able to see outsiders. Here, I was able to see the community. I was able to share my views with them and they were able to share their views with us. Only when we were brought to Melbourne did the media come to know about our existence and start reporting the problems we faced. Until then, we were told that our detention was indefinite; that we may even have to stay in the detention centre until we died.

One by one during that time many people attempted suicide. Rather than committing suicide and dying, we decided that collectively we would go on hunger strike and express our feelings to the rest of the world. We were all on the playground area. We wanted to tell the Australian people how we were suffering. So for ten days we were suffering a lot: we did not have food, we did not drink a lot. One person started bleeding when he urinated. One guy fainted. We were facing a dilemma: on one hand we didn't want to commit suicide—that's why we chose the path of going on hunger strike to express our feelings—but even on this path we were getting closer to death. We abandoned the hunger strike.

When we came to MITA, through reading newspapers and talking to other people we realised why we were really being kept in the detention centre. We realised that when that need goes away, we will be released into the community. So there was a bit of hope for the future.

We were used for a period by certain people for political gain. ASIO rejection was used to put pressure on people to not come to Australia. ASIO was only involved in refugee cases from 2009 to 2011. After that ASIO did not give any negative assessments to anyone. The detention policies had changed to offshore, to Nauru and Manus Island. The political need to torture us had ended. The Australian government portrayed us as terrorists and to reverse that image they needed a period. So they were slowly releasing us one by one into the community. Every time one got released I was very happy.

I was working in the kitchen area. I was also acting as a coordinator to distribute all the gifts that were coming for people inside. When we received a gift from outside, I'd identify people who needed it and I would distribute it to them. Through that I made friends with lots of people. We also identified who had birthdays and we would organise birthday celebrations for children in there and family members. The gifts were a variety of various different things—clothes, children's toys, things for newborn babies. Some people would let us know what they needed and we made requests to the visitors. I used to do that with the permission of the Immigration department, but the system has changed now so they can't do that anymore.

I had to come back

When they told me that I was going to be released into the community I was so happy. In the morning, at about nine o'clock, Serco came and asked me to go to property and put all the clothes there. I was going to be released at 4.15 p.m. So I did all the formalities, and went and signed the release documents and I went and loaded my bag onto the van. By this time I was at the second gate—the third gate is the actual exit. While I was at the second gate, someone came and told me, 'Peter, we want to speak to you,' and they told me that

Immigration couldn't give the release order for me to leave and I had to come back.

I couldn't understand what was happening. It was very hard for me to understand because I couldn't really get any answers from the authorities. And then after that I spent four more months in detention. That has contributed to my depression.

On 23 February 2015 I was released into the community with a three-month bridging visa. After three months, for ten days I didn't have a visa. When I went to the Immigration department they took me and kept me in custody for seven hours. When I said I wanted to use the restroom, two officers accompanied me and were waiting outside the toilet. Then, at about 5 p.m. I was released into the community. This is your law. For ten days I was living without a visa. I was the one who reminded them and then I was detained, without breaking any rules or laws. But I was kept there as a criminal and then after seven hours I became an innocent.

No courts have ever punished me for any crimes, but I am being punished by your laws. I have been identified as a slave and I have been punished. For the rest of my life I am being punished by what they did to me.

I can also tell a story

I miss being a journalist. I feel that I have lost some of the skills. I don't think I can be like who I was when I was a journalist back then, but I'm trying. I don't have the mindset to read long articles. I have memory loss when it comes to general knowledge. I'm unable to have debates with people on issues.

A good journalist has to be loyal to the community and be able to tell their stories. The journalist has to argue with and talk to various different groups of people in the community, not just the highly educated ones. Through this, the journalist is able to understand himself and understand the community and let the world know about what's happening. There is no such situation in Sri Lanka at the moment. As an ex-journalist it hurts me that so many experiences of our people are not being told. It hurts me to see the suffering of the people and still not be able to tell their story.

Since I've been in the community, I have a lot of questions from what I've been observing. I am not amazed by big buildings. What I observe are the homeless people who are sleeping under those buildings. Why do those people have to live like that? It is hurting me a lot, that question. Because of my recent experiences, I can understand how much a life is worth.

In the Melbourne CBD, I saw a pregnant woman who was homeless. What is the mother going to tell that child? We should all be hurt by this issue. So every time I go into the city I have adopted this habit of giving homeless people money whenever I see them. I know it is not going to address their problems, however, I want to do something to help their cause. I want to be able to tell their story, and why the community is ignoring such people.

I have come to the realisation that I can also tell a story to people. I continue to search for how to tell it. When I write, while it may be fiction, it tells some real life stories, some of the things that I have experienced. What I observe in this society, in this community. I am writing it and giving it some sort of shape.

Afterword

Each story in *They Cannot Take the Sky* has been carefully recorded over the course of several weeks or months. Our practice is to call and meet with narrators more than once to explain the project and so that they can get to know the person who would interview them. If someone chooses to participate, we meet again—usually several times—to record their story. Most interviews were conducted in English, but some were conducted with interpreters, and some were conducted in different languages and later translated to English.

The narrators are in control of the interview. They can answer or not, as they choose, and they are empowered to direct their testimony however they would like. We type full transcripts from audio recordings, then work with narrators to shape their words into the pieces you see in this book, by selecting the most telling themes and elements, removing repetition and correcting grammar for readability, while maintaining the person's voice. The words are the narrator's words. Some narrators have been keenly involved in editing their transcripts, while others have preferred to leave it to the editors. All have reviewed their stories.

Some narrators have chosen to be anonymous. They are concerned about being identified in the country they had fled, or by Australian Immigration officials, or both. Where necessary, narrators have been referred for legal advice. Some withdrew their consent prior to publication, out of fear of retribution. We hope they will feel safe to tell their stories one day.

Contributors

Some names have been changed

Abdul Aziz Muhamat features in the podcast *The Messenger*. His family still believes he is waiting for a visa on Christmas Island. He continues to tell his story to Michael Green, from detention on Manus Island.

Ali Bakhtiarvandi travels to Melbourne from Ballarat every weekend to take photographs of protests for the *Green Left Weekly*. He told his story to Michael Green.

Ali Haidary lives with his wife and children in Shepparton, Victoria. After arriving on Christmas Island by boat in 2009, he brought his wife and children to Australia. He told his story to Michael Green, with interpreting by Rahila, his eldest daughter.

Ali Reza grew up in Quetta, a Pakistani city on the border of Afghanistan. He boarded a boat in Indonesia bound for Australia as an unaccompanied minor. He was detained on Christmas Island before being transferred to detention centres all over Australia. He is now a permanent resident of Australia. He told his story to Dana Affleck.

Amir Taghinia waits in detention on Manus Island, feeling increasingly depressed. He is trying to study international law online, but the circumstances and facilities make it very difficult. He told his story to Michael Green there in July 2016. At that time, he had been detained for nearly three years.

Aran Mylvaganam is a proud father and, for the time being, a stay-at-home dad. He told his story to Roselina Press and Michael Green.

Ariobarzan has refused to give his refugee claim to the Papua New Guinea Immigration department. He believes that is the only way he can resist his detention on Manus Island. He told his story to Behrouz Boochani in August 2016, when he had been in detention for three years. Translation by Moones Mansoubi. Editing by Michael Green.

Behrouz Boochani is the subject of a campaign by PEN International—an association of writers with members in more than one hundred countries—calling for his release. He helped several men in detention on Manus tell their stories for this project. He told his story to Michael Green. Additional editing by André Dao.

Benjamin is still living in Nauru. He told his story to journalist Karl Mathiesen in December 2014 and Michael Green in October 2016. Mathiesen had travelled to Nauru posing as a snorkelling enthusiast and covertly spoke to refugees who had been released into the community. Additional editing by Angelica Neville and André Dao.

Donna Sherwani has finished her studies and is living in South Korea with her husband. She told her story to Dana Affleck.

Contributors

Hal-Hal arrived in Australia in 2013. She wants you to know that there is so much about her experiences she wasn't able to talk about, because those things are too painful. She believes the whole world should delete the word 'refugee' from their dictionaries and replace it with 'human being' so that all can live equally. She told her story to Dana Affleck.

Hani Abdile is a lover of life. She is one of the convenors of *Writing Through Fences*, a writing group comprised of people who have been incarcerated in Australian immigration detention. She has published a collection of her poems, called *I Will Rise*. She told her story to Angelica Neville.

Imran Mohammad loves cooking food and hosting people, and he attributes both things to watching his mother in Myanmar when he was growing up. He told his story to Michael Green and Behrouz Boochani in September and October 2016. He had been in detention on Manus Island for three years.

Jamila Jafari has begun writing and speaking publicly about her experience as a child in detention, because she thinks people seeking asylum have been politicised and dehumanised in contemporary Australia. She wants to bring back the human element in what it means to be an asylum seeker. She told her story to Zoe Barron. Additional editing by Michael Green.

Jawid arrived by boat at Christmas Island in 2001. He was nineteen years old and had spent the majority of his teens moving from place to place within Afghanistan trying to avoid Taliban violence. Many years after his release, he returned to detention to work as an interpreter and then as a social worker. He even travelled back to Christmas Island. Jawid lives in Melbourne with his wife and daughter. He told his story to Sienna Merope.

THEY CANNOT TAKE THE SKY

John Gulzari fled Afghanistan in 1999. He was detained for three months at Curtin detention centre in Western Australia. John became an Australian citizen in 2007. In 2016 he travelled to Quetta in Pakistan to celebrate his wedding. He lives in the Melbourne suburb of Dandenong, where he has run for local elections three times. He told his story to André Dao.

Lina is now studying and recently got married! She says hope sees the invisible, feels the intangible and achieves the impossible. She told her story to Michael Green. Additional editing by André Dao.

Maya left her country with her mother and siblings. An agent said that he would take them to Australia but left them in Indonesia. She is now living in Melbourne and has begun studying, while still waiting for a decision on her asylum claim. She told her story to Laura Stacey. Additional editing by Michael Green.

Mohsen is a twenty-year-old refugee from Afghanistan. He has graduated high school in Sydney and wants to become a police officer. Mohsen told his story to Leila Stennett. Additional editing by Angelica Neville.

Munjed Al Muderis' book, *Walking Free*, was published in 2014. He told his story to Angelica Neville.

Neda still likes to go bushwalking in the mountains. Every night when she goes to bed she thinks about her younger brother. She told her story to Victoria Grey. Additional editing by Michael Green.

Nima is still living in Nauru, with his partner Ashkan. Recently, he and Ashkan have had trouble getting food, because their assisted shopping visits have ended and they are too scared to go out alone. He told his story to Abdul Karim Hekmat. Translation by Sohaila Angury, Ali Ghasemi and Abdul Karim Hekmat. Editing by André Dao.

Omar Mohammed Jack recently received an international law textbook in the mail. He is studying the first chapters and has found there is no illegal way to seek asylum. It does not matter whether you arrive by foot, by boat or by aeroplane. He told his story to Michael Green in July 2016—when he had been in detention for nearly three years—with interpreting by Abdul Aziz Muhamat.

Osama Daragi is the middle of nine children. In 2010, aged 27, he fled Iraq, arriving in Australia by plane, where he spent almost a year in Maribyrnong and Villawood detention centres. He is now a permanent resident of Australia. Osama is a mechanic, and spends his spare time working on his own car, in which he hopes to compete in amateur races. He lives in the northern suburbs of Melbourne. He told his story to André Dao.

Peter is working seven days a week as a cook. He is still writing stories about his experiences in detention. He told his story to Michael Green, with interpreting by Aran Mylvaganam.

Rahila Haidary studies Arts in Perth, where she lives with her husband. Her father arrived on Christmas Island by boat in 2009, and later brought his wife and children—including Rahila, his eldest daughter—to Australia. She told her story to Michael Green.

Reza Yarahmadi arrived on Christmas Island in late 2009. After being released, Reza began visiting detention centres and campaigning for detainee rights. He was overjoyed to marry recently. He and his wife Mahsa live in Melbourne and are expecting their first child. He told his story to André Dao.

Sajjd is still on Manus Island, smoking cigarettes. He recently snuck back into the detention centre for a few days to visit friends, using someone else's ID. He told his story to Michael Green in July 2016, with interpreting by Abdul Aziz Muhamat. At that time he had been in detention for nearly three years.

Sami loves to stay fit. He is training as best he can while in detention. He told his story to Behrouz Boochani on Manus Island in August 2016. At that time, he had been detained for nearly three years. He is still there. Editing by Michael Green.

Sara was a translator and interpreter in Iran until she fled the authoritarian clamp-down. She now lives in the northern suburbs of Melbourne on a bridging visa and stays busy volunteering for a variety of community and religious organisations. She told her story to Rajith Savanadasa. Additional editing by André Dao.

Solmaz came to Australia with her son and now lives in Melbourne. She is beginning to make friends through her church and her English classes. Solmaz has told her story because she wants you to know the suffering she has gone through in search of a peaceful life. She told her story to Dana Affleck.

Taqi Alizada studies Business Management at Deakin University. He still lives in Dandenong. He told his story to André Dao.

Wahid is still working in construction in Melbourne. He married recently and the wedding was a great party. He told his story to Camilla Chapman. Additional editing by Michael Green.

Zara and her daughter **Athena** were smuggled out of their country when Athena was seven years old. They hid in the jungle in Indonesia, camping in ruins. They are now living in Melbourne, where Athena is attending school. She loves reading. They told their stories to Melissa Cranenburgh. Additional editing by Michael Green.

Acknowledgements

The stories in *They Cannot Take the Sky* were edited by Michael Green and André Dao with help from associate editors Angelica Neville, Dana Affleck and Sienna Merope.

Thank you to the photographers for the use of their work: Melanie Adams, Emily Bartlett, Tim Bauer, Rodney Dekker, Michael Green, Dominic Lorrimer, Noah Thompson and Sarah Walker.

Thank you to Grace Heifetz at Curtis Brown. Thanks also to Tom Gilliatt, Angela Handley and Aziza Kuypers at Allen & Unwin. Behind the Wire has received financial support from Amnesty International, Bertha Foundation and Vasudhara Foundation, and in-kind support from Asylum Insight, Good for Nothing, Right Now and Voice of Witness.

Thank you to Christos Tsiolkas for writing the foreword.

And special thanks to all the volunteers and supporters who have made Behind the Wire possible: Dylan Baskind, Grahame Best, Nina Blackmore, Benjamin Brooker, Tom Campbell, Giordano Caputo, Mario Carabotta, Peter Chapman, Sam Chiplin, Joel Cohen, Brigitte Dagg, Aaron Dobos, Ben Doherty, Damien Dao, Georgina Davey, Tim Denshire-Key, Julia Earley, Niall Edwards-FitzSimons, Isobel Egan, Madeleine Egan, Lauren Ellis, Rebecca Fary, Gil Fewster, Sarah Fraser, Janet Galbraith, Sam Goerling,

THEY CANNOT TAKE THE SKY

Sadie Grant Butler, Jenny Green, Richard Green, Leona Hameed, Sam Henderson, Lisa Heywood, Tom Hilton, Alyssa Huminski, Sam Kenna, Sinead Kennedy, Baqir Khan, Anne Koch, Mark Leacy, Lena Lettau, Tatiana Mauri, Nic Margan, Elle Marsh, Cliff Mayotte, Catherine McInnis, Craig McInnis, Gina McInnis, Claire McGregor, Carolyn McLennan, Bonnie Moir, Lyn Nguyen, Kate O'Brien, Rachel O'Brien, Joseph Percy, Jenell Quinsee, Hannah Reich, Sophie Ross, Jill Rudge, Anna Scharf, Sophie Schmidt, Bella Skelton, Raya Slavin, Hilary Smale, Laura Stacey, Danny Sullivan, Nik Tan, Gemma Teese, Scott Thomas, Mia Tinkler, Jon Tjhia, Aquila Van Keuk, Haiku Van Keuk, Chris Wait, Julia Wallace, Maggie Watson, Ruby Wawn, Stephen Whately, Freyja Wright Catron, Jasmine Wright Catron and Celine Yap.

Behind the Wire

Behind the Wire is an oral history project documenting the stories of the men, women and children who have been detained by the Australian government after seeking asylum in Australia. This project was founded in 2014 by a small group of writers with the aim of bringing a new perspective on mandatory detention: the reality of the people who have lived it. We made a slow and careful beginning. Eventually, a handful of connections became a network spanning the country.

As well as this book, the project comprises a website, an exhibition opening in March 2017 at the Immigration Museum in Melbourne, audio stories, videos, a series of portrait photographs and a podcast—*The Messenger*. For more information, visit: www.behindthewire.org.au.

We hope to reveal a nuanced picture of seeking asylum and life in mandatory detention—a reality that goes beyond queue-jumpers on the one hand and passive victims on the other—and show resilient, suffering human beings. We seek to place the voices, faces and perspectives of asylum seekers, which are rarely represented in public debates on refugee issues, at the centre of the discussion.

Behind the Wire Incorporated is a not-for-profit organisation, coordinated by a volunteer committee. The committee is supported by a large network of volunteers, including our narrators.